MW01612291

Für Herrn Kühl,
ein geschenk vom Franz,

Max Jansen

April 2004

This book is dedicated to Brigit, my beloved
wife and comrade who edited it with patience and care.
She supported me with good advice and enriched this
project with critical questions and suggestions.

.

JORG JANSEN

AND NEW LIFE BLOSSOMS FROM THE RUINS

A Boy in Germany 1939 to 1949

Photos: Private property

Jorg Jansen
Los Alamos, New Mexico, September 2008

Table of Contents

Prologue

Suddenly it was gone, swallowed. We did not comprehend what happened. Brigit asked me one morning in her usual way what I had dreamt during the night. I started to tell her about an unusual occurrence in the laboratory, when I stopped in mid sentence, and we both stared at each other. We could not believe it. Since our wedding in January of 1961 I had always answered her question with: "We were with masses of refugees in a big railroad station;" or "I could not find my family in some vast school building." We and family meant the Jansen family in the year of 1945. The war, the bombs, and the fleeing had always populated my dreams. And now in May of 1967, suddenly, these haunting images had disappeared. We concluded after lengthy soul searching that my old dream world had finally come to an end with the purchase of our first home in La Jolla in Southern California. A stable life had begun, and the "flight" was over after more than twenty years. Already before our marriage, I had begun to tell Brigit about my turbulent life as a boy and I continued with my stories for many years. She and our friends asked me again and again to put my recollections of those eventful years on paper. But I had to retire before I could muster time and effort to write it all down.

The driving force behind this book is my desire to tell the story of those years of my life that left a deeper impression on me and probably contributed more to the formation of my character than anything else. I want to relate this formidable experience not only to my nieces, nephews, and their children and friends, but also to all young people who may never have learned about that war or may not realize what modern wars can do to the individual and to mankind. What happened almost seventy years ago could happen again, if we do not watch out carefully. The next time it would be catastrophic. I am relating my experiences from my memory and thus from the point of view of a young boy who spent his everyday life in the middle of a disintegrating world. To put my reminiscences in context, I filled in the relevant historical events and, occasionally, thoughts from my later life. Considering how Germany managed to destroy its health and wealth twice in the same century, one wants to despair even today. Brigit and I have often compared our two countries: Here Switzerland, a small country without any mineral resources except for salt and rocks, maintains and enlarges its wealth through hard work, saving and improving its standard of living. And there Germany, a large country blessed with mineral resources, a flowering industry and agriculture, and a strong economy; it manages twice to gamble away everything, including its solid reputation in the world and a fine legacy of culture, arts, and science, just to lose it all in quick succession, dragging half the world with it into the abyss.

It all began in September

As usual, my father turned the radio on shortly before twelve noon. A voice announced the time, and then the signal from the observatory in Hamburg sounded: "Beep, beep, beep." At the last beep it was precisely twelve o'clock. Papa and Opa had already pulled out their golden pocket watches, had opened the lids, and were ready. They either smiled with satisfaction or adjusted the very pointed second hand by a smidgen. -- Time was measured with this kind of precision in my home country. Opa had often told us how he had carefully compared his watch with the clock on the platform of the Düsseldorf Railway Station, so that he could raise his green wand at the precise moment, and the train would leave on time -- . After this brief interlude both gentlemen usually listened to the short news summary, and the dinner could begin.

Not so this time! We swallowed the first words of our daily prayer, when the newscaster suddenly announced that the German troops had crossed the Polish border at 5:30 this morning. It was the first of September 1939 that would become a fateful date for Germany and the entire world. Shortly after the announcement we heard the voice of our venerated Führer: "My German citizens! After months of negotiations with the Polish government to obtain an adequate access to *Ostpreussen* (East Prussia), after never ending problems at the border, and with the increasing repression of the German populace in Poland, I had no other choice but to send our troops across the border. The Polish government simply was not willing to acquiesce to our legitimate demands. As of this morning the border crossings have been opened. Our infantry, artillery, *panzer* (tanks), and airplanes are advancing on Polish territory. I trust providence that the German People (*das deutsche Volk*) will win this war in the shortest time and that peace can be restored in Europe." This rousing speech was followed by the national anthem *Deutschland, Deutschland über Alles.* (Footnote 1). Our family sat there, thunderstruck. Opa and Papa looked very serious, and Mutti commented that this war was absolutely unnecessary and a disaster: I have lived already through one horrible war during my life, and that experience is more than enough for me". Marlis and I, who did not understand the implications of the word war, waited for Opa to say his prayer so that we could finally begin our dinner.

Only a year ago the German troops had occupied the *Sudetenland* that had been part of Germany before the First World War (Footnote 2). Hitler and Eduard Benes, the president of young Czechoslovakia, could not agree on an equitable future for the *Sudetenland* in spite of endless and heated negotiations. In 1919 the Treaty of Versailles had assigned the *Sudetenland* to Czechoslovakia, although the majority of the population was German. This unfortunate decision had remained a point of contention ever since. The fights between Hitler and Benes did not subside, until Roosevelt, Chamberlain, Daladier, and Mussolini exerted enough pressure on both parties that it came to the Agreement of Munich of September 30, 1938. The *Sudetenland* became again part of Germany. This event led to the complete breakup of Czechoslovakia: Slovakia and Carpatho-Ukraine left the union. However, in the end Hitler occupied all of it on March 15, 1939. Every move of Hitler led to new diplomatic skirmishes with Edouard Daladier and Neville Chamberlain, the prime ministers of France and England. They permitted the reoccupation of the *Sudetenland* and the annexation of Czechoslovakia as the last German expansion; but coupled with this, they guaranteed Poland's independence on March 31, 1939. The threat to the European peace grew inexorably at each step. A war with the Western Allies was unavoidable, if Hitler broke this last ultimatum.

It is true that the sudden beginning of the war caught the family by surprise; however, the political tension had existed for a long time and it had rapidly increased during the last few months. Hitler, and with him the German people, wanted to break the shackles of the Treaty of Versailles by all means. -- It was illuminating for me to read, how Churchill describes in great detail the unavoidable consequences of that unfortunate treaty in his book "The Gathering Storm" --. I have never forgotten with what overwhelming enthusiasm the citizens of Mülheim, my hometown, celebrated in 1936 the reentry of German troops into the *Rheinland*, which had been a demilitarized zone since 1919 as part of the conditions of the treaty. The Infantry Regiment 159 marched into our town with the old regimental flags, a military band including horses with kettle drums, and machine guns and canons drawn by horses. The streets were thronged by tens of thousands, the thunder of the hurrahs almost drowned the martial music. The regiment installed itself again in the old barracks across the street from us on the *Kaiserstrasse*. I remember vividly how full of pride I was during open barracks days, when we could visit the soldiers and admire their equipment. Even as a six year old I understood that we had become German again. Only a few years after the reoccupation of the *Rheinland* Hitler proclaimed the annexation of Austria, which was celebrated on March 14, 1938 with a triumphant parade of German troops through Vienna. Old Austrian flags, old German flags, and new Swastika banners all over the city. (Footnote 3).

Our family had just returned to Mülheim from a wonderful vacation in the idyllic countryside of *Osnabrück,* one day before the fateful first of September. My parents spent every year a month or so with us children in some vacation spot. These were mostly small hotels or resorts in a pretty countryside not too far from Mülheim, frequently in the hills of the *Sauerland*, sometimes a little further away. Summer vacations were always very exciting. They began months before, when Papa and Mutti made their plans. Catalogues and brochures were studied with a special eye on the price, because we could only afford one month of my father's salary for vacations in a modest place. Once my parents had found the right place and had made a reservation, the joy and excitement of anticipation began. A few days before departure a large trunk and several suitcases were packed, and the baggage carrier took them to the railroad station in his two-wheeled cart. He dispatched them early enough so that everything would arrive before us. The departure day reached its high point when we all boarded a taxi for the station. A taxi ride was an extraordinary treat that happened only once a year. Marlis

9

and I talked about it days before and after. In the train we settled down comfortably in our reserved compartment and enjoyed the long anticipated train ride. During the trip, sandwiches and homemade lemonade kept us kids from starving. This summer we were going to spend four weeks in a little resort in sandy heather and pine country. The resort consisted of two dozen cabins distributed throughout the open forest. One main building contained a large dining room, kitchen facilities, and the office. Mutti never had to cook during our vacations, so that she could totally relax with us and Papa. Marlis was ten, I was eight, Sigrid two and Heidi almost one year old. Papa was already fifty two and Mutti forty because they had married fairly late in their lives. We all enjoyed these weeks immensely: Playing in the sand, running through the forest, hiking with the parents, swimming in small lakes and rivers and playing on several huge lawns with swings, seesaws, merry-go-rounds and fountains that shot water high in the air. Unfortunately, during these wonderful weeks the clouds of war got darker and heavier. We returned home on the last day of August full of worries and foreboding; and we were not alone. The train was packed with people who had decided to journey home earlier than planned because of the increasing political tension. In spite of it all, we celebrated Heidi's first birthday in an overfilled compartment with everybody joining in; and we reached home not one day too soon.

When war broke out the next day, we learned that we had to obtain rationing cards at the office of the new Department for Wartime Rationing in the big government building at the end of the *Witthaus Strasse*. All foodstuff with the exception of fruit and vegetables became rationed. Everybody received monthly rationing cards for which one could obtain groceries according to age and occupation. All edibles were measured in calories which were tailored to specific needs. I still remember that the allotment varied from 1800 kilo calories for the average consumer to 4000 kilo calories for a miner or a worker in the steel industry. We as children received extra milk. Scientists, engineers, and similar professionals were allotted 2500 kilo calories, etc. Everybody complained and tried to hoard extra food in the last minute; but in reality we never suffered from hunger throughout the entire war. Certain imported fruits like oranges or bananas gradually disappeared; lard, sugar and meat were reduced; coffee, cocoa and tobacco products shrank to very small quantities; but

10

surprisingly, there was always enough food on the table until the last day of the war.

Fear of the war and unhappiness with the government became considerably more pronounced, when on the third of September the newscaster announced that England and France had declared war on Germany as they had threatened five months ago. My parents and their generation remembered vividly the first world war with its terror, hunger, death and aftermath. They saw already a replay of those horrible years, only this time worse. Posts were installed in our basement to provide extra support for the ceiling of the laundry room, our air raid shelter, because we feared potential air bombardments. The attic had to be emptied of all combustible material because of the danger posed by incendiary bombs. We also carried water and sand upstairs. My mother fashioned light-tight curtains from heavy blankets, which she put up in front of all windows so that absolutely no light could be seen from the outside. All street lights were dimmed; and the lights of cars, motor cycles and bicycles were covered with slotted lids that allowed only a small beam of light to pass downwards. This barely illuminated the street in front of the drivers. At night pedestrians were in as much danger as cyclists or cars, because it was pitch-black when clouds covered the sky. To avoid collisions people wore large fluorescent buttons; and street light posts as well as building corners were marked with fluorescent paint. As the most fear inducing precaution we were all fitted with gas masks, because the government expected gas bombardments from the air as a continuation of similar practices in the trenches of northern France and Flanders during the last war. Fortunately, the warring parties did not again resort to this ghastly form of warfare. As it turned out, we did not experience any air war for a long time to come.

Life goes on in spite of War

With the exception of these measures and the food rationing, life for us kids continued as before. After a short hiatus of a few weeks school started again, and, as usual after long vacations, we children barely remembered anything from the time

11

before. I was in third grade in the *Hindenburg Schule,* behind the *Oppspring* down in the *Rumbachtal.* It was named after Field Marshal Paul von Hindenburg, the hero of the First World War, who became *Reichspräsident* in 1925 (Footnote 4) It took me half an hour to walk to school, mainly through the *Oppspring,* a huge park with forest, meadows, frog and duck ponds, and walkways with benches for the older folks. I attended the *Hindenburg Schule* now after I had spent my first two years in the *Troost Schule* near the river *Ruhr* that flows below the hill called *Kahlenberg,* where our family had built a home three years earlier. At the beginning I had hated the thought of having to leave my mother and going to school. Even the beautiful traditional *Schultüte* filled with sweets and other goodies could not console me. In those days it was the custom to give pupils on their first day a *Schultüte,* a large conical cardboard container, beautifully colored and stuffed to the top. It turned out that my school fright and worry about leaving Mutti did not last very long. I got used to the other boys and girls in our class in a hurry. I guess that both, Marlis and I, were not accustomed to other children, because the *Kaiser Strasse,* where we had lived before, was a very busy street, and we were kept inside the apartment or in the yard. I started to enjoy my new life in school with all the other children. Of all the subjects I liked *Rechnen* (arithmetic) the most. The walk to school took only twenty minutes and the last portion of it went down behind a local quarry. When that steep slope was covered with ice in the winter, we slid down on our satchels. What great fun; but you had to remove your slate (writing tablet) before, because it could not handle that kind of abuse.

When the school district was changed in April of 1939, my friend Günter and I had to switch over to the *Hindenburg Schule.* From then on we were no longer in a mixed class but only with boys; and it remained that way until the end of my school years. My new teacher was Mr. Meyer, the archetype of the traditional elementary schoolteacher. He, as well as his colleagues, taught everything: The three Rs, local history and geography, botany, physical education, and music. I learned more from him than from a number of my teachers in later years. He was simply excellent; he was strict, no doubt about it, but he was also very just. Not only did he possess a broad field of knowledge, but he had also a singular ability to teach in a most interesting and exciting manner. I particularly liked our field trips

At least once a week we made an excursion into the *Rumbach* (a creek that flows into the Ruhr) valley or the surrounding fields, meadows and woods. Each time, depending on the season, we discovered something new of the flora and fauna of our home town. Soon we knew the difference between rye and wheat, oat and barley as well as between beech, oak, linden and all types of fir trees. We followed the development of the   blossoms on apple, pear, peach, cherry, and plum trees all the way to the ripe fruits; we experienced the metamorphoses of frogs, butterflies, moths, and other insects. In the class room we sang to his violin, and in the school yard we had to climb up and down on poles and ropes and exercise on the single bar. I continued to enjoy arithmetic as in the *Troost Schule*. I especially liked one exercise that he performed with us regularly. He started with a number that the class had to memorize; then he added a number, multiplied the result with another number, subtracted, divided, added, etc. I had always great fun, the faster and more complicated the better. You had to retain all the results in your memory and be ready with the answer as soon as he stopped. As a result of two years under Mr. Meyer an unusually large percentage of our class passed the entrance exam to the *Gymnasium* (the secondary school) with flying colors.

Once a week we took soap showers in a large hall in the basement, stripped to the skin, including teacher Meyer. Today it may sound peculiar that we had a shower hall in our school; but the reader should know that in 1939 showers or bathtubs did not exist in most old houses and apartments that were built earlier in the twentieth century or before. Consequently, the school provided a shower opportunity for everybody. The school was also the watchdog for and dispenser of bodily hygiene. A nurse visited the class regularly to check for tuberculosis which was the biggest killer in those years. She would rub a small amount of a tuberculin protein derivative into the skin, and you had to wait for two days for a reaction. She inspected also our head and hair for lice. A dentist came once a year to check our teeth.

On the walk home through the *Oppspring* park after school, my friends and I had to settle sometimes an account with an adversary group. Typically the fight started with throwing wood pieces and stones at each other and ended up in a general melee of fist fights and wrestling, until victory was achieved or a truce was declared. Thank God, nothing beyond a few scrapes ever happened. Did our parents have an inkling? They never said anything, unless I was late for the midday dinner, the traditional German main meal. We also engaged in harmless pranks. However, once we went too far. Conny Jentsch invited a few classmates to throw stones into windows in a new housing development that was being built nearby. Since his father was the chief architect of this very large project, Conny probably thought that he could and, of course, did impress us with this generous gesture. We fled the scene after a few windows shattered into pieces and sweated blood that we might be discovered. Luckily we got away, albeit with a very uneasy feeling. Never again!

When the frog ponds started filling up with tadpoles in the summer, I collected a bunch now and then, took them home in a water jar, fed them regularly, and hoped for the metamorphosis into frogs. It never happened, until Marlis and I discovered one day that they needed land to become frogs. We quickly built a terrarium from sand and water and, voila, we were successful. Sometimes we brought home toads that we kept in our sandbox in the garden. Unfortunately, these toads always found a way over our sand walls, which we had carefully erected, and they were never seen again. We never owned any larger animals like cats, dogs, rabbits or chickens. That was not allowed in my mother's house, neither during the war nor during the really hard times thereafter when rabbits or chickens would have greatly improved our diet.

During winter we created *Schlinderbahnen* (ice slides), in the school yard and also in our street. We formed them by taking a run and then sliding over a stretch of hard snow as far as we could. Each time the track became a little icier and longer. Eventually though, we could not lengthen the *Schlinderbahn,* no matter with what speed we raced onto it. More often than not, you fell on your behind, and ended up with some nice bruises. We also used every opportunity to skate and to sled. The *Kahlenberg Tennis Club* nearby sprayed all its tennis courts with water and thereby created one very large and beautiful ice rink. We went skating there year after year. In one of the most exciting skating games we formed a chain of six to eight kids abreast, raced down the course until the kid at one end jammed his skates into the ice and let the entire chain swirl around, ready for the next run in the opposite direction. You really had to hang on to your neighbor for the chain not to break, otherwise the outer kids would be hurled against the fence. In this manner we would skate back and forth and around, until we ran out of steam or the place got too crowded. When the chain broke on rare occasions and you were at the outer end, you could get badly hurt

Frequently we went over to the *Hockelbahn,* a sled run in the *Witthaus Busch*, a park not far from home. It was very steep and long, almost all the way down to the river *Ruhr*. The run had a sizable jump, the *Hockel*, at the end of the steep section where a pathway crossed it during the summer. If you did not watch and balance carefully, you flew, sled and all, into the snow and sometimes into the kids who were trudging back uphill and did not get out of the way fast enough. It did happen that a less well built sled wouldn't survive the impact and would fold not very gracefully under its rider. Luckily, Marlis and I owned "Davos" sleds, a Swiss product that could handle anything. The most exciting way to go downhill was with a train of sleds. We formed the train by sitting on our own sleds and holding onto the sled in front. If not properly done the whole train, on its way down, started to swing from left to right and back until some kid let go. Kids and sleds all over the place, what a thrill! Well, it is true that occasionally someone got hurt and suffered a sprained ankle or broken arm. We carefully avoided telling our parents, when an ambulance had to take somebody to the hospital. When it became dark and we were sufficiently frozen we trudged home, where Mutti put our ice cold feet and hands into a bucket of cold water and then vigorously rubbed them dry. I never forget how the thawing of my limbs tingled and tingled, and tingled. It often hurt so badly that I could have screamed; but, of course, boys don't scream.

In the summer we played almost every afternoon in the street (automobile traffic barely existed in those days): Hide and seek, cops and robbers, hop scotch, jumping rope, a kind of volley ball without net, soccer and many other games including marbles and spinning top. Down in the bushes below Buchmüller's house, we built little shelters with branches and wood scraps, where we could continue to play if a slight rain set in. Whom do I remember as my play mates? Kurt and Erika Verschoot, Hanna Jötten and her brother, Günter Rübel, Hans-Otto Bösebeck, Karl-Heinz König, Liesel Weissenborn, and some other children from the *Dimbeck* and *Witthaus Strasse*.

There was always something going on in our street. At times we would all go to the soccer field or the 400 meter track next to the *Kahlenberg Tennis Club*. There we competed with each other in running, long and high jump, and ball throwing. Somebody who owned a stopwatch measured our times for the 60 meter run. Running became my favored sport after I had seen in Leni Riefenstahl's documentary how Jesse Owens broke all records in the 1936 Olympics in Berlin. He became our athletic idol, and everybody tried to emulate him. In retrospect I am sure that Mr. Hitler did not like the idea.

On rainy days or during the winter months Marlis and I, sometimes with our friends, played, read books or made presents at home. However, we were only allowed to play after we had completed our homework. When we came home from school around one o'clock the family ate dinner, our main meal. After dinner Papa would return to his office which was located in our house next to the main entrance. Our next task was homework, which had to be done very thoroughly, because Mutti inspected it every day without mercy. Anything that did not meet her standards had to be corrected, or completely redone. She was a strict school mistress.

Inside the house, the whole family wore house shoes. Ours were placed at the back entrance where we had to put them on before we could set as little as one foot inside the door. Children never entered the house through the front door, always through the garden gate and back door. If we were ever caught with street shoes in the house we were scolded or lost one or the other privilege, even if we just had to go to the bathroom. I remember a few times, when it was simply too late to take our shoes off we rushed down to the laundry room in the basement and dashed for the obliging floor drain. Naturally, friends brought their own house shoes, which we reciprocated in their houses or apartments. -- When Brigit and I visited Japan in 1983, it did not take us long to realize, how much more advanced the Japanese were in these matters. Everybody, including the guests, wore slippers inside, not only in private homes, but also in hotels, temples, and even in the university buildings. One always found lots of shoes or slippers in an entrance area which was one step lower then the adjacent corridors. If you went to the bathroom you changed yet into another set of slippers of a loud color, like green or orange, so that they would not be mixed up with the house slippers . --

We only had to help in the house each day after supper, when Opa, Marlis, and I washed and dried dishes. This was accompanied by singing songs that all three of us enjoyed. Mutti did not ask Marlis and me to handle other chores, because she always employed a young woman as help in house and kitchen. For a while she had even two girls when Sigrid and Heidi were very young. -- This was possible because of a social program that the government had started years ago. According to the socialistic principles of the *Third Reich*, after all it was a "socialistic" *Reich*, girls over fourteen who no longer attended school had to spend a year in social services. That included helping mothers with many children, working on a farm, or in a hospital, etc. -- I would like to remind the reader at this point, that in the thirties of the last century a family with four children was highly unusual in Germany and, for that matter, in most of Europe. All my friends came from families with one or two children; three were already very rare. The population of the industrialized European countries had stagnated already before the First World War. It actually declined even further during and after that horrible cataclysm because of the enormous war losses, the ensuing economic misery, and the complete lack of new housing. Nobody desired more than one or two children. However, Hitler and the *Third Reich* needed more children in view of the planned German expansion to the East and associated potential wars. That led to a host of programs to foster larger families. My mother, for example, received the *Deutsche Mutterkreuz* (German Mother's Cross) after the birth of Heidi. I still have a photo where she proudly wears the medal, sitting in our garden, together with my father. I believe that she was very happy with so many children.

On Saturday or Sunday afternoons our parents frequently strolled or hiked with us through the *Witthaus Busch*, along the *Ruhr* or into the *Rumbachtal*. When we returned, Mutti always served coffee and a cake that she had baked the previous day: *Streusselkuchen* (a cake that was sprinkled with crumbs of sugar, butter, cinnamon, and ground almonds), *Guggelhupf* (bund cake), *Marmorkuchen* (marble cake), and all sorts of fruit pies with whipped cream in the summer. The coffee was made of roasted barley because we children were not allowed to drink real coffee; and real coffee was highly rationed and therefore saved for adult visitors. Sometimes we went on longer hikes over the *Auberg,* or to *Mintard* on the other side of the *Ruhr,* or to the *Icktener Bauernhaus,* or all the way to *Kettwig* on this side of the river. From there we would return with one of the white passenger boats that cruised up and down the river. As a destination for these hikes, my parents picked always a garden restaurant, where we could get coffee or hot chocolate and cake, the typical German afternoon fare. Since we had to use rationing coupons for the cake, as soon as the war began, Mutti took frequently her home-baked cake along. The restaurants almost always had swings, merry-go-rounds, or seesaws in the back on grassy grounds. We children got excused as soon as we had eaten the last piece of cake, so that we could enjoy what we had been looking forward to. I liked these family outings very much. We could walk or run in front or behind our parents or we could hold their hands. As long as Sigrid and Heidi were babies, Marlis or I could occasionally push the baby carriage as a special treat. Sometimes Mutti would start a song and we all would fall in. She knew a lot of songs from her years in the *Wandervogel* (migrating bird) after the First World War. The *Wandervogel* was one of many youth organizations that blossomed probably as a reaction to the misery of the war and the following hard times. Young people like my mother and her friends hiked through the forests, fields, and meadows of the German countryside singing and playing their guitars, which were adorned with colorful ribbons. I read recently that the *Hitler Jugend,* Hitler Youth, absorbed after 1933 many of these and similar youth organizations into their ranks, some voluntarily, some under pressure. Young people continued to hike through the country singing the same songs, however, with a new complement of military and political songs, and sometimes in uniform.

As our life continued quietly at home the war developed with all its might outside the country. Poland was overrun in four weeks during the *Blitzkrieg* (lightning war) as it became known later. The Polish army was no match for the highly motorized German troops. The Poles defended their soil bravely with all possible means, including cavalry squadrons against *Panzer* regiments. All in vain! The guarantors, Britain and France, did not have a chance to mobilize and send help in time. However, Stalin took the opportunity to invade the eastern part of Poland, thus splitting the country in two with his confederate Hitler. Already before the *Blitzkrieg*, on August 22, 1939 the foreign ministers von Rippentrop and Molotov had signed the Non Aggression Treaty with the explicit aim "to destroy the British Commonwealth". It included a secret clause that allowed the Soviet Union to annex Eastern Poland and the Baltic States Estonia, Latvia, and Lithuania in case of a German-Polish war. Thus, between Russia and Germany, a new border was drawn through Brest Litovsk. Only twenty years after Poland had been resurrected in 1919 as the result of the Versailles Treaty and President Wilson's new order of Europe, it now disappeared again. Once before It ceased to exist as the result of the Congress of Vienna in 1815 after a number of divisions between Russia, Germany and Austria in 1772, 1793 and 1795. Hitler converted the German part into the *"General- gouvernement Polen"*. As I read many years later in the historic literature and especially in Mitchener's "Poland", the Poles suffered more under the war than any other nation in Europe. An important part of Hitler's policy of expansion to the East had been to convert the Polish people into servants and slaves of the Germans. The implementation of that policy was ruthless and thorough. First the intelligentsia was suppressed or eliminated and all institutions of higher learning were closed. Then the population was stripped of their civic rights, which allowed the occupiers to treat them in most inhuman ways. For example, if a Pole committed an act of sabotage or, worse, killed a German soldier, the whole family was rounded up, driven from its home, and sometimes executed as a warning for everybody else. Cases have been reported, where the population of an entire village was killed and its houses destroyed. The Nazi government was intent upon demoralizing and subjugating the Poles and especially the Polish Jews.

After the victory over Poland our family like everybody in Germany hoped that Hitler's goal had been accomplished and that the war would be over, so that normal life could be resumed. I discovered recently that Hitler did actually make a peace offer to the Western Allies on October 6, 1939. However, it was roundly rejected by Chamberlain and Daladier. We will never know whether Hitler really wanted to quit or whether this was just another of his ploys. Thus the war did not come to the hoped-for end; but it came to a pause, and for some time it looked as if both parties did not know what to do next.

Our family got quickly used to the new lifestyle that

included rationing cards, war propaganda, blackouts, and preparedness for air raids that did not come. The most important change in Marlis' life occurred when she entered the *Lyzeum*, the secondary school for girls. I was as excited as she because I was eager to know what one learned at the *Lyzeum* and in a broader sense also at the *Gymnasium,* the secondary school for boys. Marlis practiced and demonstrated words and sentences of her first foreign language, English,, which made her very proud and me quite envious. Naturally, I wanted to learn it as fast as possible too. -- It is not a surprise from a geopolitical point of view that in 1937 the German government substituted English for French as the first foreign language to be taught in school. Even Hitler had recognized the importance of that language for the future of Germany. Both my parents had still begun with French, and I believe that my father knew only French. English had replaced French already around the turn of the century as the diplomatic language because of the rapidly growing Anglo-American influence in the world. Now belatedly the German schools followed suit.--

I remember another geopolitical, or should I say modern, adjustment that was made during the first war years. We had learned to write in the traditional German script, that was known by the name of *Sütterlin*. In 1941 we had to change and learn the Latin script which was then employed by all western nations. Again, the National Socialistic Government had decided to adjust to the rest of the western world. From then on we used the Latin script in school; and my father used it at work as was expected from all German civil servants. Only Mutti continued to use her old German script until the sixties. I always enjoyed reading her letters in her beautiful precise handwriting, slightly inclined towards the right with strong up and down strokes. My sister Marlis and I can still read and write the old German script, but Sigrid, Heidi and also Brigit have difficulties with it. Soon it will be forgotten altogether.

Six months later the hope for an early end to the war was shattered. The Führer had decided on a surprise attack on France. Listening to the news on May 10, 1940 we learned that "the German army had crossed the borders to Holland and Belgium". I was impressed how upset Opa, Papa and Mutti were. They remembered, as in a recurring nightmare, how the war with France had started full of glory in a very similar way only 26 years

20

earlier and how it had ended full of misery four years later. But, the Führer always knew best. The rapid daily advances through Holland and Belgium were reported in the *Wehrmachtsbericht*, the army bulletin, that had become an integral part of the radio news. Holland surrendered five days later after a devastating air raid on Rotterdam which demolished the city and the harbor. The Belgian king, Leopold III., had decided to fight on, convinced that Britain and France would come to his support. The Fort Eben-Emael in eastern Belgium, considered to be invincible and the strongest fortress of the world, was overrun in a few days. As the *Panzer* rolled westward and the promised help from the Allies did not materialize, Leopold capitulated on May 25. The motorized German columns reached the coast in the shortest time and turned south into France. They had followed precisely the Schlieffen Plan (Footnote 5), which the German army failed to adhere to in 1914. In the weekly newsreel, that was always shown in the movie theaters before the main feature, we saw the advancing *Panzer* regiments, listened to the thunder of the artillery and the ear splitting screaming of the *Stukas*, dive bombers. We were awed by the surrender of entire French armies and by the never ending stream of refugees who were overtaken by the German infantry. Chaos reigned on all roads. Throughout my father and I had stuck little flags into a map that was hanging on the wall in his office. There position showed the daily advance of the army.

My friends and I were very proud of the German troops and their victories. Our daily conversations revolved around *Panzer, Stukas, Jagdflugzeuge,* and *U-boote* (Tanks, dive bombers, fighter planes, and U-boats). We knew the names of all the famous fighter pilots such as Mölders and Galland. We were intimately familiar with all war planes: The single seat fighter Messerschmitt 109, the twin engine bomber Messerschmitt 110, the dive bomber "Stuka" Junkers 87, the twin engine bomber Heinkel 111, etc. Without doubt, the Stukas were our favorites. I always got goose bumps watching the newsreel when a squadron of Stukas flew over enemy territory and when one plane after another rotated over its right wing in order to dive onto a target with a hellish scream. Next to the physical destruction of the bombs, the psychological effect on the French troops must have been devastating. After six weeks of pounding and after the wide sweep through Belgium and along the coast, that included the routing of the British at Dunkirk, the *Deutsche Wehrmacht* was closing in on Paris. That city was in a state of utter chaos and decided to surrender to avoid destruction. The French government had given up all hope and had fled to reestablish itself in Bordeaux. The military command had capitulated, and the German infantry, artillery and *Panzer* columns paraded down the Champs-Elysées past the *Führer* and his generals. The war was over. Or was it? We could breathe once more after the signing of the armistice in Compiegne on June 24, 1940; in the same place where an earlier armistice had been signed on November 11, 1918. The entire family listened to Hitler's patriotic, rousing speech on the radio: Fatherland, honor, heroism! "Finally the German people have abolished the dishonorable Treaty of Versailles. We are now again a nation that the rest of the world has to reckon with." The German national anthem! End! I am absolutely convinced that at that historic moment the vast majority of the German nation was still solidly behind Hitler. In such a short time he had managed to annul a shameful treaty that had been more than a thorn in the side of every German for 21 years. Not surprisingly, on August 3, 1940 Hitler made another peace offer to the British Government, which the new prime minister Winston Churchill promptly rejected.

The family Jansen discussed now excitedly the question of what would become of Alsace Lorraine. Would there be again a German *Elsass Lothringen* as it had existed before 1919? My father and his four sisters had been born and raised in that lovely province. My grandfather who had been a Prussian civil servant was assigned to the *Elsass* sometime after 1871. He worked for the German government in the administration as a high customs official until 1919. I found records indicating that the family had lived in three different locations: in Kolmar, Schirmeck, and Strassburg. -- The reader may remember that *Elsass Lothringen* had been at the heart of the Franco-German conflict for over thousand years, ever since the second division of Charlemagne's empire (Footnote 6). -- Papa and his sisters Martha, Agnes, Clara, and Johanna spoke German, French, and the Alsatian dialect fluently. They often described to us how they spent their youth in this beautiful country with forests, meadows, fields, rolling hills, and mountains. I was most impressed when they told us about the storks that built their aeries on top of farmhouses, barns, and churches, because I had never seen a stork in my life. -- I had a wonderful opportunity to experience and enjoy their home country myself when I made a long bicycle tour through France in 1956. *Alsace Lorraine* was truly beautiful; and the stork aeries still rested on top of the roofs of farmhouses and churches. Also, their ubiquitous *Gewürztraminer* was a true delight. I sipped this delicious white wine many an evening in the local *Wirtshauses* (inns). --

When my grandfather got called back to Prussia in 1919, my aunt Martha and her husband Menne Thal remained in Alsace. The rest of the family moved to Koblenz, at the confluence of the *Mosel* and *Rhein,* where Opa assumed a new responsibility as the director of the *Katasteramt,* the German government department that kept, and still keeps, track of all land ownership, subdivisions, and land transfers. Because of this venerable institution, that had its roots in Roman times, there was and is no need for something like Title Insurance as it is practiced in this country. My grandfather retired after the sudden death of my grandmother and moved with his two youngest daughters, the twins, to the small quiet town *Brühl* near *Bonn.* Our family visited him many times before he died in 1936, surrounded by his daughters who had taken care of him until his death. I remember him as a tall, somewhat rotund gentleman who was always well dressed and enjoyed good food and the occasional glass of good Rhine wine.

Regiment 159 on the parade through Mülheim (1936)

Hindenburg Schule (1940)

My classroom (1940)

The author in elementary school (1940)

Mutti and Papa celebrating the "Mother Cross" (1938)

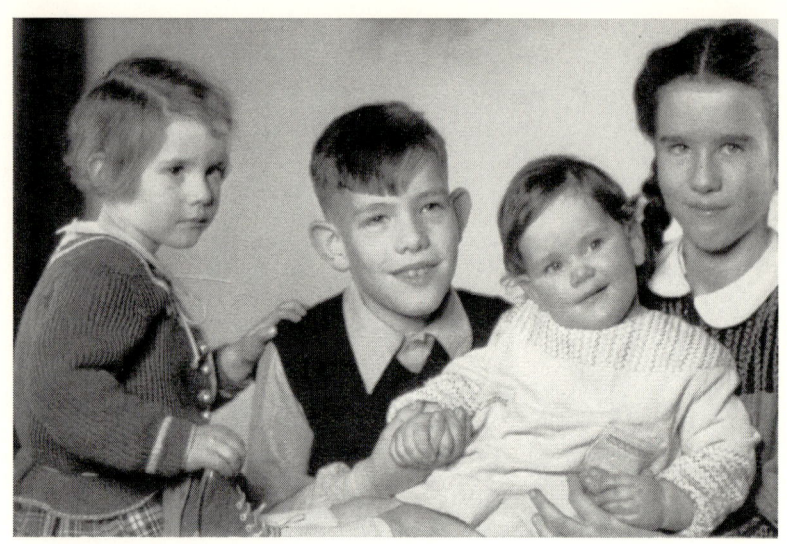

The Jansen siblings (1940)

Opa Jansen with his three daughters and Mutti (1929)

Engagement of Uncle Helmut and Aunt Mali (1939)

Photo above: Langemarck Oberschule, formerly Königliches Gymnasium (1911)

The author in his brand new uniform (1941)

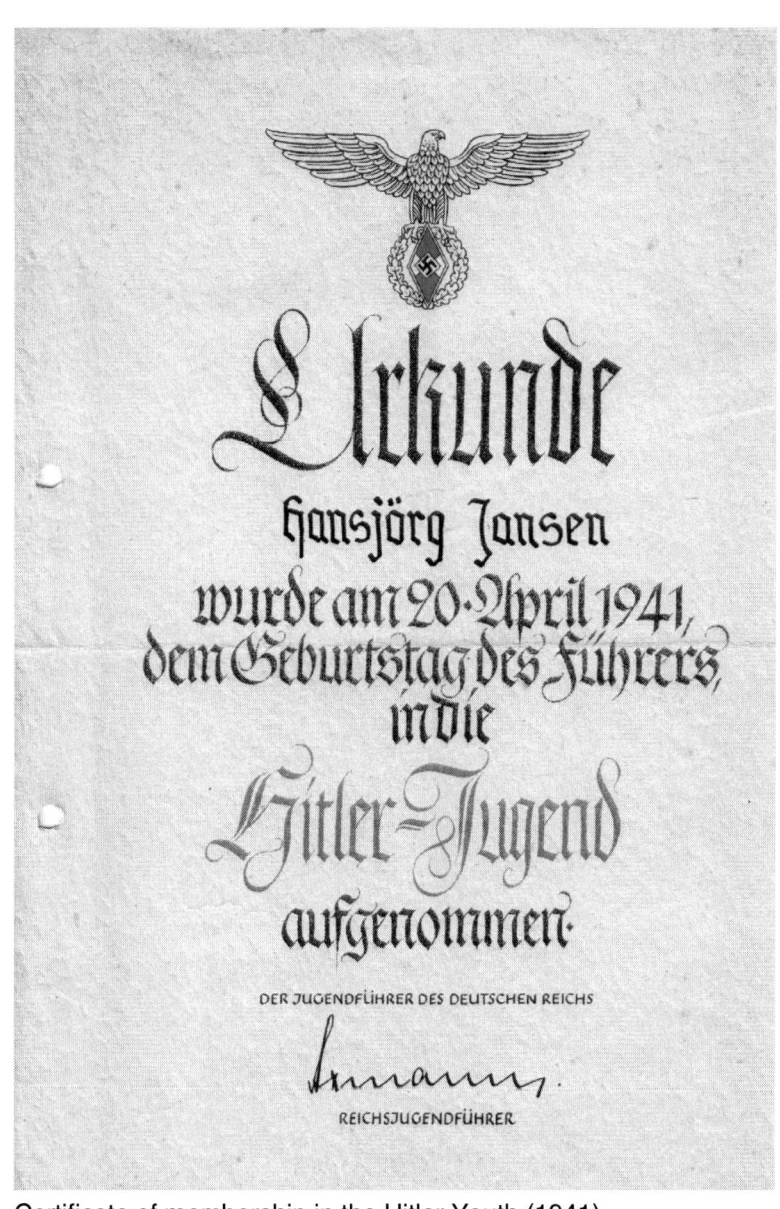

Certificate of membership in the Hitler Youth (1941)

Hitler Youth marching band (1939)

Hitler Youth in front of the town hall on Hitler's 50th birthday (1939)

My war itinerary during the years 1943 - 1945

(1) Mülheim-Ruhr, Ruhrgebiet, May 43
(2) Katzenelnbogen, Hessen, May to Oct. 43
(3) Prag (Praha) Czechoslovakia, Oct. 43
(4) Lazne Bielohrad Czechoslovakia, Oct. to Dec. 43
(5) Waldenburg (Walbrzych), Schlesien, Dec. 43 to Feb. 45
(3) Prag (Praha), Feb. 45
(6) Ronneburg, Thüringen, Feb. to Sep. 45
(7) Aurich, Friesland, Sep. 45
(8) Mülheim-Ruhr, Sep. 45

Bombs, School, Hitler Youth

During the fall of 1940 the war took a more serious turn for the people in the *Ruhrgebiet* (the Ruhr Basin) the heart of the German heavy industry with coal mines, blast furnaces, steel mills, and heavy equipment factories in every town. The immense Krupp Works in Essen (Footnote 7) had forged the weapons for Germany and the world for almost a century. Thyssen made steel in close proximity to the coal mines. Siemens and the AEG built huge electric generators, transformers, and motors. Mannesmann sold seamless steel pipes all over the world, and Stinnes operated fleets of river barges and ocean freighters to transport it all. When you stood on the *Kahlenberg,* a hill overlooking Mülheim, you could discern at least a hundred factory chimneys, all belching clouds of varying colors into the air. When my mother placed the bed linen on the lawn for sun bleaching, and the wind blew from the wrong direction, they were covered with soot particles before they were dry. As a matter of fact, there was so much industrial pollution in the air that we didn't get sunburned all summer while swimming in the Ruhr. When I visited Pittsburgh for the first time in 1961, saw its blast furnaces, and walked over its cobblestone streets with now abandoned streetcar tracks, I felt right at home.

The Germans and the British began to bombard each other from the air. The predictions, based on the last year of the previous war, came true. The new weapon of choice became the long distance bomber. In May 1941 the *Luftwaffe* (German air force) had dropped bombs "by mistake" (according to reports after the war) on *Freiburg im Breisgau* in the southwest corner of Germany. This was an opportunity for the German propaganda machinery to lay the blame at the feet of the enemy. Then a German plane dropped bombs on East London in August, whereupon the Royal Air Force (RAF) attacked Berlin. On September 4, 1941 Hitler gave a speech in the *Berliner Sportspalast:* "If the English government continues their air raids on German cities, we will level their cities to the ground." As if on command the bombing intensified immediately: Munich In November, Coventry and Mannheim in December. The raids on the *Ruhrgebiet* were still very limited. I read recently that the RAF had not yet developed the necessary precision bombing gear.

34

Therefore, they had to resign themselves to scattered bombing that rarely hit the desired targets. Soon Mülheim and other industrial centers in the Ruhrgebiet were surrounded by tethered blimps with dangling steel cables (barrage balloons) that were supposed to stop the enemy bombers. Furthermore, antiaircraft guns, *Flugabwehrkanonen* or FLAK, were installed at many strategic locations to protect the heavy industry, the steel mills, coal mines, and railroads of my hometown. Nothing had happened in Mülheim for a year, until bombs fell during one night only a few blocks away from our house. First thing next morning, I believe it was a Sunday, Marlis and I reconnoitered the neighborhood and found already a number of people milling about on "our" athletic fields on the *Kahlenberg*. We discovered about half a dozen bomb craters in a neat row, starting in the farming fields on the other side of the road that skirted the athletic fields, continuing through them, and ending in the garden of a house on the *Jahn Strasse*. The last bomb had ripped open one wall and the staircase of the house, so that one could look into all three stores. Nobody got hurt because the bombs were still fairly small in those days. Workers were already in the process of supporting the staircase and the wall remnants with wooden beams. It took only a few weeks until the house was repaired and the craters had been filled. These people were lucky; the damage happened so early in the war that it got fixed fast and at the expense of the government.

The memory of the early bombing raids brings back the Passek story. In the apartment house where my friend Günter lived, resided also an American family by the name of Passek. Mr. Passek came from Pittsburgh where he worked for Westinghouse as an electrical engineer. He had been assigned to *Siemens* in Mülheim on some collaborative program between *Siemens* and Westinghouse. Günter, a few friends, and I played often with Passek's daughter Annemarie. We visited her apartment frequently and admired her American toys which were so elaborate and numerous compared to our own. As the bombing raids became more frequent Mrs. Passek became more and more unhappy about her family's unusual fate. Here they were stuck in Germany and had to endure the air raids of their British friends like all their German neighbors. She bemoaned her misfortune in front of us children and all the neighbors in the local stores. Everybody heard daily how unfairly she had been treated, everybody understood and indulged her, and everybody was a little amused about the irony of it all. All laments did not do her any good; her husband continued to work for *Siemens* until he got called back by Westinghouse when the United States entered the war.

My parents developed a greater respect for the air war after the *Kahlenberg* bombing. We transformed the laundry room in the basement into a real bomb shelter. In addition to reinforcing the ceiling supports, a concrete enclosure was built over the light shafts for the basement windows. Beds, lounge chairs, a table, and chairs were carried into the basement; water was stored, candles and a flashlight were kept ready on a table. The blackout was taken very seriously by everybody with or without government edicts; the neighbors let each other know if only the most minute light beam shone to the outside. We children had to place our clothes neatly on a chair next to our beds, so that we could jump into them in record time, and even in the dark, as soon as the sirens started to scream. Marlis and I were responsible for the "Little Ones". That was how we called our younger sisters Sigrid and Heidi. We had to get them dressed and take them into the basement in a hurry. We knew inside out the waxing and waning howls of the sirens that tore us from our warm beds at the approach of the British bombers. The family spent typically between two and three hours in the basement depending on the path that the overflying bombers took. We slept mostly through the whole time until we were awakened by the steady droning of the sirens, indicating the end of the danger. Then quickly back into our beds. For the time being the air war had almost no impact on Mülheim; and absolutely nothing happened in our suburb that would have changed our daily lives.

In April 1941 at the end of the fourth grade, the starting date of the school year was shifted from spring to fall. Consequently our next school year began in September . Would it not have been nice, if we had been given all this time off. But alas, the school authorities thought otherwise. We had to stay for another five months in elementary school until the new school year began. Finally, after the summer vacations, the all important day had arrived. I entered the *Gymnasium* together with a number of my classmates. A new school life commenced in the Sexta (fifth grade) of the *Langemarck Oberschule* (secondary school).

The National Socialistic Government had changed the name from *Humanistisches Gymnasium* to *Langemarck Oberschule*. The choice of that name was not an accident. Langemarck, a village in Flanders near Ypern, was the scene of a battle on November 10, 1914, where 20,000 Allied and German soldiers died. On the German side, a number of young, eager volunteer regiments suffered enormous losses. More than ten thousand insufficiently trained gymnasium graduates were slaughtered, literally as canon fodder. For the National   Socialist propaganda, however, "Langemarck" became the symbol of the German youth's love of country and willingness to die for it.

Let me inject here a few words about the German school system of those years. Every child had to enter the *Volksschule* (elementary school) at the age of six. After four years the pupils had four choices: They could remain in the *Volksschule*, or they could enter either the *Gymnasium* for boys, the *Lyzeum* for girls, or the Middle School. To get into the latter schools, they needed a recommendation from their teacher and had to pass the respective entrance exams.

The majority of the school population continued in the *Volksschule* for four more years until the age of fourteen. This was followed by an apprenticeship at big and small companies, at stores, trades, offices, garages, etc. for another four years. The apprentices had to attend classes in their respective disciplines one day a week at the *Gewerbeschule* (vocational school) in addition to classes given by all big companies and some of the smaller enterprises. This schooling coupled with the practical apprenticeship was the requirement by all trades and other skilled professions for becoming a journeyman and potentially later a master of a trade.

The middle school lasted six years until the age of sixteen. It prepared the pupils for those professions that did not require an university education, such as clerks, secretaries, nurses, lower civil servants, merchants, etc.

The *Gymnasium* and *Lyzeum* lasted nine years until the age of nineteen. They paved the way for the university or professions that required a higher degree of learning. The grades had Latin names and were counted "backwards" from the highest to the lowest. Presumably, the goal of every pupil was to reach the first, the best, the Prima. You began the school in the Sexta (the sixth). Then you advanced to the Quinta (5.) and so forth through Quarta (4.), Untertertia (lower 3.), Obertertia (upper 3.), Untersekunda (lower 2.), Obersekunda (upper 2.), Unterprima (lower 1.) and finally Oberprima (upper 1.), altogether nine grades. A good percentage left the *Gymnasium* after six years. The rest aimed for the *Abitur*, the final exam, the hurdle that had to be overcome to enter a university or any of the higher professions. About 10% of the total school population made it into the *Gymnasium* and *Lyzeum*, of which 30 to 40% entered ultimately the universities.

As a measure of how times change I like to include here an interesting tidbit. It appeared in our school's annual report of 1928/29 (12 years before my time):

"In regard to smoking and visiting restaurants, the school together with the parent council made the following decision:
  a) The pupils of the upper grades may smoke in public
     if they do not wear their school caps; however,
     neither on the walk to and from school, nor during the
     ride in streetcar or railroad.
  b) The pupils of the "Primas" (12. and 13. grade) may
     visit all restaurants of good repute."

Another sign of the changing times in Germany of the thirties can be found in the annual report of 1933/34. The National Socialists had taken over in 1933 and began immediately to "reform" the German youth, and, of course, their teachers. The topics of the teachers' papers below speak for themselves. The annual report of 1933/34 included amongst other items the following:

  * Studienrat Dr. Heinen gives a paper on "National
    Socialism and the Youth".
  * Studienrat Dr. Elsässer gives a paper on "What is
    Aryan?"
  * A National Socialistic Course for the "Primas" was
    held during a retreat in the Eifel Mountains from Dec. 8
    to 22, 1933.

The *Langemarck Schule* was a beautiful, stately building on the *Von-Bock Strasse* directly opposite to the *Lyzeum* and the Middle School. My first *Klassenlehrer* (principal teacher) was

Dr. Breuer who taught us mathematics, a new subject that was not taught in elementary school. There the same class had simply been called *Rechnen, i.e.* addition, subtraction, multiplication, division and fractions, now it metamorphosed into mathematics. Dr. Ludwig taught the first foreign language, English. Now I could compete with Marlis. I will never forget: "Jim in camp. The sun is high in the sky, etc." We learned history and in the second year Latin from Dr. Hahn. His nickname was "Gallus". Although he had a deep and thorough knowledge of his subjects he was a very bad pedagogue. We got away with just about anything. I remember vividly an incident in the classroom which gave the class a wonderful thrill and poor Gallus a bad shock. He always brought several big card board mounted posters into the history class. They showed famous historical scenes like the coronation of Charlemagne in the dome of Aachen or Martin Luther affixing the fifteen theses to the door of the *Münster* in *Wittenberg*. He placed the relevant poster of a size of four by three feet on top of the lower sliding blackboard right above his head. Knowing that the position of this heavy poster was not very stable, we made it the object of a bombardment with little paper balls. When Gallus, who sat behind the lectern, did not look, another paper ball would hit. It did not take long until the right succession of balls brought the poster to wobble and fall with a bang on his bald head. The ensuing deadly silence in the class room was unbearable. Everybody sat absolutely quiet with a hand in front of his mouth, barely able to suppress the laughter. Dr. Hahn stormed out of the classroom and, of course, came back with director Brüggemann. The ensuing punishment was terrible, but it was worth the fun.

However, in general, discipline and obedience governed our lives. Each morning before class we had to line up in the school yard, three in a row, one class behind the other. When everybody was assembled, our director stepped through the big entrance doors at the top of the wide staircase and gave the signal to enter the building. The boys of the *Oberprima*, the highest grade, entered first and we the *Sextaner,* the lowest grade, came last. Once in the classroom we had to stand next to our desks until the teacher entered and greeted us with "Heil Hitler", to which we responded in unison, "Heil Hitler." After his "Sit down!" we could take our seats. After each break the class stood again to attention, until the new teacher bade us to sit

39

down. We had a healthy respect for our teachers with the exception of Dr. Hahn. They represented the absolute authority; no question about it. They were so much more knowledgeable than we pupils that the very idea of criticism never entered our minds. The utmost respect was also due the boys from the *Oberprima* or *Unterprima*, giants who towered above us and gave orders. They wore long pants, white shirts, and neckties, and had their classrooms on the top floor. It seemed to be an eternity before we would be in their shoes in nine years. The number of subjects increased, as we changed from the *Volksschule* to the *Gymnasium.* English, music, art, and geography were added. Each subject was now taught by a different teacher who came to our classroom. Only for subjects like music, art, science, and physical education did we have to go to the respective rooms. Also the homework became more diversified, so that each boy kept a little calendar in which he wrote the assignment and its due date for each subject. In this manner the parents knew what homework had to be accomplished on any given day. Mutti always checked our calendars and made sure that her children had done all homework before they were allowed to play.

Our leisure activities had not changed much. However, I occupied myself more and more with handicrafts. I did a lot of work with my coping saw, I built bridges, cars, trucks, airplanes and buildings with my *Märklin* kit (similar to Meccano). I enjoyed cutting out and gluing together war planes and ships. Messerschmitts, Stukas, Spitfires, and Fokkers were hanging from the ceiling in my room. Destroyers, u-boats, and battleships were anchored on the chest of drawers. It took an enormous amount of patience to cut hundreds of little parts from the printed cutout sheets and glue them painstakingly together. To assemble a battle ship with its tiny gun turrets and barrels, with its complicated bridge and other equipment took months. Apparently I had the patience and skill. At the same time, Marlis excelled in arts and crafts in the *Bund Deutscher Mädchen* (BDM), the Hitler Youth organization for girls, which she had joined already in 1939. Her group spent the months before Christmas making toys for kids of poor families and soldier's families. At home, she and I made presents for our parents, siblings and relatives for their birthdays or Christmas. The few *Pfennige* from our savings box would not have purchased much. Talking about saving, Marlis and I saved every penny and nickel that we got from aunts and uncles or sometimes from Opa, if we had done something nice. Mutti had instructed us very early, how to save and how to enter each tiny amount in a little notebook with date and description. Occasionally she would take us into town to the savings bank where we emptied our metal savings boxes and deposited the money into our own accounts. The air raids remained sporadic throughout 1940 and 1941. The British concentrated their air raids on industrial installations and railroads, because they did not yet have enough bombers. Naturally, our big neighbor city, Essen, was a favorite target for attacks. I believe that all air raid planners loved the huge *Krupp* Steel Works. Very little happened in Mülheim in spite of *Thyssen*'s blast furnaces, *Mannesmann*'s steel mills and the heavy electrical equipment factories of *Siemens* and *AEG*, let alone the numerous coal mines. Unfortunately, however, we had air alarms whenever the bomber formations crossed Mülheim or got near it. The number of times when the wailing sirens rushed us into the basement increased. The thunder of the *Flak* kept us awake until the *Entwarnung,* the all clear, signaled the end of the danger

It seemed that Hitler's next goal was to invade England. That would give him a free hand for the expansion to the East where we Germans would acquire all the "needed" *Lebensraum* (living space). The archives show that plans were developed first for July 16, 1940 and later for October. I am not certain to this day, whether he really wanted to take this step. Nevertheless, air supremacy over England had to be obtained before anybody could think about an invasion. The famous "Battle of Britain" ensued during the months of July and August 1940. The *Luftwaffe* did not win this decisive battle, in spite of all the promises that the *Reichsmarschall* Göring had made. The British fighters fought brilliantly and had the advantage of short flight distances from their nearby air bases. Also, the RADAR system, which had been invented shortly before the war, had been perfected and proved to be the decisive weapon, not only during the Battle of Britain, but throughout the entire war. With its RADAR the British Royal Air Force could detect and pinpoint the position of any advancing German bombers and fighters during day and night. Surprisingly, I found out about the Battle of Britain only many years after the war. It was never mentioned in the *Wehrmachtsberichte*, probably because the *Reichsmarschall* did not want to advertise his failure. Hermann, as he was called by everybody, had clearly underestimated the resolve of the British. He actually declared in a speech, "My name will be Meier, if a British air plane ever flies over German soil." Well, in no time he was called Meier. On October 12, 1940 the German High Command abandoned the idea of an invasion.

After I had reached my tenth birthday I joined the *Deutsches Jungvolk* (German Young Folk) in the spring of 1941. That was the name of the branch of the Hitler Youth for all boys under fourteen. Becoming a member of the Hitler Youth was not voluntary, as some people may think. It was as mandatory as attending school. Every German boy or girl had to join the organization by law. My parents bought me a uniform that made me very proud. The summer issue consisted of a light brown, almost yellow, shirt with long sleeves, and black corduroy shorts with a broad black leather belt. A triangular black bandana was worn under the shirt collar with a small triangle showing on the back. In front, the two ends of the bandana were inserted through a yellow brown leather knot that held them together. We also wore a black cap that could be folded flat and put under the right shoulder strap. After half a year I received my *Fahrtenmesser,* a knife for hiking and camping, that was sheathed and fastened to the belt. A thin black leather shoulder strap completed the uniform. It was hooked to the belt in front and back and worn over the right shoulder. During the winter months we wore dark blue, heavy woolen shirts and ankle length knickerbockers. A woolen visor cap of matching color with extendable ear flaps kept head and ears warm.

Every Wednesday and Saturday afternoon we had *Jungvolk* duty that took place on the *Kahlenberg* sports grounds. For those afternoons we did not have to do any school homework, a benefit that we very much appreciated. It was certainly not improving our academic performance, but I guess that the arrangement had been worked out between the minister of education and the minister for youth affairs, i.e. the *Hitlerjugend.* I was assigned to a *Jungenschaft ,* the smallest organizational unit which consisted of ten boys. After we had assembled, our leader, the *Jungenschafts Führer,* reported to the next unit leader up the ladder and so forth. Four *Jungenschaften* made up a *Jungzug ,* and four *Jungzüge* one *Fähnlein.* I remember that our *Fähnlein* had the number four and consisted of about 160 boys between 10 and 14 years old. To complete the hierarchy, four *Fähnlein* made up one *Stamm,* and five Stämme one *Bann.* Our *Fähnlein* was part of the *Bann* 159 that, of course, had the same number as the Mülheim Infantry Regiment. I estimate that the Mülheim *Bann* comprised approximately 3000 to 4000 boys and a similar number of girls who were organized in the same way.

Most of the time we assembled as a *Jungzug* of 40 boys in three rows with the tallest boys up front and the shortest at the end. Because of my height I always ended up in the front row. We learned to form straight rows, make turns to the left, to the right, rotate 180 degrees and back, stand to attention and at ease, and march and run as a column -- exactly as in the army! A good deal of time was spent with athletic activities: We practiced running over short and long distances, high jump and long jump, and throwing small balls the size of a tennis ball, but heavier and harder. The older boys (fourteen to eighteen years old) in the *Hitler Jugend* practiced throwing dummy hand grenades instead. Other exercises included climbing wooden walls, walking and running over beams, crawling under low wire mesh, and advancing on knees and elbows through the grass. We called that *robben.* for it describes how a *Robbe* (seal) propels itself on the ground. Little did we realize that we were undergoing pre-military training. We also played *Fussball* (soccer) the German national team sport, handball, and volleyball. Once a year we participated in the nationwide *Dreikampf,* triathlon, for boys and girls in the large sports arena at the *Südstrasse.* That important day began with marching bands, mass athletic presentations, folk dances and, of course, speeches by high ranking *Hitler Jugend* officials. The competition began as soon as referee committees had been formed and had taken their positions all over the field. We competed in three disciplines: sixty meter run, long and high jump, and ball throwing. Each event was executed three times and received a certain number of points. All points were added for the final result. To my chagrin, I never reached the highest points, because, I simply could not throw that little ball far enough. Must have been lack of muscle. However, I could compensate somewhat with excellent results in running and jumping. At the end of the day, the winners were announced and the event closed with the singing of one of our many patriotic songs:

"On the pole before us flies our flag,
into the future we march man by man;
we march for Hitler through night and through need
with the flag of the youth for freedom and bread.

On the pole before us flies our flag.
Our flag is the symbol of a new time,
our flag leads us to eternity.
Yes, the flag is more than the death."

We learned a myriad of songs during our Wednesday and Saturday afternoon meetings. They were a mix of folk songs, soldiers songs from the middle ages to modern times and Party songs. They ranged from "Oh, you beautiful *Westerwald*" (a mountain region east of the Rhine) to "Wild geese are flying through the night", to "Forward legionnaires", to "Good night comrades, behold this day", and to " Yonder the valley". It amazes me how many I can still sing today. Years after the war, when I was a student at the *Technische Hochschule* in Aachen, a group of friends and I used to make weekend bicycle trips to the *Rursee*, a huge reservoir in the *Eifel* Mountains. There we sat around the camp fire and sang the old songs. However, by now American popular and folk songs had become part of our repertoire. Somebody always brought a guitar along, and we could sit there for hours next to the fire, happily mingling the old with the new.

What did the *Jungvolk* do during the winter? We marched, we went sledding or ice skating, we had huge snow ball fights, and we spent a good deal of time in our den. This was a large garage that some benevolent parents had offered to the *Fähnlein*. There we would often make Christmas presents for poor children: Wooden hobby horses, little carts and autos, and all sorts of toys. At other times, our leader or one of us would read stories, or we learned new songs.

Brigit has asked me often how we were indoctrinated in the National Socialist ideology. The answer is, that I do not remember a direct indoctrination comparable to the Chinese youth memorizing every word of Chairman Mao's little red book. The only material that we had to learn by heart was the life of the *Führer* and many songs that glorified national socialistic or patriotic ideas. I believe that a concerted indoctrination began

44

only in the *Hitler Jugend*, i.e. at the age of fourteen. However, considering Brigit's question from a more general point of view, the entire idea of a Hitler Youth is indoctrination. Although we did not learn catechisms, we were formed with the help of ideals, uniforms, marching, athletics, songs, rallies, etc. As teenagers we simply absorbed everything that happened around us without giving it much thought. Family is good, sports are important, old people have to be helped, one must be obedient, death is preferable to losing freedom, and Germany must become strong again. On national holidays the entire city was full of flags and banners with political slogans. On *Führer's* birthday the family Jansen decorated the balcony towards the street with a large flag and a bust of Hitler. The neighbors hung flags from the windows or flew them from flagpoles, and some displayed large Hitler pictures or banners with political slogans. We listened with our parents and Opa to speeches of the *Führer* or Dr. Goebbels. It was exciting to help my father to put on his splendid party uniform and especially the long black boots. When he came back from a rally or some meeting, I always assisted him with getting his boots off, which was by no means an easy task.

A few days after the *Kristallnacht* (crystal night) on November 11, 1938 Marlis and I went to town with Mutti for her weekly shopping. We stared at the shattered show windows of the few Jewish stores and the burned-out synagogue, all of which had been destroyed by the *Sturmabteilung* (storm division) generally referred to as the SA, *Hitler's* storm troopers. Although the sights and the idea of destroying property filled us with horror, we could not relate to Jews as individuals, because we had no Jewish friends, classmates or neighbors. Being a blue collar town, Mülheim had only a tiny Jewish population. But there is no doubt in my mind that we were constantly absorbing the never ending hate propaganda against the Jewish part of the population. We heard it untold times in Hitler's and Goebbels' speeches that we Germans belonged to a superior race, and that the Jews and Slavs were inferior. The Germans had therefore a right to more *Lebensraum* , living space, which meant, of course, a right to expand to the east. It was never said that Himmler had the right to kill millions of Jews.

Instead of attending our regular Wednesday or Saturday meetings, we frequently had to solicit contributions for one or the other cause. For these occasions, we were sent off in teams of two. Each pair received a can with a slotted lid and a depiction of the collection's purpose. Most of the time we were also furnished with a box of buttons or little flags that we fastened to people's lapels for their contributors. It was important to find a busy street corner or a square in our neighborhood where the chances of meeting many pedestrians were the highest. Most people put a few coins into our cans, some people said that they had already given, and some ignored us. These collections were normally very successful, unless we ended up in the wrong place at the wrong time, or the weather did not cooperate. Sometimes we had to go from house to house and apartment to apartment, especially if the collection was for the NSV, the *National Sozialistische Volksfürsorge.* The NSV was a government supported organization that provided an array of social services for the poor, the sick, and the old. Certain afternoons were dedicated to helping old people to carry loads from a store across the street and up the staircase to their apartment. Hauling up coal from the basement or carrying out the trash could be another assignment. Occasionally we had to collect leaves, stalks or flowers of medicinal plants that Marlis and I dried in the attic and delivered to a collection point for the infirm and also the soldiers at the front.

In the 1990s recycling became one of this country's bigger concerns; in the 30s and 40s it had been already an important part of my life. In those years anything that still had any value was gathered and reused. Hermann Göring was in charge of the recycling campaigns. As usual, somebody had come up with a song: "Rags, paper, bones, and iron, yes that's what we collect for Hermann." Long before Hermann's campaign, the "ragman " had been coming by as long as I could remember. As a matter of fact, ragmen had probably been around since the beginning of industrialization. From afar you could already hear him playing catchy tunes on his fife. This gave you time to gather everything up and have it ready at the door. Mutti was usually ready with bundled paper, cardboard, rags, metal scrap, and other materials. When we stepped into the street, the rag man stopped his horse and cart, got out his scale, and weighed everything carefully. Then Mutti got paid per weight and type of material; and we children received occasionally a candy. That took care of the inorganic waste. All the organic waste went on our compost heap with the exception of potato peels and the likes. Marlis and I carried those in old potato sacks on our scooters to the farmer at the far end of our street. I still remember my fear of the geese, that stood almost as tall as we, and did not want to let us into the farm. They were very aggressive, hissing, flapping their wings, and trying to bite us with their yellow beaks. Usually, Marlis and I negotiated ahead of time who would enter first through the huge gate, armed with the biggest stick we could find. Once inside we delivered our gift to the farmer who boiled the peels and fed them to his pigs. On the way out we fled in front of those beastly geese. Because all the trash was thus disposed in one way or the other, only the ash from the furnace was left over. It was filled into "ash cans", not "trash cans" (!), that we hauled down the front steps and to the curb once a week. During the winter even the ash was made use of by strewing it over the icy sidewalk And today, sixty years later, the industrialized world is gradually waking up and relearning the art of recycling in order to protect our forests and mineral resources.

In spite of everybody's hopes, the war had not come to an end. On September 27, 1940 Hitler signed a treaty of mutual support with Italy and Japan. The archives show that on July 21, 1940 he gave orders to *Generalfeldmarschall von Brauchitsch,* the chief in command of the army, to develop plans for the invasion of Russia. In December the date for the invasion was fixed for May 15, 1941. -- Ironically, Stalin trying to protect his eastern flank, signed also a non aggression treaty with Japan on April 13, 1941. -- However, things did not work out as planned. This time our Italian friends got in the way. Mussolini wanted to expand the Italian sphere of interest by conquering the Balkans. Unfortunately his troops did not succeed against the British who were supporting the Greeks. So, Hitler was obligated to help his ally. He sent German troops to Greece, which were really needed for the planned massive invasion of the Soviet Union. Consequently, the date for the invasion had to be postponed by two months to July 21, a date much to close to the onset of the Russian winter. This fateful decision led to the failure of the entire Russian campaign. Hitler with an unwarranted self-confidence repeated Napoleon's classical mistake of invading a country of such immense size and formidable winters.

Naturally, all these plans were secret, so that our family, and I presume the entire nation, was aghast when Hitler announced his *Barbarossa* plan (footnote 8) at noon on July 21, 1941 over the radio. As two years before, we heard again the great demagogue and orator: "My German citizens! The threat of the huge Russian Red Army has increased steadily during the last months. The Bolsheviks are ready to destroy our fatherland. Therefore, having no other choice but to preempt the Soviet aggressor, I have ordered the German Army to cross the Russian frontier as of   six o'clock this morning. We have to protect Germany against these red hordes. International communism is not going to rest until it reigns first over Germany and then over the entire world." The national anthem. End.

Hitler had two main reasons for the invasion. First, he absolutely hated the Communists based on his experience during the early years after the first world war, when the National Socialists and the Communists were both vying for dominance over Germany. -- The reader should remember that during the decade after the first world war storm troops of the Communists and of the National Socialists were fighting each other to the death in the streets of all major German cities. The national government was much too weak to do anything to stop the chaos. My mother told us many times of her experiences in Düsseldorf where the Communists, the National Socialists and other factions from the left and the right, were battling each other. They frequently wore uniforms and helmets, and used machine guns and canons left over from World War I. The civilians had to duck and stay out of the line of fire. Once when she and her friends were attending a dance, a band of Communists with red arm bands and rifles at the ready burst in and forced them out of the hall, all the time pelting them with insults like "bourgeois swine", etc. --

Second, as I have mentioned already, Hitler believed that his Germans needed more *Lebensraum* (living space) which they should obtain at the expense of the Polish and Russian peoples. He called the Slavic people *Untermenschen* (subhumans), who had to be governed by a superior race and had to support it as serfs and servants. I would not be surprised if plans had been already formulated enticing German settlers to go east by giving them free land and government support. After all, German settlements had already existed in Russia since the eighteenth century, when Catherine the Great (1729 to 1796) had invited settlers to colonize the land (footnote 9).

48

When my parents and Opa heard the news they were incensed and more than seriously worried. Although they had not been in favor of the war; they had accepted Hitler's reasoning at each escalation. But now for the first time Hitler's arguments for further war were no longer good enough. There was simply no compelling reason for an invasion of Russia that would be endorsed by everybody. Furthermore, all Germans had learned in school about Napoleon's ill fated invasion of Russia, which was the beginning of his downfall and the defeat of France by the European powers. However, whether you were incensed or worried or totally opposed, whatever the Führer said was done. Anybody who uttered concerns, let alone opposing views, in public had to suffer the consequences by losing his job, spending time in jail or concentration camp or worse. Dictators do not tolerate critique.

Again, as in the Poland and France, German *Panzer* and *Stukas* wore down the Soviet might. Huge pincer battles ensued, in which entire Russian armies were encircled and captured. In a few weeks millions of Russian soldiers became prisoners-of-war. The advance happened so fast and furiously that the German army reached Moscow in barely four months. And then it got stuck; supply lines were far too long, the Russian winter began, and the troops were exhausted. The advance came to a halt on October 6, 1941 twenty miles before Moscow. The delay of the *Barbarossa* campaign by two months had now formidable consequences. The army was not at all prepared for a winter war in driving snow and temperatures of -50 to -60° F. Neither the soldiers nor the vehicles could handle it. Thirty percent of 500,000 vehicles were beyond repair, and forty percent had to be refurbished. The lives of approximately 900,000 German soldiers were lost; one of them was Uncle Helmut, Aunt Mali's husband. Father Winter had been the best friend of Russia for centuries; and he still was.

The German population rallied around its freezing sons, brothers, and fathers. An enormous collection of warm clothing went on for weeks. We boys and girls carried and carted everything imaginable from apartments and houses and delivered the goods at collection points throughout the city. The heaps mounted from day to day; overcoats, especially fur coats, heavy socks and knitted caps, woolen underwear, fur lined boots, mittens and gloves filled halls after halls. We helped to

49

sort, pack, and ship it. This helped the German men at the front, but it did not affect the war. The predicted early victory did not materialize; instead a long drawn-out war of attrition set in. As Papa and I had begun during the military campaigns through Poland and France, we had stuck again little flags into the large Russian wall map in concert with the *Wehrmachts- berichte,* the daily military news. Those flags had moved briskly east in the beginning; now they stood still for the first time.

As the war raged in Russia, and I had just made my first experiences with gymnasium life, I suffered an accident that put me out of commission for two months. Each Saturday morning after school a few friends and I went to the city indoor swimming pool in town. We had recently invented a game, where you had to catch each other by racing around the pool with the condition that you could only cross the corners by diving into the water. The pool manager was not very fond of our game and us squealing boys, but he tolerated it until he sometimes lost his temper and threw us out of the pool hall. Then he gave us ten minutes to get dried and dressed until we had to present ourselves at the main door. It was during one of these abrupt exits that I slid on the tiled floor. With my bent knee I hit the bull nose tile of the bottom step of the staircase leading to the change rooms. My knee split open - what a nasty wound! The manager quickly applied a bandage and sent me to the next hospital. With Günter's support, I limped the two miles to the hospital where the doctor gave me a good scolding as he was stitching the wound together. Günter took my satchel home and told my parents about the mishap. Thus I was forgiven for arriving late for the Saturday dinner and still got my warmed-up pea soup. Everything went well until Sunday night, when the knee swelled and the fever started to climb. Next morning, with a fever over 102° F, my parents took me back to the hospital where the doctor opened up a very badly infected wound.

I was kept in the hospital because of the severe danger of blood poisoning; and I spent the next two months in the children's ward with the leg in a half cast and the wound washed twice a day. That was the only treatment available in 1941, for antibiotics did not yet exist. The survival of the leg depended entirely on avoiding movement, continuously cleaning the wound, and on my healthy constitution. Had there been penicillin nothing would have happened in the first place and I would have been up and running again in less than a week. Thanks to the dedication of the wonderful sisters I still have my leg, albeit with quite a scar. I was a patient in the Catholic Hospital -it was closest to the pool- where all the nurses were nuns and were called "sisters". They not only took excellent care of our bodily needs, but also would pray with us each morning and each evening. During many a night the sirens howled their fluctuating wail, and shortly thereafter the *Flak* started to bellow. Unfortunately, I was always the last kid to get into the basement shelter, because the sisters had to wait for an available gurney before they could take me down. In the meantime, through the window above my bed, I watched the exploding *Flak* grenades and the white fingers of the search lights in the sky. I was always scared and felt deserted. Finally one of the sisters would wheel in the gurney, heave me onto it, hurry through the corridor, pick up five or six bundled babies from the maternity ward, place them around me, and race with us to the elevator. In the basement I felt safe again. Nothing serious happened during those two months. Only once, a window was shattered and had to be replaced. Somebody from the family or my friend Günter brought my daily homework, so that I would not fall behind in class. What a happy boy I was, when the knee had finally healed and I could learn how to walk again. The leaves were already falling from the trees, when my parents took me home.

War kills Family and Friends

Our family, relatives, friends, and neighbors remained untouched by the war until 1941. However, that changed rapidly with the increasing air raids and the huge eastern war effort. The first bad news reached us when Uncle Karl Beerman, the husband of Papa's youngest sister Clara, telephoned on the morning of March 1, 1941. There had been an air raid on *Köln,* Cologne, during which Aunt Johanna (we called her Aunt "Hans"), who lived with the Beermans, had been killed. Aunt Clara, his wife (Aunt Hans' twin sister), was severely wounded. A bomb had fallen alongside the house, hit a balcony, got deflected, and fell through the light shaft directly into the basement where all inhabitants of the three story apartment

51

house had sought shelter. Uncle Karl, who was on leave as a major of the infantry, had remained in the apartment and did not get hurt. When he heard the bomb explosion and the screaming from the basement, he ran and almost fell down the staircase that no longer existed. When he finally reached the basement, he found most people dead including his sister-in-law. Aunt Clara, being terribly maimed, barely hung on to life. She died three days later. Papa was absolutely devastated. He took the next train to *Köln* where he found her still alive. We children were totally frightened; the air war had become reality. I believe that Papa never recuperated from this blow of losing his twin sisters. His worries about his own family mounted steadily; and I remember well how excited he got during every air raid. I believe that his weak heart developed its first "crack" in those days and ensuing months.

Because the government was very concerned about the demoralizing effect of these air raids on the civilian population, it made every effort to minimize any publicity. Therefore, Uncle Karl was not allowed to mention the real reason for the deaths of my aunts. It had to be disguised not to upset the general public. Instead, the obituary read as follows:

"Our dear sister, sister-in-law and aunt, Miss Johanna Jansen, passed away suddenly and unexpectedly on the first of March. Johanna Jansen had been 48 years old and had been decorated with the Medal for War Service 1914/18. She was a very good comrade. Today, my dear wife Mrs. Clara Beerman, was taken away from us after a short, serious illness at the age of 48 years. In the name of all grieving family members, Major Dr. Karl Beerman, *Köln* on the fourth of March 1941."

A few months later, Kurt Thomas, the son of my parents' best friends, was reported missing on the Russian front. Uncle and Aunt Thomas waited and hoped; but no news came of definite death or survival. They hoped for many years, even after the war, that he might return from Russian imprisonment, but all in vain. I have always thought that it was much worse for the family if a soldier was reported missing rather than dead. Parents, wives and children waited from year to year in a state of gnawing uncertainty, where hope came and went until it finally slowly vanished. The death notice, on the other hand, was a terrible blow in the beginning, but it was definite; and the certainty made it much more tolerable for the family than the indefinite wait.

52

Next we lost Uncle Helmut, the husband of Aunt Mali, my mother's sister. She had met him before the war in a seminary in *Ostpreussen* (East Prussia) where he was working as pastor. He then took over the parish of *Hochweiler* near *Militsch* in *Niederschlesien* (Lower Silesia) close to the Polish border. How proud was I of my new uncle who wore a smart lieutenant's uniform, for he had been already assigned to the army. Especially his dagger impressed me. It had a beautiful hilt that was much more ornate than my ordinary *Jungvolk Fahrtenmesser* (trekking knife). Aunt Mali's engagement was one of the last family gatherings before the war. Uncle Eugen, Mutti's brother, and Aunt Fanny came from *Düsseldorf*. Uncle Ernst, the youngest brother of the Family Krämer, came from *Gerresheim*, a *Düsseldorf* suburb, with Aunt Herta, and their three boys. Aunt Grete, Mutti's girlfriend, also arrived from *Düsseldorf*. Aunt Mali and Uncle Helmut were married later at his mother's in *Waldenburg* in *Schlesien* (Silesia), and they went on to live in *Hochweiler*. Uncle Helmut fell as army pastor in the Winter of 1941/42 shortly after the German advance got stuck before Moscow. Their marriage only lasted two years.

Two years later In the night of May 29, 1943 we lost eight close relatives of my mother. During a major air raid on *Wuppertal* 611 RAF bombers had dropped first explosive and then incendiary bombs on the borough of *Barmen*, thus creating a firestorm that destroyed the city center and let few people escape. Opa's brother Georg and two of Mutti's cousins and their children perished during that night.

The   air raids increased in frequency and intensity throughout 1942. According to British archives the first massive bombardment of a German city, *Köln* (Cologne), took place on May 31, 1942 . One thousand planes dropped their bombs primarily on the center of the city, essentially obliterating it. The increasing number of attacks forced our family more frequently into the basement shelter. Although Mülheim was rarely the target, we had alarms because the bombers overflew our town in search of the bigger cities of the *Ruhrgebiet* (Ruhr Basin), which was the center of the German heavy industry. Normally we would remain in the basement from the moment when the sirens imperiously howled their warning until the time of their all-clear droning at the end of the danger. However, when it was obvious that the action took place over *Essen, Oberhausen* or *Duisburg*, we were sometimes allowed to go outside and watch the spectacle. Thousands of *Flak* grenades exploded in the night sky like gigantic fireworks. The white beams of the searchlights danced their macabre ballet like long legged ghosts. When one of them caught a bomber it was immediately joined by others. Massive *Flak* explosions ensued, until the plane plummeted towards earth with a tail of fire. Frequently the planes would explode on the way down. Other times a plane escaped from the probing fingers into the clouds. To make this performance even more spectacular, frequently brilliant white flares on little parachutes -we called them "Christmas Trees"- descended slowly and illuminated the world below. To watch these fireworks from afar was one thing, but listening in the basement to the incessant bellowing of the *Flak* and the howling of the bombs, was quite another thing. By far the worst horror was listening to the fall of a screaming bomb and waiting for the impact. No matter how often it happened, I was always scared. People invariably said: "If you hear the bomb do not worry, it will hit elsewhere." True, but little consolation when you heard them hurtling downward with this earsplitting howl. If a bomb hit the ground in the neighborhood, the entire house shook. The British had recently developed a new type of bomb that could be timed to blow up above ground. We called it *Luftmine* (air mine). It generated a huge pressure wave that could push in walls and thus destroy houses close by and that busted windows and light structures over quite a radius. Since it was very difficult to get window panes repaired, my parents simply left the windows and doors open so that the pressure wave could pass through with minimal damage.

Opa never joined us in the basement. He had an absolute faith in God; and if Mutti urged him to come down when the air raid came closer he would always answer: "If I get harmed or killed then it was God's will." And with this he stayed in his room night after night or he would walk around the house to observe the sky and report back to the rest of the family what he had seen. Sometimes he climbed the steep ladder to the attic to make sure that everything was all right up there. Often he picked up incendiary bombs -eighteen inch long sticks with a hexagonal cross section of two to three inches diameter- and hurled them through the attic window into the garden where they could not do any harm. Thus he saved our house many times, especially at one occasion when one of those bombs crashed through the attic floor and landed in my parents' bedroom. My respect for Opa deepened with each bombing attack. That man was an absolutely fearless hero.

If an air raid lasted longer than two or three hours (I do not remember exactly), school was delayed by one hour the next day. On the way to school my classmates and I usually picked up fragments of *Flak* grenades or bombs. Everybody amassed quite a trove whose value steadily increased over the years. My collection comprised a few shoe boxes of high, medium, and low value. We traded all the time. Ignitors were most valuable; then came pieces of copper guide rings from *Flak* grenades, graded by length and quality of shape; followed by bomb fragments of an unusual shape or large size; small *flak* grenade and bomb pieces were at the bottom of the scale. One could trade several beautiful bomb fragments for a number of guide ring pieces or an ignitor, and so forth. Once I found a guide ring that was almost complete. Splendid ! As the air war became more intense, the British often dropped canisters filled with liquid phosphorous that spread out and burned on impact. When we boys discovered these black spots on the pavement after an air raid we rubbed our shoe soles in them so that we could produce flames in the school yard by striking the ground hard. Naturally we thought this new game was great, however not so our teachers and parents. A few years ago, when I mentioned to a British acquaintance of my age how we had collected the debris, he grinned and confided to me how they had done exactly the same thing as boys. He added that their most highly valued prize was a little parachute that supported the magnesium flares as they drifted towards earth. I had never found one.

Papa worked as a civil servant for the German equivalent of our Social Security Administration, where he held the position of an inspector. Already before the turn of the century, Bismarck had created the *Allgemeine Deutsche Altersversicherung* (General German Retirement Insurance), which had been obligatory for every German ever since. It functioned in the following way: Each employer had to make contributions to the Retirement Insurance of his employees by buying stamps of certain values from the government and handing them out with the weekly pay envelope. The employee pasted them into booklets that he collected and maintained during his working years. When he retired at the official retirement age with 65 he presented his booklets to the responsible government in exchange for a pension of a certain value. An easy system that depended, however, on the honesty of the employer and on the worker's understanding of its workings. My father's job was to ensure through random checks that the companies, stores and other small businesses abided by the law. His base was an office in our house where he worked with a few assistants. Every Thursday, people would sit in the waiting room to present their questions and grievances to my father. Several times a week he visited employers in the region and checked their books. He told us often how an employer tried to give him a little present here and there. Without success, Prussian civil servants could not be bribed.

As the younger inspectors joined the army the older men had to take over their duties. My father, who was then fifty five years old, had to extend his base over the entire *Niederrhein* (Lower Rhine) region. As the job became ever more demanding, the indications of a heart problem increased. No more smoking, - my father had been a heavy cigarette smoker like most men of his generation- no more coffee, no extreme physical exertions. Our family doctor Tünsmeyer checked him up more frequently and proposed a reduction of his work load. Not possible in the middle of the war. He finally ordered a hospital stay of several weeks for observation and complete rest. Mutti made a plan to take Papa and us to a quiet place in the country as soon as he left the hospital. The suitcases were packed for a departure on the day after his discharge. Unfortunately, Papa did not stay in the hospital until the train would leave. Instead, he came home. Fate wanted it that there had to be an unusually intensive air raid during that night. The *Flak* made its usual racket; but then bombs began to fall close by with their terrible howling and impacts that made the house shake repeatedly in its foundations. Suddenly, Papa made a movement with his head as if he wanted to say something and then he lay there very still. Scared and full of fright we forgot the bombs and worried about Papa. Mutti shouted for Opa who was upstairs as usual. He came rushing down, listened for Papa's breathing, looked at his eyes, and broke the terrible news: "Adolf is no longer alive." Mutti raced up the stairs to call Dr. Tünsmeyer, who arrived shortly after the end of the air raid. As we children sat there stunned and terrified, he examined my father and confirmed his death, caused by a massive heart attack. Mutti sent us all to bed and stayed with Papa in the basement the rest of the night.

It was only during the next day when I began to realize that in the future my father would no longer be with us. I cried and cried, when the men from the funeral home carried him from the basement into the entrance hall and laid him into his coffin. One last look at his peaceful face, and the lid was closed. On the day of the funeral we were visited by friends, acquaintances and neighbors; many relatives arrived by bus and train; our home was overflowing. Mutti had rented several streetcars that took us all to the crematorium in *Essen*. A large throng filled the auditorium, where friends, colleagues, and party members gave eulogies. I was awed by all the people in black or military or party uniforms, by the orators, the mass of flowers, and the flags on both sides of the podium. When the last words of praise had died down, the coffin rolled slowly through a door in the back of the stage. Papa had left us for good. Marlis was thirteen, I eleven, Sigrid five and Heidi three years old; Mutti was forty three. Luck had it, that there was no air raid during that day, so all the guests returned safely to our home. There everybody talked, ate, and drank. Sometimes I heard somebody even laugh when one of Mutti's cousins told a funny story. That felt good. In the evening the house emptied, and only Mutti's sister Tante Mali and her best girlfriend Tante Grete stayed behind. Now both sisters had lost their husbands.

On the next day we held a family council to plan our near future. The planned vacations in the Harz Mountains were canceled; instead we were going to stay with relatives in the country. Opa, Marlis and I would visit our Grand Uncle Willy in *Bergneustadt;* and Mutti together with the "Little Ones", Sigrid and Heidi, would visit her Uncle Karl in *Altenhundem*. With the suitcases already packed we could leave immediately, away from nights in the basement with sirens, Flak and bombers. The month in *Bergneustadt* on the farm of Grand Uncle and Aunt Schneider and their daughters -- the sons and husbands were all at the front -- became an unforgettable time. Marlis and I helped in the house, the garden, and the fields. We got excited when we were told to herd the cows which we tried to milk without success. We ran and hiked through meadows and forests or strolled through the little town. Once we took the train to visit the rest of our family in *Altenhundem*. There was only one event that disturbed this quiet idyll. During the first night when I slept in the same room with my grandfather, I was awakened from this noise coming from Opa's bed. It swelled to a crescendo, then it abated, then it started all over again. I was scared. What on earth was going on? Was Opa very ill, or was he dying? Out of desperation I woke him up and learned that he had been snoring. How was I to know, who had never heard anybody snore.

After our return, I entered my second year in the *Gymnasium*, the *Quinta*. There, I began to learn the second foreign language in addition to English. Dr. Hahn, who taught us already history, instructed us now also in Latin, the language that I enjoyed more and more as I got older. We also moved into the next classroom down the corridor. *Jungvolk* meetings on Wednesday and Saturday afternoons continued, so did playing with the neighborhood kids in the street. The air alarms did not abate; on the contrary, they happened now occasionally also during the day. One day Mutti sat me down at the living room table and told me that from now on I had to take on some of Papa's duties. She explained that in the future she would discuss all the plans for the family with me, and we would make all the financial decisions together. Suddenly, with my eleven and a half years, I had been elevated to co-head of the household. This gave me quite a scare, but it made me also very proud. From that day on Mutti and I discussed all important issues and made the necessary decisions. As the only son, I was drawn into her confidence, although I was not the oldest child; and I believe that I never disappointed her.

Since money matters were frequently the issue, I would like to say a few words about the finances of our family. Together Papa and Mutti made all the yearly plans, balancing income with expenditures and savings. He was responsible for all major expenses, paying the bills, making the savings deposits, and keeping a ledger in his small, regular hand writing. She received a monthly allowance for the household that took care of food, clothing, utilities, etc. I remember that she frequently managed to generate a surplus that she saved for special occasions. Being very frugal and meticulous she entered every expenditure down to the *Pfennig,* the cent, in her household book. If one of us children was sent to *Buchmuller's* grocery store at the *Dimbeck* corner to buy a few items, we had to return with the exact change. My mother knew the price of everything in the store by heart. In case the numbers did not add up, which meant that we had not watched carefully enough, we had to go back to the store and either return the amount we owed or, worse yet, ask for the pennies -and they were usually just pennies- the store owed. I hated this humiliation like the plague, but in these matters our mother knew no mercy.

After Papa's death, Opa and I continued to stick little flags into the big map of Russia, following the news of the battles. In the North the flags had not moved since the previous winter of 1941/42. However, they kept moving towards the South East, the Caucasus with all its oil fields. Hitler needed oil badly in order to support his motorized advances. He also wanted to cut off Stalin's access to these oil fields. The German oil reserves had fallen to 800,000 tons, although the chemical industry at the *Rhein* and *Saale* rivers had increased the production of synthetic fuels (Footnote 10) from 4 million to 6 million tons. Yet the production was not keeping pace with the growing need to fuel the expanding war. Getting to the oil fields became a must.

During the same year General Rommel fought his *Panzer* battles in the desert of North Africa carrying out Hitler's and Mussolini's plans to gain control over the Mediterranean Sea and above all the Suez Canal. I was astounded when I found in the historic archives that Mussolini's grandiose plans encompassed the whole of Africa and extended all the way to India; quite an ambition. In the beginning, Rommel's *Afrikakorps* had been very successful until he overextended his supply lines, and the equipment suffered badly from the harsh climate. He was beaten by General Montgomery at El Alamein on October 24, 1942. A lengthy retreat followed until Montgomery reached Tripoli in January 1943. The *Afrikakorps* surrendered in May. To add to the calamity, the United States Armed Forces had landed in Algeria and had met up with the British Forces.

The ultimate disaster befell Germany, when it got dragged into the war with the United States, after Japan declared war on the US only hours after Pearl Harbor. Japan, Italy, and Germany had entered into a treaty on September 27, 1940 that automatically committed each partner to support the others in case of war. Without doubt, war with America became the downfall, because nobody could match the industrial might of the US. Immediately after the declaration of war the Americans increased their support of Britain; and much more war materiel reached the island in spite of the continuing buildup of the German *U-Boot* fleet. The air war intensified too, because the American planes had joined the British planes in the bombardment of German war installations, industry, cities, and railroads. To top it all off, the USA had made a treaty with the Soviet Union to supply it with war materiel via Murmansk and Archangel.

Seven Months in Camp

As the bombing raids mounted in 1942 and 1943 the school authorities started a campaign to send pupils from the threatened areas, i.e. big cities and industrial centers, to places in the countryside. A new administrative department was created with the name of *Kinderlandverschickung* or *KLV,* meaning "sending children to the country". It was interesting for me when my friend Derek Davis, with whom we used to ski in Durango, told Brigit and me that he and his English classmates were also sent to the country when the air raids on London got worse. However, he lived with a farmer's family, where he went to school and helped on the farm. The only difference between their and our system was that they were sent as individuals and we as a whole school.

The *Langemarck Schule* decided in the spring of 1943 to send pupils from the first three grades to the KLV, if their parents were interested. After our family had agreed that I should go, I signed up together with another fifty five boys. A number of teachers were assigned to us, and the big trip into the unknown began. At the beginning of May we boarded the train to *Katzenelnbogen* in the *Taunus* Mountains near *Limburg* at the river *Lahn.* Dressed in our yellow-black uniforms, we carried our suitcases, rucksacks, and school satchels. We were all very excited and sang and played on the way through the beautiful *Rhein* valley. This was my first and definitely not my last trip through that lovely country side. -- Brigit and I are still enjoying the train ride up and down the *Rhein* when we travel between *Frankfurt* airport and *Mülheim* during visits to my sister. -- After a train change in *Koblenz* at the confluence of the *Rhein* and *Mosel* we got off the train in *Diez* on the *Lahn* from where we marched the rest on foot. When we arrived shortly before sunset in the tiny town of *Katzenelnbogen* and saw this really old castle looming above us, our excitement knew no bounds. We were going to be quartered in this fairy tale castle towering way above the town! It was a real medieval castle with high walls arising from the steep rock formation, a steep access road paved with cobblestones, an enormously thick wooden gate with steel reinforcements, and a real drawbridge. The walls of the main hall measured five feet in thickness. I liked to sit or lie in the deep window recesses to look over town and country. When the windows were open we would throw little paper zeppelins and air planes out of the window and watch how the wind carried them up and away until they became tiny specks in the sky. I could not have imagined anything more thrilling and romantic than the castle of *Katzenelnbogen*. That peculiar name, meaning cat's elbow, belonged originally to the count who owned the land and the village and had built the castle centuries ago.

The three grades, Sexta, Quinta, and Quarta were distributed over three bedrooms. We, the Quinta, moved into a room with sixteen bunk beds of which I picked a lower bed in the middle of the room. After we had stacked and hung our clothes in lockers in the corridor, we took our first supper in the big hall, which also served as the main classroom. Before each meal, we hold hands, somebody recited a poem or a saying, and afterwards everybody joined in the chorus: "Good appetite". After dinner we helped clear the tables; and the dishwashing team disappeared into the kitchen. We pupils had been organized into rotating teams to help the kitchen staff prepare the meals, set and clear the tables, and wash the dishes. The principal teacher introduced the camp leader who would be in charge of our lives after school. Oddly, I neither recall his name nor the names of most of our teachers. However, I do remember Dr. Elsässer who was going to play a role later in my KLV life. "Mucki" (his nickname) was a strict but just teacher and he liked to hike with us through the fields and woods. He smoked a pipe constantly, but he never had enough tobacco because of the rationing. We were impressed to watch how he filled his pipe occasionally with dry leaves picked from the bushes. The emanating odors were something else; but apparently that did not disturb him as long as he could smoke his pipe. The faculty consisted of a principal and six teachers; the staff was made up of the camp leader, the head housekeeper and her helpers, the cook, and the nurse. They all took care of our minds, souls, and bodies apparently well enough that homesickness was rare.

The camp leader woke us up at 6:30 a.m. and swiftly pulled your blanket if you did not jump out of bed right away. After we had washed ourselves, brushed our teeth, made the beds, and cleaned the room he came back for room inspection. All the beds had to be made in exactly the same way. If a bed did not pass his inspection it was pulled apart and the delinquent had to remake it properly in a few minutes. Occasionally, he inspected the entire room and if he found only one speck of dust under a bed, the boy who was on cleaning duty was already under the bed and had removed it before you could count to three. At 7:15 a.m. we had to stand in formation for the morning inspection that took place in the gorgeous old castle yard with its cobblestones, ancient walls and trees. Two boys raised the flag and somebody recited or read the motto of the day. After breakfast, lessons were held till one o'clock, followed by dinner. The distribution of the mail from home after dinner was always the highlight of the day. If I could manage I sneaked upstairs to our bedroom, where I could read and reread in peace my letter from Mutti and my sisters. When a boy received a package from home with a cake or sweets, he had to share its contents with his room mates. That could be tough for the recipient, but was considered fair by the management, because some boys seldom or never received a package. After we had done our homework in the main hall under the supervision of a teacher we either had time off or our camp leader would take over. We hiked through the nearby forests or over the dirt roads between the fields. Often we practiced athletics on the town's soccer field. Occasionally our camp leader conducted a clothing inspection when we came back to the castle. He usually gave us fifteen minutes for cleaning up before the inspection. Our uniforms had to be in top shape. Woe, if anything was still dirty, a button loose or missing, or the shoes not shiny. Those deficiencies had to be remedied immediately.

Regarding cleanliness and order, you quickly learned their meaning, unless your parents had hammered those virtues into you already during your younger years. Naturally, our lockers in the corridor had to be in perfect order, too. The shirts, underwear, pants, and sweaters had to be folded to exactly the same width so that the stacks had precise vertical corners. During an inspection, our camp leader took only one brief look at a locker, as the owner was waiting with bated breath for the verdict. Sometimes only a minor correction was required, occasionally a complete remake. One of my classmates, Hellmut Kemper, was a bit of a free spirit and the word "order" had not yet made it into his vocabulary. During one such inspection the camp leader took only one look into his locker, and shirts, pants, underwear, and handkerchiefs flew out in one swoop and landed in small heaps on the floor. Everybody chuckled, because Hellmut always talked big and had the biggest mess everywhere. With a very red face he spent the next twenty minutes bringing his locker into the prescribed shape. Little experiences like this one made us teenagers learn in a hurry what mothers had often not managed to achieve in years.

Some evenings were reserved for the mending of our clothes. The nurse and the head housekeeper taught us to darn socks, sew on buttons, and fix tears in shirts or pants. They made the rounds during our mending hour, being very helpful in their friendly ways. It was then that I learned many tricks that helped me often later in life. Frequently, we had an hour or two of free time that we spent writing letters, reading, or playing games. I learned to play chess and *Skat,* a kind of bridge for three people, that were played at every opportunity, and, as I found out after the war, were played by all the boys in every KLV camp. I enjoyed *Skat* with the accompanying camaraderie; but I really liked chess because of its intricate forward looking planning. Surprisingly I never played these or other games again during my life except for some social occasions. We had probably overdone it, and other matters became more important in later years.

Once, I managed involuntarily to become a patient in our little infirmary. Two friends and I were returning from the athletic fields when we could not resist an open barn door. We sneaked quickly into the barn, mounted a ladder to the hayloft, and tumbled around in the hay. What an incredible thrill! Unfortunately we had overlooked the fact that there are farmers where there are barns. Suddenly the farmer loomed in the doorway and threatened to report us to our principal. To avoid humiliation and punishment we jumped out of the upstairs window before the farmer could apprehend us. I did not land right and sprained an ankle, yet managed to escape with my comrades in the last minute. I barely made it to the castle, and after the ankle had swollen badly and turned red and blue I reported to the infirmary. Our friendly nurse treated the swelling with aluminum acetate and ordered bed rest for a few days which I thoroughly enjoyed.

Besides soccer, handball, running, and jumping we had to learn how to box. I believe that it was our camp leader's favorite sport. He and many of the older boys liked it, but I and some younger boys hated it. First those stupid gloves were much too large and heavy, secondly I was always totally exhausted after a match, and thirdly I absolutely disliked any sort of contact sport and still abhor it today. Therefore my boxing career was of the shortest duration. As much as I loathed boxing I definitely enjoyed target shooting. It probably tickled my interest in mechanical and technical things. It became a challenge to eye the target over the front and rear sights and to make corrections for ballistics and wind for longer distances. We learned to shoot lying down, kneeling, and standing up with or without support. My target score was up there with the best. We were also trained in disassembling, cleaning, oiling and reassembling the rifle locks. -- It may sound peculiar that I dwell on this shooting experience, because in this country practically every boy learns how to shoot at an early age, and often possesses his own BB gun. But in a country like Germany almost nobody had a rifle or knew how to shoot. Hunting had been the privilege of the aristocracy since the middle ages. When I was young, big landowners and their friends or business partners hunted in their own forests, and poachers were severely punished. My classmate, Lothar Buchloh, was the only boy I knew who would occasionally accompany his rich uncle on a hunt. Not having grown up with it, I never picked up hunting or, for that matter, fishing in all these years that I have lived in this country. The only fishermen whom I remembered were old men sitting on little stools along the *Ruhr* and dangling their worms for hours in the river. The only thing that I ever saw them catch were tiny fish that were definitely not worth eating. Moreover, the *Ruhr* was probably the most polluted river in all of Germany in those years, which was not a positive recommendation for eating its fish. Today, however, after decades of successful anti pollution efforts the river is clean, and the old men on their little stools catch bigger fish that can actually be eaten. --

Many times our camp leader took us into the countryside

where he taught us to find our way with the help of map and compass. We learned to understand topography, judge distances, and find the points of the compass by day and night. We became acquainted with the finer points of map design including symbols like a single farmhouse, a tall chimney, a salient tree, or anything that helped the orientation. We could translate the elevation contour lines into real topography, differentiate between paths and roads of different quality, etc. We learned how to judge distances by estimating with an outstretched arm the separation between the images of our thumb as it jumped from right to left when one closed right and left eye in succession. We also practiced climbing tall trees in a forest in order to establish line of sight with a distant landmark that allowed us to align the map with the help of the compass. In day time we found the points of the compass with the help of the sun's position and a watch, or by moss growth on the prevailing weather side of a tree. During the night, we oriented ourselves easily, having learned how the constellations moved across the night sky throughout the year. Unfortunately, cloudy nights could spoil the game. I enjoyed these exercises tremendously, especially when they enabled me to find a rendezvous spot somewhere in the countryside. In retrospect there is no question that this was all part of pre-military training; but for us boys it was great fun.

During the warm summer months, we spent a lot of time in a swimming pool that was located in a meadow near town. There I learned to dive from the high dive and I earned my swimming certificate that consisted of rescuing a person, retrieving a heavy rock from the bottom, and swimming 45 minutes without interruption. The pool was very nice except for one horror. Since it had only one ladder we mostly slid down the sides to get into the water. These slanted (45°) concrete walls were covered with algae and slimy leeches which sucked themselves to the walls. Well, not everything is perfect.

The big blow came on June 23, 1943. Our principal told us before the midday dinner that a major air raid had hit *Mülheim* the night before. The center of the city and the industrial areas were devastated. He would give us more news as soon as he could find out more details. First there was a deadly silence in the hall, and one could have heard the proverbial needle drop. Then everybody talked and shouted simultaneously: "Is my family still alive? Is our house or apartment destroyed? Which borough has been hit the hardest? Why *Mülheim* that had been spared for so long?" The suspense lasted for several days until our principal obtained better news and the first boys received letters from home. Luckily nobody's relatives or friends got killed, but many homes and apartments were destroyed or severely damaged. The city streets were full of rubble, the railroad stations had disappeared, and Thyssen, Mannesmann, Siemens, and AEG had suffered badly. The suburbs were mostly intact. -- I read recently in the British archives that 499 British bombers had participated in the raid, and had dropped 500 tons of bombs. Only 35 air planes were shot down, and 202 civilians perished. -- Finally, the long awaited letter from Mutti arrived: "Do not worry, nothing happened to us, the house has suffered only some damages to roof and walls. I decided for us to leave town and not to wait for the next bombardment. The girls, Opa, and I are taking the train to my Uncle Karl in *Altenhundem.*" There it was, the enemy had finally found Mülheim. For three years people had recited a little ditty: "*Mülheim im Loch, sie finden es doch* (Mülheim in the hole, they will find it in the end)." And now unfortunately this had become true.

    -- Little did we know at the time how the American and British Air Forces had divided the pie. During the Casablanca conference in January 1943 Churchill and Roosevelt had come to an agreement about the air war. The RAF would concentrate on massive night attacks on German cities, and the USAF would bombard strategically important industries and railroad centers during the day. The "Battle of the *Ruhr*" had been planned for the period of March through July 1943. The RAF flew 18,000 sorties and dropped a total of 58,000 tons of bombs. *Essen* alone suffered eight massive attacks between March and April, while one single attack took care of Mülheim. --

    One week later I received another letter from Mutti: "I do not want to continue to risk our lives every night in Mülheim. Therefore, I have decided to move the family to *Waldenburg* in *Schlesien.*" The province of Schlesien (Silesia), was after *Ostpreussen* (East Prussia) the easternmost province of Germany. Because of its location the western bombers could not reach it, and thus it remained untouched during the entire war. Uncle Helmut's mother had died recently in *Waldenburg* and left a furnished apartment behind. When Aunt Mali heard that Mutti wanted to get as far away from the *Ruhrgebiet* as possible, she rented the apartment immediately for Mutti and the girls. Miraculously, the authorities allowed our family to move in, even though they were not local residents, not a small feat, for apartments were unbelievably scarce.

Although the rest of our family had moved to the East, I remained in the KLV camp, where life continued as usual. The routine of that everyday life was dramatically interrupted one day by an unusual strike. We certainly could not complain about our food in the castle. It was plentiful, varied, and nutritious. Of course, some boys did grumble here and there; but altogether we liked it. This state of affairs was disturbed, when the frequency of one disagreeable dish increased steadily: *Pellkartoffeln* (potatoes boiled in their skin) with mushroom sauce. And again, *Pellkartoffeln* with mushroom sauce. We complained mildly, without success. The same disgusting sauce continued to appear on the table. One day the older boys from the *Quarta* decided to tackle this problem with a hunger strike. They threatened us younger boys from the *Quinta* and *Sexta* with terrible reprisals if we did not cooperate. So during one fateful dinner, nobody touched the *Pellkartoffeln,* and we stared with hungry eyes at the steaming serving bowls and our empty plates. When the teachers at the head table had finished their meals and saw the full serving dishes on our tables, all hell broke loose. The Speaker of the *Quarta* explained that we simply would no longer eat this awful food, and that was it. Well! We were dismissed immediately to do our homework; and then our camp leader announced an afternoon march. Did we ever suffer! Marching in formation, running in formation through thick and thin, mostly through dirt, crawling through wet meadows, jumping up, standing to attention, falling into puddles of mud, running our little lungs out. After a few hours we marched back to the castle, shaking with exhaustion, soiled, and, above all, indescribably hungry. Having arrived in the courtyard, we got half an hour to clean up, followed by a thorough inspection by camp leader and principal. Whose uniform was found wanting, was ordered to do a more thorough cleaning job. The rest of us trudged off for supper in the great hall. What did we expect? Surely not anything other than *Pellkartoffeln* with the same old disgusting mushroom sauce warmed up. Without one word everybody dug into the food and swallowed it whole. The glorious strike had ended in a whimper. Nobody mentioned it again; however, *Pellkartoffeln* and mushroom sauce gradually disappeared from the menu.

Far from the peaceful world in our dream castle, the luck of war had definitely turned against our country. The consequences of the American entry into the war, the colossal defeat at Stalingrad, where an entire army under *Feldmarschall* Paulus surrendered on February 2, 1943, and the end of Rommel's North Africa campaign were clear signs that offense had turned into defense. And, after the *Pellkartoffel* strike was over, on July 9 our principal announced even worse news: "American troops have landed on Sicily. The Italian and German troops are defending the island heroically; and the Führer left no doubt that they would throw the enemy back into the sea." Although I was still putting my trust in the productions of the propaganda machinery, I started to develop an uneasy feeling way inside.

When the harvest began, anybody whose academic standing was good could volunteer to help on a farm. I liked the idea and reported right away to the principal; yes, I could work for a farmer. Promptly, a classmate and I were introduced to a farmer whose farm house was not far from the castle. The first day on the farm began at six o'clock with cutting grass and clover. The farmer mowed with his scythe, and we boys raked the fodder and stowed it on the small horse drawn wagon. Back at the farm, we helped feeding the animals, then had breakfast with the farmer's family and the maids. All the young men were fighting in the East and the South. Afterwards, everybody boarded the large wagon that was drawn by a pair of big horses and took us to one of the fields outside the village. Rye, wheat and oat were the first crops of the harvesting season. The farmer hitched the horses to the mowing machine and cut wide swaths into the grain stalks. His wife, the maids, and we boys collected the bundled sheaves and set them up in small groups. Group after group, row after row. At noon, I sank dead tired into the shade of a tree where we ate our lunch. A short rest, followed by a long afternoon's work. At the end, my classmate and I climbed slowly on the wagon and were taken back to the farm house, exhausted but full of accomplishment. I always liked the trip home the best; the hot sun was sinking, a cool breeze sprang up, and supper was beckoning. However, the stables and pens had to be cleaned first, and cows, horses, and pigs had to be fed and watered before it was our turn. Afterwards, when everybody had assembled around the huge table in the dining room, the farmer's wife and a maid brought soup, steaming potatoes or dumplings, meat, and vegetables from the kitchen. I was quite surprised when they laid down the silverware but no plates. Instead of plates there were plate-like depressions that had been carved into the thick tabletop in front of each chair. The soup and afterwards the rest of the meal was ladled into these "plates". What a very practical custom! After dinner the maid simply scrubbed the table, which was then ready for the next meal. The food was delicious, and I ate my fill. Barely returned to the castle, I fell into my bed into a deep, deep sleep.

The most exciting job for us novices was the threshing in the fall. *Katzenelnbogen* owned a community threshing machine that was wheeled from farmhouse to farmhouse during the threshing weeks. On the evening before the great day, the thresh master showed up with his machine and directed all the preparations. Threshing day itself began at five o'clock. I was stationed way up in the loft of the barn from where I had to throw down the dry bundles so that the next person could pick them up and feed them into the machine that threshed them with a lot of clattering and dust. Up there I almost died from the heat, noise, and dust. Clatter, clatter, clatter, all day long. I was very happy when the last bundle had been swallowed by that infernal machine. After cleaning the stables and feeding the animals with our last bit of energy, my classmate and I stumbled into the dining room where all the participants had assembled around the large table. Talk and laughter filled the room, because everybody was happy that the grueling job was finished and that the grain was ready for the flour mill. The threshing day was definitely the most exhausting day of my farming career. Our last job that fall was the potato harvest with its long days in the field. The farmer walked slowly behind horse and plow, pushing the plowshare deep into the soil in order to bring up every last potato, furrow after furrow. His wife, the maids, and we boys followed the plow bent to the ground and collected the potatoes in baskets. Each basket was emptied into gunny sacks that, by evening, stood in long rows in the empty field. This job was literally back breaking; and every night I knew exactly how much I had done. At the end, the sacks were loaded onto the wagon, and the horses took potato sacks and the tired heroes back to the village.

My farm work ended with a bit of sadness, because I had really enjoyed the outdoors and being able to help in field and yard in spite of moments of exhaustion. It was hard to say good-bye to the farmer's family who had been "my" family for many memorable weeks. It was difficult to return to my classmates and the daily routine of the castle. I also learned to my dismay that new plans had been made for our school during my absence. The government had decided, that time had come to close all schools without exception in all major cities that were exposed to ever increasing air bombardments. Every child had to be evacuated. All schools from areas like the *Ruhrgebiet* and big cities like *Hamburg, Berlin, Köln, Frankfurt* or *München* were moved into KLV camps in areas that were considered to be safe from air attacks. Our other classmates from the *Langemarck Schule* had already been moved to *Lazne Bielorad* near *Jicin* in northern Czechoslovakia, which had become in 1938 the *Reichsprotektorat Böhmen und Mähren* (the German Protectorate Bohemia and Moravia). Since *Katzenelnbogen* was no longer considered safe because of its proximity to *Mainz* and *Frankfurt*, we were to join the rest of the school in *Bielorad*. At the beginning of October we packed our suitcases, rucksacks, and satchels and took leave from our dream castle and the extraordinary time that we had lived within its enormous old walls. I could not shake the melancholy feelings as I marched with fifty-five other boys to *Diez* from where the train rolled east towards a somewhat uncertain future. - Brigit and I visited *Katzeln-bogen* fifty years later. The medieval castle still towered above the sleepy little town. It had been converted into a hotel where we spent the night in one of the upper rooms. Was it perhaps the same room where I had lived with my Quinta for one long summer? The window sills in the dining room were still five feet deep and just as impressive as then -.

The first stop after a long train journey was Prague where the whole crew was lodged in a splendid hotel for a week. Another impressive event! None of us had ever stayed in such a large, elegant hotel that even featured a swimming pool in the basement. We spent most of our time playing cards or chess, writing letters home, reading, or swimming. Maybe the teachers organized some classes; I have no clear recollection. Because I knew somehow that Prague was a beautiful historic city, I wanted to visit its famous sites. After I had talked my friend Günter into joining me, we ventured outside. We left our uniforms behind and wore civilian clothes after a consultation with our principal who knew better. For several days we strolled through the old town admiring the magnificent buildings, churches, and squares. We spent hours watching the astronomical clock on the old town hall with its complicated calendar that included sun and moon phases. We were fascinated by the beautifully colored figurines: Death on one side of the clock inverted the hourglass every hour. Kings, dukes, and bishops appeared one after the other in a window above the clock during the ringing of the hourly bells, each stopping and turning to the onlooker for a brief moment. We marveled at the statues of saints and heroes when we crossed the *Vlatava (Moldau)* on the Charles Bridge; and ultimately we found our way to the *Hradçany Castle*, the huge fortress on top of the hill overlooking the ancient city. As we visited the *Hradçany's* churches, palaces, and fortifications we came across an old tourist guide who wanted to show us two boys something very special. With a huge rusty old key he let us into the treasure chamber that contained the crown jewels. Entering the vault we were absolutely stunned. We had heard of such treasures only in fairy tales. But here they were: Golden bracelets and necklaces studded with diamonds, pearls and other precious stones, gleaming and glittering crowns, tiaras and diadems, gorgeous jewels of any kind, formidable swords and daggers adorned with carvings and colorful semiprecious stones. Günter and I, who had never seen anything like this before, were utterly speechless and listened to every word our guide told us. Although I do not remember the provenance and age of all those treasurers, it was an unforgettable experience. How lucky we were! The old man, who explained the history of each jewel in great detail, had probably been touched by two young boys exploring the formidable *Hradçany Castle* on their own. -When Brigit and I revisited this wonderful city in 2000 and wanted to visit the same treasure chamber, tourists were no longer allowed in the vault. Too many onlookers and too much resulting damage-. In the middle of this terrible war, Prague became a lasting, lifelong memory. Unfortunately, these fabulous days were gone too soon. Also, unfortunately for them, most of my classmates had wasted this week with games or doing nothing, enclosed in the womb of the hotel. Soon our principal announced the departure, and again a train took us further east.

The journey ended in *Lazne Bielorad,* where the rest of our school had lived in a beautiful old hotel since the big June attack on Mülheim. It was nice to see our other classmates again, with whom we were going to share our lives from now on. My room was comfortable with a high ceiling, a french door with a balcony, and only eight bunk beds; however, the mattresses had been replaced by straw bags which were not easy to get used to. *Lazne* (spa) *Bielorad* was a small sleepy resort town in the district of *Jicin.* Three big resort hotels were located at the nicer end of town, surrounded by parks, lakes, and forests. Normally they would be filled with well-to-do guests who were "taking the waters", as people used to say. Now the German government had confiscated them for the preservation of the German youth. The pupils of the *Langemarck Schule* were housed in an attractive three story building from the turn of the century with a beautiful lobby, big dining hall, wide corridors, and high ceilings. The daily routine followed the same schedule as in *Katzenelnbogen,* except we were now about 150 pupils with a correspondingly larger teaching faculty. Classes took place in the hotel and in a small school near the center of town. I can still see the coal fired stove in our classroom in that school that was lit every morning by the Czech custodian.

Sometimes I went with a few boys to the local bakery to buy some bread which the Czechs called "chleba". That bread provided extra nourishment, because here we were hungrier than in our previous KLV camp. Since there was less food in this camp, we watched with eagle's eyes that everybody got the same share. When we received our two slices of bread with margarine and jam for breakfast, the heels were always in great demand, because they were usually a bit larger than the slices. Therefore they were apportioned in a strict cycle around the table. Dishwashing duty had the enormous advantage that occasionally an extra piece of bread or cup of soup could be obtained from the nice kitchen ladies. We named the owner and chief physician of the hotel "Stalin", because of his round face, bushy eyebrows, and thick black mustache. Rumor had it, that he supplied the villagers with part of our food. We were also afraid of him when he checked for tuberculosis or administered vaccines against one or the other disease. Most likely these ideas and

72

fears sprang from our vivid imagination, and "Stalin" was a nice man who in reality liked us boys. Unfortunately, we could neither understand him nor the personnel in spite of a number of Czech words that we had picked up. I forgot them all except for "chleba". To this day, one unbelievable event remains before my eyes. It was a Sunday afternoon, and we eight roommates were bored out of our minds. As usual, we played *Skat* or chess, read, wrote letters, or darned socks. Suddenly, Hellmut had the glorious idea of lighting a match fire. Excitedly we collected all the matches that we could find and built an artful match tower in the middle of the table. (I wonder from where we got all these matches.) This was going to be an experiment with the objective of finding out how high and how long the flame would burn. One of us was selected through a drawing of matches, of course, to light the match tower. Wow, I had never seen such a tall and beautiful flame. As we were silently watching the rapid growth of the flame and just when it reached the ceiling, the door opened and in came one of the house maids. Maybe she had a seventh sense. Before we could say pooh, she ran down the corridor screaming at the top of her lungs all the way. Guilty as never before, we extinguished the fire, removed remaining wood pieces and ashes, opened the windows, and pursued our previous activities as if nothing had ever happened. Too late, the stupid fire had burned a shallow hole into this beautiful oak table of the last century. The door flew open and in rushed our principal followed closely by "Stalin". The ensuing thunder left little to our imagination, and the punishment for us eight experimenters was so devastating and humiliating that any thought of heroism disappeared in a hurry. However, as the news of our experiment spread rapidly through the hotel, we became instantly the heroes of the day and maybe of the month.

As we continued our daily school lessons, performed athletics, hiked through the woods with our new camp leader singing and learning more songs and receiving more pre military training, Germany started losing the war in the East, in the air, and in Italy. In spite of the propaganda machine running at full speed, even the most optimistic war reports could no longer hide the fact that the German army had been moving slowly westward since Stalingrad. The Soviet military might, supported by the vast resources of Siberia, a huge reservoir of army recruits, and significant shipments of American supplies and equipment, was increasing from month to month. The US army was slowly advancing through Italy; our great Italian allies and friends had surrendered on the third of September 1943; and the air bombardments in Germany got worse and worse. My days in Bielorad were numbered, because my mother had begun the complicated process of extricating her son from the KLV camp and from *Böhmen und Mähren.*

At the beginning of November Mutti had written a long letter to the authorities explaining her plan to remove me from the camp and reunite me with the family in *Waldenburg.* In principle this should have been possible, for *Waldenburg,* lying so far east, did not belong to the cities that were considered unsafe. As I wrote a little earlier, my mother had decided to move to *Schlesien* (Silesia), although it lay very far away from the *Ruhrgebiet,* and she would leave neighbors, friends, and her other siblings and their families behind. But living closer to her sister in these tough times made her decision easier. Our grandfather had decided to stay with his brother's family in *Wemlighausen* in the *Sauerland.* Mutti and the girls had lived since July in *Waldenburg* only thirty miles from the border with *Böhmen and Mähren.* They had already got used to their new life; and Marlis and Sigrid attended the local schools. My mother had reached her main goal: No more suffering with fear and horror through nights of bombing raids!

Her correspondence with our principal, Dr. Elsässer, and the authorities of the Protectorate went back and forth with little success. Always the same infuriating bureaucratic answers: "The children are not allowed to leave either the KLV camp or *Böhmen und Mähren.* It is true, *Waldenburg* is not the *Ruhrgebiet,* but one does not know whether she would not move back to *Mülheim.* This is a difficult case and one needs to get permission from highest quarters. And so on." The German bureaucracy churned slowly. Finally, shortly before Christmas, Mutti felt that the way was clear and she could pick up her son in *Bielorad.* I was waiting for her at the railroad station with one crying and one laughing eye, because I liked the idea of being again with her and my sisters, but I also loathed to leave the camp with all my friends and classmates. After all, I had enjoyed life with them since May. We too had become a family with strong ties, and it seemed hard to leave all that behind.

When Mutti finally stepped from the train it was

wonderful. We both were very happy to see each other again. She met Dr. Elsässer with whom she had negotiated by mail for some time. It is astounding, that I do not remember where she stayed and what we did specifically to get me out of the camp and, more difficult yet, out of *Böhmen und Mähren*. The official permission did not arrive and did not arrive, and Christmas got nearer. In the end Mutti and "Mucki" came up with a plan. (At their first meeting, my mother had addressed him as "Dr. Mucki", thinking that that was his name, because in my letters I had always referred to him with his nickname. So, when she called him Dr. Mucki I just about died; but he stood there with a pleased grin on his face and introduced himself to my astounded mother.) He proposed that I take leave for the Christmas vacation in order to bypass the convoluted bureaucracy. Even to obtain the vacation permit, Mutti and I spent a whole day in *Jicin* running from office to office and obtaining signatures and stamps on documents. Mutti had to promise that she would send me back on the sixth of January. As the ultimate irony, we realized later when we were ready to leave, that among all the papers there was no official permission to leave the Protectorate.

That small oversight did not faze my mother. I packed my suitcase and my satchel, took leave from classmates and friends, and off we were to *Schlesien* two days before Christmas. The train chugged through the most beautiful mountains, forests, and villages all covered by deep snow like in a precious fairy tale. All compartments, the corridors, every square foot of the train were packed with people and their luggage, civilians mixed with soldiers on leave. A real pre-Christmas mood had spread through our compartment, with food and drink and many tales making the round. When we got closer to the border the adults made plans to get me across in spite of not having the proper permission. They stuffed me into a corner under military coats and gear where I became invisible. Then came the border, border control, military police, documents, questions, answers, and everybody in the compartment talking and gesticulating. It worked beautifully! Nobody noticed me; and suddenly I found myself again on German soil. The whole compartment celebrated this success. A few hours later we arrived in *Waldenburg*. Into the streetcar and the last stretch on foot through ice and snow to *Cochius Strasse* 19. A tumultuous reunion with Marlis, Sigrid, Heidi, and Tante Mali. After eight months I was back in the middle of my family.

75

The "Church Hill" in Mülheim before the war (1938)

The "Old Town" before the war (1938)

Mülheim is burning (June 23, 1943)

Löhberg at the market square (1944)

Lower Wall Strasse (1944)

Löh Strasse (1944)

My friend Günter, drafted two months after his 14. birthday (1945)

No War in Waldenburg

Waldenburg is located about 30 miles north of the *Riesengebirge*, which separates *Schlesien* from *Böhmen und Mähren*, and about 50 miles west of the river *Oder*. To my surprise, the town was a coal mining center like *Mülheim*. It was surrounded by a friendly, hilly countryside with woods, meadows, and fields. There were no iron ore deposits in the region and therefore no steel industry. Actually, most of the mines were not far from our house; and I believe that the mines dominated the economy of the region. *Cochius Strasse* 19 was a four story brick building, where the red bricks had darkened with time. I guess it had been built around the turn of the century like most of the other houses in the street,. A wide stone staircase led from the entrance door to the apartments. Ours occupied only half of the second floor, because the original single apartment apparently had been subdivided in the past. We lived on the right and Fräulein Zielchen on the left. The tiny entrance led into a small kitchen, from where one reached the living room and the bedroom. Mutti and the girls slept in the bedroom, and I slept on the sofa in the living room. All rooms had double windows with blanket rolls on the sills in between to keep the icy winter wind out. A huge *Kachelofen* (tiled stove) built into one corner, dominated the living room. It extended all the way from floor to ceiling with a wooden bench around it. These tiled stoves were prevalent throughout the East and represented one of the most efficient heating systems I have ever experienced. The combustion chamber was filled every morning with ten soft coal briquets. They smoldered all day and heated the beautifully painted tiles through an intricate system of flues. To keep the system going overnight, a new briquet wrapped into wet newspaper was placed on the embers before bedtime. This burned extremely slowly during the night so that the remaining embers ignited the new briquets next morning. It was always very *gemütlich* to huddle together on the bench when we came home from the icy and windy city outside.

A large dark table with six chairs formed the center of the room. On one side next to the wall was the sofa on which I slept. In front of one of the two windows stood a white Jesus statue on a pedestal. Obviously Uncle Helmut's parents had been very religious. After all, he had become a pastor. We children who had not been brought up under the mantle of the protestant church never knew what exactly to do with this statue. It did not quite fit into our world, but we knew that it had a mysterious meaning for Tante Mali who was as religious as her father. She always wanted to take us to church on her visits; and sometimes we went along. Tante Mali was very different from my mother, her brothers, and my father; and she was the only sibling of the Krämer family who actively maintained the faith of her parents. Since Opa's life was totally immersed in the protestant-lutheran faith, he would not allow Papa to marry his daughter Berta, my mother, without joining the protestant church. Papa, who had grown up as a catholic, albeit a very liberal one, accepted the condition, and as a consequence the Jansen household remained essentially neutral, and my sisters and I grew up without exposure to the protestant faith until the demise of the *Third Reich*.

As one entered the small kitchen from the main door, there was a stove with its hot water storage bin to the left. It was coal fired and had four cooking openings that were covered with a number of concentric rings with a small plate in the center. Depending on the desired amount of heat and the size of the pot or pan one removed the appropriate number of rings starting with the plate in the middle. In this manner Mutti controlled the heating of the food. The briquets were stored next to the stove together with the briquet carrier and the ashcan. It became one of my first tasks to take the ash into the basement and haul up the briquets. Food was prepared on a table next to the stove. There was a tall kitchen cabinet on the other side with glass doors in the upper part, through which one could see all the plates and glasses. The bedroom was packed with a large armoire, the wash stand, and several beds in which Mutti and the girls slept. Water for the wash basin was brought in a large jug from the kitchen. The toilet was located at the staircase landing, a half story below the apartment, as it was the custom in older apartment buildings. Those toilet closets with a window to the outside were never heated. This had the advantage that nobody held long sessions in this multifamily facility.

We celebrated a beautiful Christmas. Again at home with my beloved sisters, Mutti, and Tante Mali, who was visiting us as in old times. We sang our Christmas songs as in Mülheim, however, without Papa's and Opa's baritone voices. I remember that Opa knew every verse and every word of all Christmas songs by heart, which was not exactly the case with his grandchildren. The *Kachelofen* spread a cozy warmth throughout the room; and Mutti and Tante Mali prepared the festive dinner. From *Hochweiler,* our aunt had brought a carp that became the center piece of the table. The *Schlesier* enjoyed their carp at Christmas, while the *Rheinlander* were accustomed to eating their goose. -- I had an opportunity to see the carp ponds myself when we visited Tante Mali the next summer in *Hochweiler.* The carps were raised in shallow ponds that were simply emptied out by opening a lock when the time came to "catch" the fish. The carps stayed in the lower section of the pond, until all the water had been drained; then they were removed with net and shovel into a wagon. -- Santa Claus still brought Christmas presents in spite of the war. Most were home made; but some came from so called "exchange shops", which had sprung up everywhere. There you could exchange your own merchandise for something of equivalent value that somebody else offered. The items had tags that indicated a choice of things that the seller was interested in. I believe that Marlis got skis and ski boots through such a trade. I received the skis and boots that had belonged to Uncle Helmut. They towered over me with their length of 210 cm. The boots were so large that I had to wear three pairs of heavy socks.

The family enjoyed the time after Christmas together. Mutti and the girls showed me Waldenburg and environs, which they had already explored during summer and fall. The town was covered with deep snow. It snowed frequently and was truly cold. The temperature hovered often around -40˚F; what a change from the mild *Rheinland* where temperatures in the worst winter were never below +14˚F. I learned in a hurry to wear the warmest clothes. No longer knee socks with shorts that we wore heroically at home through most of the winter. Instead, long woolen pants, a heavy sweater, and a long overcoat constituted my new attire. It was below my dignity to wear the full length knitted, woolen stockings with short pants which were worn by the Silesian boys of my age. These ugly brown or black stockings were fastened to a knitted undershirt, the kind that we had worn as very young children. Silesia was a different world! Its climate was truly continental, similar to the climate of Poland and Russia and no longer influenced by the Gulf stream that kept the West European climate moderate.

I enjoyed my new home town; but the thought of having to return to *Bielorad* never quite left me. Officially, I was here only on a leave of absence and, to top it all off, I was illegally in Germany. The departure date when the leave of absence ran out came closer and closer; and still no letter from the camp. That meant all the promises by the authorities had come to naught. Little by little it became clear that I had to return to the KLV camp. Everybody was depressed, when suddenly one early morning a telegram arrived from Dr. Elsässer: "Hansjörg's stay in Waldenburg has been granted. Documents will follow by mail." We danced with such abandon that one of us stepped into the full chamber pot. A minor inconvenience when we had so much to celebrate.

After the vacation, Mutti took me to the Gymnasium where we were received by a Dr. Kaufmann who was the class teacher of the Quarta. He inspected all my report cards, asked many questions about my schooling at home and in the KLV camp, and finally decided to put me into the same grade as in the camp. Pretty soon, I realized that I had to work very hard to catch up with my new classmates. Since their learning had not been interrupted be air raids and KLV camp, they were way ahead of the boy from the *Ruhrgebiet*. The school was located in *Neustadt* (New Town) on the other side of the central valley where Marlis and Sigrid went to school. I had to walk through town past Marlis' school and up on the other side through a large park. It took 35 to 40 minutes if I walked briskly; in snow and ice it took easily an hour. There were thirty boys in my new class who all came from Waldenburg and environs, many by streetcar or train. Classes started punctually at eight o'clock, no matter how much snow had fallen during the night. The only acceptable excuse was a verifiable train delay. This happened very rarely, because all trains and streetcars were equipped with huge snow blowers that kept them running under even the worst circumstances. After we had hung our coats, caps, shawls, and gloves on the hooks on the wall opposite the windows we were ready for class.

Dr. Kaufmann was as strict as Dr. Elsässer and he was also as fair and human as his western colleague. I cannot recall clearly the other teachers with the exception of our physical education teacher who impressed me the most. He was small, wiry, and extremely demanding. White-haired and probably in his sixties this man taught us *Turnen* (gymnastics) and he demonstrated every exercise by his own example. A classmate who came from *Köln* (another "Westerner") and I were speechless and we shuddered. The feats that he and all our other classmates accomplished on the single and double horizontal bars, the beam, the table and the floor mats were sheer acrobatics in my view. They performed every imaginable exercise including somersaults coming off the single bar with such an ease that left us boys from the *Rhein* totally overwhelmed. The two of us could not even succeed with one single upswing; we hung from the high bar like sacks of potatoes. It was unbelievably humiliating and turned the gymnastics lesson into an ordeal. Of course, I got an F in my report card. Incompetent! I will always remember this gymnastics teacher who managed at his age to go through a routine of daring exercises and finally jump from the high bar, where jump and landing were meticulously controlled. The tough "Easterners" were clearly way ahead of us soft "Westerners".

The German lessons gave me my other big problems. Unexpectedly, it turned out that the German of Silesia varied remarkably from the German of the Rhineland, especially in its daily usage. Once I made a real mess of retelling a story that the teacher had read to us, because I "mistranslated" a few key words that were unknown to me. When I received an F, I was so incensed and unhappy that I went to see Dr. Kaufmann and explained the whole misunderstanding. He laughed heartily and gave me mercifully a B in recognition of my language problems. -- The reader probably knows that the Germans spoke and still speak as many dialects as there were provinces, kingdoms, dukedoms, counties, and other realms. The only people who speak naturally "High German" live in the Hannover area. Everybody else has to learn it in school; and even then many differences in use and meaning of words remain. -- .

Even though the family had escaped from the air war, the war as a whole was being lost in the East and South, no matter what Dr. Goebbels said in his eloquent speeches. The war had been going on already for four and a half years. My hometown was destroyed; all big cities within the reach of the Anglo-American bombers where either destroyed or heavily damaged; my father, two aunts, one uncle, eight cousins, uncles, and aunts of Mutti were dead; the young Thomas was still missing. Millions dead at the front and at home, and the country full of prisoners of war and foreign workers (voluntary and involuntary) who kept industry and agriculture going. Times were no longer good for Germany. Ever since the gigantic battle and defeat at Stalingrad and the invasion of Italy the excitement and support for the war were gone. People had become numb and ever more interested in their own survival, only hoping that the war would end soon and hopefully still come to a tolerable ending. The intensity of the propaganda increased from month to month; each defeat was metamorphosed into some sort of victory or necessary "alignment". We read everywhere on big posters or banners: "We Germans are fighting for the final victory" or " Wheels (that meant the railroad) must roll for the victory," etc. The newsreels from the front were always rosy. The chasm between fantasy and reality grew steadily. Looking back, I do not think that we ever talked at home about this whole business of the propaganda, the government's various efforts to convince us of the need for continuing to sacrifice, and the disparity between truth and fiction. It would have been too dangerous for my mother to talk with Marlis and me about such subjects. Did any of her visitors ever criticize the speeches of Göring, Goebbels, or Hitler? Maybe the adults really opened up amongst very good friends and relatives when we were not around. I just do not know. As *Hitler Jugend* teenagers we were, of course, dangerous. Not that we would have said deliberately anything against our parents or their friends, but we could have easily talked or slipped without realizing the consequences. It must have been difficult for all parents and especially for those who were in basic disagreement with the regime. Possibly many people, our family included, did not discuss the issues because everybody hoped desperately that in some way Germany would still win the war. The trust in the Führer was no longer absolute; but most people hoped that he would still come up with some new and yet undisclosed weapons to win. I do not remember when the V1s and later the V2s were unleashed against Southern England, but I do remember that many thought they would bring about the victory. Maybe in their desperation they kept hoping against hope for better and bigger surprises.

In spite of these concerns, life in Waldenburg continued in its quasi peaceful routine. I got well acquainted with most of my classmates in school, but I never developed a real friendship with any one of them. I think that the same was true for Marlis. We must have felt that our family was a tiny island in an alien world; therefore, we were oriented totally inward. Mutti organized as many outings, hikes, and movie visits with us as she could. Marlis and I went skiing in the surrounding forests trying out our new gear. We would take the streetcar to one of the suburbs, walk a mile or so, put on the skis, and find ourselves with many other kids in winter wonderland. Waldenburg received many feet of snow, for it was snowing all winter long and little melted because of the extremely low temperatures. The streets were covered with packed snow; and huge mounds of snow, which were mostly taller than I, separated the sidewalks from the streets. However, between snowstorms the sun was beaming from an azure sky in this dry eastern climate. On days like that we put on our ice skates and skated up and down the *Cochius Strasse,* that was frequently iced over. In spring and summer Mutti took us on hikes into the neighboring countryside, or she would invite us to an afternoon coffee and cake in *Bad Salzbrunn,* a well known resort and spa nearby that was easily reached by train. Once she took me to my first operetta *Das Land des Lächelns* (Land of Smiles) by Franz Lehar. I liked it so much that I sang *Dein ist mein ganzes Herz* (Yours is my Whole Heart) for weeks.

During Whitsuntide vacations we spent a week in *Krummhübel,* a small resort in the *Riesengebirge,* where *Rübezahl,* a giant mountain troll, resided and did his good deeds for the poor and innocent, took from the rich, and punished the evildoers. I am sure that he is still roaming those mountains today. From *Krummhübel* we undertook many hikes into the mountains and once went to the *Schneekoppe,* the highest mountain of the *Riesengebirge,* which stretches between *Schlesien* and *Böhmen.* In the upper reaches we found ourselves above the tree line, where the *Schneekoppe* itself loomed large and bald, but not steep compared to alpine mountains. As much as I cherished these excursions, there was one thing I really hated. Like at home, we took our food along in my mother's big leather handbag. Did we not have any rucksacks? Nothing worse than lugging this heavy awkward thing all morning long up the mountain. But, in the end everything was great when we reached our destination, a *Baude* (mountain chalet) unpacked our sandwiches and enjoyed them together with the ubiquitous barley coffee. We actually called this thin brew *Blümchenkaffee* (little flower coffee), because one could easily see the little flowers that were often painted on the bottom of coffee or tea cups. As I wrote earlier, *Bohnenkaffee* (real coffee) was not for us kids, and apparently never had been for children. -- Already during Johann Sebastian Bach's time it was frowned upon. He actually wrote a Coffee Cantata, in which a father forbids his daughter to drink this dangerous drink. But she likes her coffee so much that she refuses to quit. He threatens that he will not get her a husband unless she gives up her bad habit. Finally she succumbs to her father's admonitions, gets her husband and - - - resumes to drink her coffee. -- During the war, coffee was highly rationed, and Mutti always saved it for special visits of her siblings or for *Kaffeeklatschs* with her friends. Not surprisingly, in the *Ruhrgebiet* a special coupon on the rationing card for 100 gram of coffee and for a pack of cigarettes was made available after a heavy air raid. Keep them happy!

Once Mutti and I made a trip to *Breslau*, the capital of the province of Silesia, because she had to take care of some business with the provincial bureaucracy. It was a very beautiful, elegant city along the shores of the river *Oder* with huge parks and promenades along the river, old churches, and an outstanding town square surrounded by colorful, gabled Renaissance buildings. In addition to the surrounding houses, more buildings and a remarkable city hall had been built in the center of that huge square, which was called the *Rink.* All cities and towns in *Schlesien* featured a *Rink* in the center. I am not sure, but it could mean *Ring,* because the houses "ringed" the square, Unfortunately, *Breslau* was totally devastated in the spring of 1945, when Hitler declared it as a "fortress" which had to be held at all cost. He declared several East German cities as "fortresses" presumably to protect the fleeing masses from the advancing Red Army. As bad as this order was for that beautiful city, it was a godsend for us, because it gave us an opportunity to flee unscathed. I read recently that *Breslau* only surrendered in May 1945.

I soon as I arrived in *Waldenburg* I continued the mandatory *Jungvolk* duty. Our meetings took place on Wednesday and Saturday afternoons in Sigrid's elementary school in the center of town. We marched frequently into the adjacent woods, where we practiced our pre-military exercises, went on cross-country runs, or played games. Soccer and track and field activities took place in the sport stadium near my school. During the winter months we mostly met in a classroom, where we sang, read, played, and built toys for children of poor families and soldier families. As in Mülheim we had to make collections for one or another charitable cause, and we had to help old or invalid people. After a few months I became a *Jungenschaftsführer,* the leader of the smallest unit in the *Jungvolk* hierarchy. I was now responsible for ten boys, and as a sign of my rank I wore a white/red cord on my uniform. In my new position I had to organize the activities of my small troop, make plans, lead the singing, lead small projects, and report my unit to the higher ranking leader at the beginning of our twice weekly meetings. Furthermore, I maintained a little notebook, in which I had to enter the presence or absence of the boys and whether or not they had a written excuse from their parents, exactly as the teacher did in school. In a certain sense Jungvolk duty was not so different from school. Instead of teachers we had leaders, although they were only a couple of years older than the boys in the unit. We had to be punctual, we followed orders, we participated in all activities with more or less enthusiasm, depending on the individual. Before the war the older boys of the *Jungvolk* and the *Hitler Jugend* went a few times during the year on overnight trips or spent a week in a camp with tents, bonfires, and swimming in a lake, or climbing a mountain; but the worsening war made those excursions impossible, so that my comrades and I never made this wonderful experience.

Sometimes on the morning of a Sunday or a National Holiday we would participate in a parade, where all the *Fähnleins* and *Stamms* of *Waldenburg* got together for a big event. Usually some prominent dignitary had come to visit. Weeks before we began to practice marching in rows of six and goose-stepping with precision. It took a lot of practice to keep rows of six straight; but they had to be absolutely even. On the day itself after our leaders had inspected uniforms, flags, and music instruments, we were organized outside the center of the city into columns with six boys to a row, *Jungzug* after *Jungzug, Fähnlein* after *Fähnlein,* and *Stamm* after *Stamm.* Ahead of each *Stamm* came the flags and banners, followed by the drum and bugle corps. Then, singing our songs, we marched through the city streets bordered by throngs of onlookers. Closer to the tribune the tension mounted. Would we do as well as or better than the others? The parade reached its high point when we passed the tribune where the out-of-town dignitary stood, his right arm outstretched to salute us. For hundred feet everything had to be perfect, the rows straight, the distances between rows the same, heads to the right looking at the visitor; and sometimes in goose step. Not easy! A few times I was elected to carry the flag of our *Fähnlein* in front of the *Stamm,* a much desired honor. I had to wear a special belt with a receptacle for the flag pole. The flag had to be carried perfectly vertical, which required quite a balancing act especially if a wind blew. It may be difficult for today's reader to imagine the deep impression which a parade like that made on us teenagers. What a Sunday morning and, going back to an earlier chapter, what a clever indoctrination!

Frequently the *Jungvolk* went to a movie theater on Sunday mornings, where we watched a patriotic, historic film. These films dealt typically with famous figures of German history. I recall titles such as *"Bismarck, Fredericus Rex, Schiller, and Hitlerjunge Quex".* I enjoyed these performances, because the films were usually of a high quality and very interesting for a teenager. They were regular movies and not especially made for us. The historic figures were always played by prominent German actors. Looking at these Sunday morning events from today's perspective, it is clear that the Sunday morning was not only chosen because it was the only time available, but also to compete with the church services. This clash between the expectations of the churches and of the party came to the surface now and then. There was absolutely no problem in our family; but difficulties must have existed in other strict catholic or protestant families. I remember *Jungvolk* comrades who did not always show up to our meetings, were not beyond a snide remark here and there, or did not participate in Sunday morning events. Nobody rebelled or criticized openly, God forbid; but one could not miss the occasional passive resistance. As teenagers we certainly did not discuss party ideology and religion. First, we were too young and inexperienced to conduct a debate, and secondly, the subject was taboo like so many others. However, even I with my thirteen years had no difficulty noticing a conflict.

I learned after the war that problems had existed between the churches and the National Socialistic regime from the very beginning. Hitler did not have the nerve to attack the churches directly, because that would have cost him the support of the German populace. A shaky relationship emerged, which both sides tolerated, yet was everything but friendly. Regarding the Catholic Church, Hitler and Pope Pius XII. agreed in the Concordat of July 20, 1933 that neither party would interfere with the other. This Concordat and the attitude of Pius XII. have been endlessly discussed and heavily criticized since the end of the war in view of the persecution of the Jews. It took sixty years before Pope Johannes Paulus II apologized in Jerusalem for the questionable conduct of the Catholic Church. As for the Protestant Church, it was not as tightly organized as the Catholic Church and therefore not as powerful. Therefore Hitler tried to convert it slowly into a state church, the "German Protestant Church" under a *"Reichsbischof"* (State Bishop). That attempt did not succeed at all; a *"Kirchenkampf"* (church fight) ensued as a consequence of state efforts to suppress the church. Ministers and pastors lost their positions and were persecuted or jailed. The government tried to interfere with and undermine the church. All in vain! Hitler could not break the resistance of the faithful in the twelve years of his reign. All the propaganda aimed at the parishioners to leave their church failed.

Earlier, I had already touched upon the question of the indoctrination efforts by the National Socialistic Party. The indoctrination worked simply through our social environment. We listened to the adults and the radio, we saw newsreels in the movie theater, looked at pictures in magazines, we read the ubiquitous posters with their exhortations and slogans, we knew who the enemies were and why they were our enemies, we were proud of our uniforms. Belonging to a *Fähnlein* meant having comrades and being part of a whole. We learned soon that the word "we" was more important than the word "I". We inhaled political content with our songs. On the other hand, I did not even know about "The Book" *Mein Kampf* (My Struggle). I was probably too young. However, I read *Mein Kampf* after the war when I found the book accidentally in a drawer of my father's former desk where it seemingly had been forgotten. I perused this unusual, demagogic book in secret, because books like that were forbidden by the Military Government. After reading the book I had, and still have, a hard time understanding how anybody who had read it could follow a man like Hitler, unless he belonged to the same fanatic extreme right in the first place. It remains an interesting question, how many Germans had actually read *Mein Kampf* before the decisive elections in the early thirties.

Our family lived mostly in harmony in spite of the tight quarters in our tiny one bedroom apartment. On one hand this depended on Mutti, for whom the family meant everything; on the other hand it was the result of living in a foreign world where we were totally dependent on each other and ourselves. Everybody had his or her duties, and everybody made a contribution to the well-being of the family. My jobs included the cleaning of everybody's shoes, hauling coal from the basement, taking the trash down, and keeping the fire in the *Kachelofen* going. My sisters had to assist in cleaning the apartment, preparing the meals, and cleaning up afterwards. We all helped with the dishes, shopping and with the big monthly laundry in the basement. Fridays we all took our baths as in Mülheim with the difference that now the bathroom was in the basement and was used by all tenants. This arrangement was typical for all apartment houses that actually had a bathroom; other people who lived in houses without a bathroom took their weekly baths in a public or private bathhouse. The custodian, Herr Urban, kept track of bathing and laundry times, so that people did not interfere with each other. He heated the water in a coal fired boiler and called my mother, when the water had reached the right temperature. I forgot, to how many freshly filled bathtubs we were entitled, but we kids usually used one bath water two. For the daily wash in the morning, Marlis and Sigrid used the basin on the washstand, and I used the sink in the kitchen. Mutti's and Heidi's turn came after breakfast when we three had left for school. As in Mülheim, we returned from school between one and two o'clock. After the midday dinner we did our homework on the big dining table under close supervision of Mutti. If you had to read aloud, recite poetry, or learn vocabulary of a foreign language, you had to retire to the kitchen or bedroom. In the afternoon we played our games either in the street or in the living room.

One evening my mother asked me whether I would like to continue my father's habit of reading to her when she mended clothes. I was very pleased to take on this task and read to her after I had made my sofa bed and crawled into it. I also emulated my father by falling asleep after a little while. Mutti turned off my reading light, removed the book, and continued her work into the night. I remember that Papa once had received a bookmark as a gift that said: "Here I fell asleep." Maybe I should have received the same when Brigit and I revived the custom and I promptly fell asleep after some time, specially if I had a tough day at work. Unfortunately we had to give up this beautiful arrangement about ten years ago when I dozed off already after the first pages. Today I am just reading for myself and still happily falling asleep in a hurry.

We kids were always looking forward to the few occasions when Mutti would take us to the movies. Not only would we get to see a movie but we would also see and hear what had happened in the rest of the world. In the days before the advent of the omnipresent television a newsreel was always shown before any movie. That gave people the only opportunity to observe in action what they could only read in newspapers and magazines or hear on the radio. Naturally, military events took up most of these news, and without fail the German actions were always shown in a positive light whether the armies were winning or losing. The rest of the newsreel was dedicated to scenes from politics, sports, the arts, and other important events. It was on the newsreels where I had witnessed the impressive extraordinary Party rallies in *Nürnberg* with tens of thousands of marchers, with forests of flags, and with the *Führer* ascending slowly over a flight of stairs to the podium from where his oration thundered into our ears.

In spite of all the good news in the newsreels, the papers, and the radio it became clear that the war was being lost. The eastern front moved slowly, ominously in the wrong direction. Or were the maps off? The trains were still bearing huge signs: "Wheels have to roll for the victory"; but what had happened to the victory after almost five years? Listening to the magic words of our *Führer,* victory was always around the corner and the only thing we, the people, had to do, was to have absolute trust in him and his sense of providence. He knew exactly what was right for *sein Deutsches Volk* (his German People). No matter what opinion anybody had about Hitler, he had a singular ability to excite his listeners with his overpowering speeches and charisma. Every time when something went wrong, he gave a speech over the radio explaining to his Germans how things were not really that bad. However, his Germans had to work and fight harder, and had to make more sacrifices in order to achieve the final victory over the evil elements of this world. His *Volk* had known for years who those elements were: The Communists who wanted to remake the world in their image, the Bolsheviks under Stalin who wanted to conquer Germany, the Zionists who wanted to control the media and finances of the world, and the Anglo American Plutocrats. Next to Hitler, his minister of propaganda was also an excellent orator of no lesser quality than his master. Dr. Goebbels had been schooled by the Jesuits where he probably acquired his skills of the written and spoken word.

Nobody could afford to doubt the *Endsieg* (final victory). Anybody who got caught making disparaging remarks had to suffer the consequences in the form of fines, job loss, jail or worse. Saying the wrong words in public was assiduously avoided; however, the number of biting comments or disparaging jokes about our leaders increased all the time. I do not remember a single joke about Hitler himself, but Göring and Goebbels were always the laughingstock. Herr and Frau Goebbels are visiting the Görings. Frau Göring opens the door and welcomes her guests. "Where is Hermann?", asks Goebbels, whereupon Mrs. Göring says: "Wait a moment, I have to check his wardrobe." When she returns she says with a smile: "He is getting the coal from the basement, because his miner's uniform is no longer hanging in the closet." (Göring was a very vain man who loved his uniforms.) In the *Rheinland* we called Joseph Goebbels "Jüppkes", the diminutive name in dialect for Joseph.

Tante Mali visited us frequently because she lived not too far from *Waldenburg*. She had moved with *Onkel* Helmut to *Hochweiler* close to *Militsch* near the Polish border where he had become the village pastor. As the widow of the pastor she participated energetically in the affairs of the congregation. *Onkel* Eugen, the older of my mother's brothers, visited us occasionally when he was on a business trip from Russia to Düsseldorf. He had followed in the footsteps of his father and had become a civil servant of the *Reichsbahn*, the national railroad. Opa had worked all his life for the *Reichsbahn* where he had advanced from switch man to station chief. -- As an interesting aside, in *Westfalen*, the province of Westphalia, it was the custom, maybe law, that the firstborn boy inherited the farm, the girls received each a dowry, and the other boys could work on the farm as farmhands or fend for themselves elsewhere. Opa did not want to stay on the farm. So he found a job with the *Reichsbahn,* where he started from scratch as a switch man, whereas his older brother became a very well-to-do farmer. I do not recall the professions of his other brothers. Opa worked first in *Velbert*, where my mother was born, later in Düsseldorf. After the First World War he participated in the campaign against the French occupation. As a faithful Prussian civil servant he followed orders and sabotaged the French trains by sending them in the wrong direction or derailing them when they transported coal from the *Ruhrgebiet* to France, as part of the odious reparations that had been imposed upon Germany by the Versailles Treaty. Unfortunately his machinations were discovered, but he was lucky that the German authorities managed to extricate him from the French and transferred him from the occupied *Rheinland* to *Westfalen*. Customarily saboteurs were shot If caught by the French authorities. -- Back to Onkel Eugen who was responsible for certain elements of the the railroad infrastructure in the Soviet Union. He always brought us eggs, butter and bacon, real delicacies in those times. When he discovered that little or no salt was available in Western Russia he always took sacs of salt along in order to barter it for farm products that were scarce in Germany. He also brought the latest and actual news from the front, and they were mostly depressing, but, in this way, we could get a more accurate picture of the real state of affairs.

The rapidly mounting German losses at the eastern front resulted in the enlisting of older and younger men. In school, that meant that first all boys who were seventeen and older had to join the *Wehrmacht* (Armed Forces). Then the sixteen year olds and towards the end also the fifteen year olds became Flak (anti aircraft canon) helpers or had to perform other military duties. In that way our seventh grade became the highest and last grade in the school. This lasted until our summer vacation in July 1944 after which we too were thrown into the war machinery. But before I relate my duties and experiences of that new way of life I want to tell the story of our last family vacation before everything started to collapse.

Tante Mali had invited the entire family to *Hochweiler* where we stayed at the house of the *Gräfin* (countess) von Fürstenstein who had become a friend of my aunt. What an unbelievable world, so totally different from the rest of Germany! Sometimes you had to stop and reassure yourself that you were not in a fantasy land. The train from *Waldenburg* stopped at a tiny station seemingly at the end of the world. As we stepped off the train we discovered a carriage with two horses that stood ready to take us through the village to the estate of the *Fürstensteins*. There Tante Mali introduced us to the countess who welcomed us graciously. She lived in the mansion all by herself, because her husband fought as an officer on the Russian front. They had no children. After she had shown us our rooms we were allowed to discover the rest of house and garden by ourselves. For us four kids this was like an enchanting dream; a very airy, light colored, rambling two story building with long corridors on whose walls family portraits were displayed. Sofas, sideboards, easy chairs, and large vases complemented each other. We carefully made our way through room after room, all furnished in light colors, pictures on every wall, and books to the ceiling in the large downstairs study. The well tended flower garden was surrounded by fields, meadows, lakes, and forests which all belonged to this huge estate, including the little village of *Hochweiler*. We were in seventh heaven for the next four weeks. However, one paradox baffled me. How could everybody live here in seeming peace when the rest of the country was engaged in a devastating war. Did they sense that they were all sitting on a powder keg about to explode?

I was impressed and confused at the same time by the social order of this world which was totally alien to me. The *Graf* (count) represented everything in one person: He owned the estate, the village, the church, and above all the villagers. From my point of view they were serfs, albeit well kept. They did not own property, lived in small nice houses, bowed low before the *Gräfin* and ---- kissed the hem of her skirt. The *Graf* owned the land, he was the sole employer, he was the village mayor and the local judge. In the church his family had their own beautifully carved regal pew. They were simply the absolute rulers in a well established feudal system; very difficult to understand for a boy who lived in a socialistic, bourgeois country. Coming from the *Rheinland* I could not believe that such social order, characteristic of the last centuries, did still exist in modern Germany. Close to the next village lay the castle of a duke who was probably the superior of the count. Also, the former country seat of the last German Kaiser was located not far from there. We had stepped back in time into a fairyland, where an aristocratic feudal society still reigned as if time had stood still.

The contrast between the incessant air bombardments in the West and Berlin, the slow but steady retreat in Russia, and the idyllic peace of man and nature in Hochweiler was extraordinary. Without people realizing it, it was the *"Ruhe vor dem Sturm"* (Quiet Before the Storm) which Theodor Fontane describes so vividly in his book about the occupation of *Brandenburg* by Napoleon. For our family too, this lovely, peaceful summer on *Gräfin* von Füstenstein's estate was the last "quiet before the storm". However, one extraordinary event shattered the lovely summer weeks like an earthquake. On July 20, 1944 we heard on the radio that a serious assassination attempt on the life of the Führer had taken place. Colonel Klaus von Stauffenberg had smuggled a bomb in his attaché case into Hitler's headquarters and in to the operations center where the Führer met with his top brass for the daily briefings and strategic plans. A miracle had happened; finally, somebody had dared to blow up the Supreme Leader of the *Reich* and the Chief of the *Wehrmacht*. Looking back, it was extremely unfortunate that this assassination attempt failed in spite of careful nationwide planning by a large group of German patriots. By the time the bomb went off, Hitler had moved away from the attaché case that Stauffenberg had left close to a table leg. The colonel had to be out of the compound before the explosion to avoid being apprehended by the officers and men of Hitler's body guard. Having killed or severely wounded Hitler, his foremost task was to notify immediately the conspirators, so that they could launch the nationwide surprise attack on all the key leaders of the regime.

It was a tragedy for Germany that the Supreme Leader suffered only minor wounds and remained functional. He lost no time to go on the national radio, where he talked about providence and his determination to eradicate all the traitors and lead the country to the final victory, the *Endsieg*. The reaction to the news was very ambivalent. On one hand, Hitler meant just about everything to all the young and many older people. Was he not the symbol of the new, successful Germany? Had he not preached again and again in his sermons that fate had chosen him to restore Germany to its former glory and to turn it into a real world power? On the other hand, the war had lasted too long by far, and Germany was losing it rapidly. The populace had suffered dramatically from the incessant air bombardments and the huge military defeats, which had resulted in a staggering loss of human life. People were no longer enthusiastic, they were tired, worn out, and had lost confidence in the leadership. *Gräfin* von Fürstenstein was not shy and even in front of Marlis and me she expressed her disappointment and unhappiness. We caught a glimpse of what became widely known after the war. The aristocracy which had furnished the officer corps for centuries had never accepted the idea of an Austrian corporal leading Germany and its *Wehrmacht*. They were no friends of the corporal. Hitler must have been very aware of this, because he had made strenuous efforts to train ideologically inspired officers and attach them to all military organizations. They acted somewhat as a fifth column. I find it almost unbelievable, that all the aristocratic officers and generals followed his orders until his death. But they had sworn their oaths of allegiance to him and, as true Prussians, believed in unconditional military obedience. And their ingrained belief in honor did not allow them to break that oath.

Soon we learned from the news, that a ring of "conspirators and traitors" had been discovered who had planned this assassination for a long time and who had been waiting for the right opportunity. Had they been successful, all senior party officials would have been arrested and executed upon the prearranged signal , and the armed forces would have taken over. Unfortunately, this did not come to be, and instead, all conspirators, who were the true patriotic heroes, where identified and shot immediately. I have asked myself many times what would have become of Germany and Europe, if this conspiracy had been successful even at this late hour. Of course, it would never have come to a war, if Hitler had been killed in 1938 or 1939. (A number of assassination attempts have been reported; in particular in the autumn of 1938 General von Beck rallied his fellow officers against Hitler, unfortunately without success.) But even in 1944 it might have come to a compromise with the Allies. Millions of people in all European countries would have survived and Germany might not have become the pariah of all nations of the world for the next fifty years. But the assassination failed, the country was further sucked into the abyss of devastation and death, and Germany became the symbol of horror and human wickedness not to be forgotten for generations.

The Great Migration West

At the end of the summer we returned to Waldenburg by carriage and train; and Marlis, Sigrid and I went back to school where I began my eighth grade, the *Untertertia.* We had barely embarked upon the new school year, when the principal announced one day that school instruction had been suspended for our class, so that we could participate in the struggle to save our fatherland. Marlis had been sent already to the *Ostwall* (east wall), the brand new eastern fortification, to provide support for all the men and women who were digging a huge trench and building an equally huge earthen wall. In the last minute Hitler had decided to build a wall at the eastern German border similar to the *Westwall,* the famous Siegfried Line. The only difference was, that it had to be built in a hurry and did not include concrete bunkers, tank obstacles, or anything that came close to a modern fortification. It was simply an embankment of earth of the kind that the Romans had built almost two thousand years earlier filling the vulnerable gap between *Rhein* and *Donau* (Danube). The East Wall was a rather desperate effort in the hope it would stop the advance of the Russian tanks. Tens of thousands of people slaved for months at this enterprise which in the end did not hold up one single Russian tank.

I was assigned to the local post office where I did all sorts of paperwork which was so uninteresting that I do not recall any details. However, the next assignment was more than exciting. As the winter of 1944/45 approached some of my classmates and I became part of a team that directed the intense traffic in the center of town. This traffic did not at all consist of automobiles as one would assume today, neither did it flow in all directions. No, it was an extremely unusual, unidirectional traffic going only from East to West. Slowly but steadily the peaceful atmosphere of Waldenburg had undergone quite a change. Refugees from the East on their trek towards the West had started to trickle into and through our town. It had become my job to help directing this stream of mankind at one key intersection at the east side of town. A small rivulet increased to a river in a few months. Our team advised the refugees, extended any possible help, and primarily directed them to collection camps where they could get some rest and receive food and medical attention. These camps had sprung up all over town: Schools, gymnasiums, large halls, warehouses, etc. Marlis was working in one of those camps after her return from her *Ostwall* duties. She and other girls took care of the refugees until they were sent further to the West to make room for newcomers.

Directing this torrent of people was one of my most memorable experiences of the war and actually of my life. They came on foot, they drew little hand carts behind them, they came with large covered wagons. They came from all countries east of Germany. In the beginning they were Bulgarians, Ukrainians, and Rumanians. Most of the women and girls were wearing beautiful dresses, colorful wide skirts, frequently several on top of each other, white embroidered blouses with colored vests or jackets, headscarves, and boots. They were mostly seated on their big wagons, while the men were walking alongside. The men were controlling the horses or oxen which steadily pulled their load. -- The covered wagons remind me of the Conestoga Wagons with which the American settlers crossed this continent in the nineteenth century, albeit with completely different expectations and great hopes for the future. -- To brake these heavily loaded wagons on their way downhill, the men used massive wooden beams that they jammed between the wheels and the chassis. Most everybody knew some German, so that I could understand their questions and give rudimentary instructions. The first wave of fugitives was followed by a wave from Hungary, Poland, Slovenia and Slovakia. When I considered that many of these refugees came from places as far away as six hundred miles, and that they had already trekked for weeks or months, I was gripped by a horrifying recognition of the force that pushed them relentlessly west. Pretty soon I learned from conversations that they all shared a deep seated fear of the Russians. Nobody wanted to fall into the hands of the Red Army. They were scared of the Russian retributions, for their countries had fought the Red Army on the side of the Germans. They were fleeing from mass executions, raping, pillage, and other horrors. I had become witness to a modern *Völkerwanderung,* comparable to the vast medieval east-west migrations, that were caused then by the pressure of the huns and other far eastern tribes and now by the all consuming Soviet steamroller. Untold millions left their possessions, farms, homes, and countries behind.

The Silesian winter of 1944/45 began with a vengeance

99

with deep snow, ice-cold days, and even colder nights. That made our task more demanding; we alternated every hour and sought shelter in a nearby house where we took our shoes, gloves and caps off to warm up in front of a tiled stove. Sometimes the lady of the house gave us hot soup. The human river continued to swell from day to day and week to week, a sign that the front came closer regardless of the official propaganda. The rising fear that nothing could be done against the Soviet onslaught did not prevent us from hoping that our troops would stop it at the border. Surprisingly, we did not experience any air raids in those months in spite of the fact that the front was only a few hundred miles away. Nothing ever happened during the rare warnings of the sirens.

I like to interrupt here and tell of an event that would be easily considered fantastic had it not really happened. It could have channeled my life for the next months or years into an altogether different direction. In the middle of all this turmoil, we still attended our *Jungvolk* meetings. No more marching through town with drums and bugles, no more athletics. Instead we huddled together to talk about ways and means to help the people and defend the fatherland, because we could not tolerate the thought of the Red Army on German soil. One Saturday late in November we had a meeting of all the leaders of the diverse organizations within the *Bann* , probably fifty boys between thirteen and fifteen, when the *Bannführer* suddenly proposed that we should all volunteer for the *Waffen SS*. -- As I explained earlier, for us boys that branch of the army ranked higher than all the others. If you thought about volunteering, it would be first for the elite troops of the *Waffen SS*, unless you wanted to join the Air Force or the Navy. -- After our *Bannführer* had talked long enough about the need and honor of protecting our fatherland and had sufficiently stimulated our youthful enthusiasm he asked who wanted to volunteer. We all jumped up because nobody wanted to show less courage and heroism than the others. The mood in the room was explosive. We all crowded around a table that was covered with the required volunteer forms. By signing these, we had demonstrated that we were ready to defend our country with rifle and *Panzerfaust,* bazooka, against the Red Army. I walked slowly home that night thinking about what had happened and full of pride that I had participated in this momentous event. However, when I got home I knew better then to divulge the news to the family.

Christmas was imminent, and Mutti managed to celebrate with us a quiet Christmas with the now traditional carp, diverse cookies, and a real tree. This year Tante Mali did not visit us. We had lost contact with her, because she was already on her way west with a refugee trek as we learned much later. Mutti believed that the family life should go on as usual in spite of all setbacks. Thus we continued a more or less normal life, no matter what happened around us. We could not change anything anyhow, because the government and fate determined our future. The surprising fact was, that we still had enough to eat and to heat with, since the production and distribution of food stuff and coal continued to work without a hiccup. Mutti had to be inventive, but we never went hungry. Since the food rations for children and teenagers were relatively high, the family had always enough. My mother also traded her cigarette coupons occasionally for some special food. The Christmas feast allowed us to temporarily forget the stealthily increasing fear.

The neighbors and other acquaintances had started to talk more and more about the front: "Where was it in reality? Had the *Ostwall* stopped the Russians? Would there be air raids? What should we do if the situation worsened?" Gradually nothing else interested us any longer. We did not care anymore whether Berlin got bombed for the hundredth time, how the *Ruhrgebiet* or *Mülheim* suffered worse devastation, whether American troops had landed in France, or whether they were already on German soil, or whether Dr. Goebbels still talked about the final victory or what he had coined as the "Total War". Our interest was now focussed on the immediate future of the family and *Waldenburg*, especially as the refugee stream took on a different color. At my intersection I no longer noticed Hungarians or Slovaks. They had been replaced by Poles and ever increasing numbers of Germans.

There was another horrifying development that left me dumbfounded. I observed that occasionally German military personnel was mixed in with the refugee stream. What in the world where the soldiers or officers doing here? Were they not supposed to be at the front defending us? And how about the military trucks that were loaded with everything but military equipment? Here I had just volunteered to join the army, and there parts of the army were streaming westward. One day a platoon of German MPs joined us and watched the goings-on. They came in their jeeps with automatic rifles and hand grenades and wore metal breast plates around their necks which said *Militärpolizei* (Military Police). I was absolutely delighted when I saw how they stopped all military personnel whether on foot or in army vehicles. They checked everybody's papers and let those through who had legitimate documents. Others were arrested right there on the spot. Occasionally they hauled some officers unceremoniously from their trucks or cars, tore off their epaulettes and other insignia of rank and shoved them into one of the jeeps. When my classmate and I asked what was going to happen to them, the MPs told us that these deserters and traitors would be summarily executed. Did I ever feel relieved when I realized that there was still something like justice in this world.

Now I have to complete my earlier story. In the middle of all the excitement of the last weeks I had, probably conveniently, forgotten that I had signed the induction papers for the *Waffen SS*. Therefore, I was terrified when one morning the induction order arrived in the mail: "Report immediately to the Military Command Headquarters in town." Here it had finally come into the open. Well, the explosion of Mutti left no doubt where she stood. I had never seen her in such a state of fury: "This is unheard of. Nobody has the right to draft children. This is the ultimate insanity, etc., etc." I wanted to sink into the floor; after all, I was responsible for this draft order, but fortunately her ire was directed at the military authorities and not at me. Immediately she rushed with me to the local military headquarters, where she let some high ranking officer have it: "How come that you can draft children willy-nilly without any knowledge or agreement by their parents? He has barely turned fourteen, (actually I had signed up when thirteen) and no matter what papers he has signed, this whole affair is completely unacceptable and unheard of. You will let this child go and right now!" The poor officer did not even make an attempt to defend his position, he just wanted to quiet her down and probably get rid of us as fast as possible. He admitted that there must have been an error and tore up the induction notice. Mutti departed full of triumph with her son in tow. Thus nothing had come of my ambition to join the army; and I do not recollect whether I was relieved or unhappy. At that stage I most certainly did not argue with my mother. Anyway, my enthusiasm to sacrifice myself for the fatherland must not have been overwhelming. After the war I learned from friends and classmates, who were only a few months older than I, that some of them got actually drafted but luckily never made it to the front. Back at my intersection I had begun to inquire daily where precisely the refugees were coming from. By now they were mostly German, but still from the eastern shore of the *Oder*. Pretty soon the Russians would cross the river, and the fleeing masses would come also from lands on the western side; and then it would be our turn. Talking with neighbors and acquaintances, it became clear that nobody was going to remain in *Waldenburg*, because the fear of the Russians, of enslavement, rape, and death was much too great. We too began to develop plans for the unavoidable flight. We decided to obtain a small hand drawn cart that we could load with suitcases and sacks, so that we could join the "mass migration" to the West. The thought of marching, possibly hundreds of miles, in the middle of the Silesian winter with my younger sisters, who were only six and eight years old, was almost as frightening as the thought of enduring the horrors of a Russian occupation. Then the miracle happened! During the twenty months in *Waldenburg* Mutti had become good friends with a young couple, Hanni and Walter Kobel, who lived in the apartment below us. They were originally from *Höxter* on the *Weser*, from where Dr. Kobel, a medical doctor, had been transferred to a hospital in *Waldenburg*. *Tante* Hanni, as we called her, had a little daughter Renate and was expecting a second baby. *Onkel* Walter had made every effort in the last weeks to find a place for his and our family on one of the military hospital trains that were continuously passing from the front through our town. Finally his good relations with the military medical staff panned out; and we could make new plans for the escape. He assured Mutti and his wife that his plan would definitely work and furnished them with the necessary documents. We should quit worrying because we would be evacuated at the right moment in a military hospital train. The waiting began. Marlis and I were still doing our duties and helping the refugees who were all Germans now and came already from the western shore of the *Oder,* only fifty miles away.

Little by little *Waldenburg* emptied out. One observed less traffic and fewer people in the streets. During the last two weeks before our departure, the place turned into a veritable ghost town, which did not lessen our anxieties one iota. Day and

103

night the *Stalinorgeln* (Stalin Organs; huge cannons with multiple barrels) thundered in the East and lighted up the sky during the night. The Red Army was stalled in front of *Breslau,* the capital of Silesia, because our troops were fighting desperately all along the eastern front to protect the slow exodus of the German population. As I mentioned earlier, *Breslau* had been designated by Hitler as a *Festung*, a fortress, that had to be defended without regard to losses. That was a tall order for the army that was already completely exhausted and demoralized; but the front held long enough for millions to escape. Unfortunately the once beautiful *Breslau* was essentially destroyed in the process. We had definitely given up the idea to flee on foot and had now pinned all our hopes on Uncle Walter's plan. Scary!

There was enough food. The basement storage bins of all the families who had left our house already were filled with potatoes, winter vegetables, canned fruit, and many other edibles. Surprisingly, a few stores were still open for us stragglers. We began to carry all valuables that we could not take along into the basement, thinking, of course, that we would return after the war. All paraphernalia relating to the Third Reich were eliminated except for one picture of Hitler that we did not have the nerve to destroy. We hid it very carefully in one of the basement rooms. Amazingly, Mutti permitted this although she should have known better. Next, we packed those belongings that we could readily carry, each of us a suitcase and a backpack. We planned to wear a few layers of clothing for additional warmth and to have extra clothes available.

We had daily conferences with Aunt Hanni who was talking in turn to her husband on the phone, which was still working, as were the electricity and water. One day she announced: "Be prepared, our turn will come on the eighth of February." Was that really true? What were we going to do if that did not work? Tension and fear increased from day to day. The city was so empty now, that one rarely encountered other human beings, except for the refugees. Terrifying! Rumors still abounded: "The front is only fifteen miles away. The entire *Waldenburg* county is already encircled with the exception of an escape route through Czechoslovakia." Better not to listen to anything. The thunder of the advancing *Stalinorgeln* was already enough; but hope kept the family going.

104

We got out just in Time

Finally, finally we got notified at 2:00 a.m. on the eighth of February 1945 as promised: "Be at the railroad station at 6:00 a.m. when the hospital train is expected." Did we ever move. Everything had been planned to the last detail. On this ice-cold winter morning, Mutti, the expecting *Tante* Hanni with her two year old daughter Renate, Marlis (16), I (14), Sigrid (8), and Heidi (6) left the *Cochius Straße* 19, where we had lived for twenty months in peace and harmony. Those times were gone, the future was shrouded in a dense mist, and we had no idea that we would never come back. With the little children and the luggage the trek to the railroad station was slow and arduous, but we reached it at the very first glimmer of dawn. A large crowd had already gathered in front of the tall iron gates to the platforms; and the military police had a hard time to maintain order amongst people who were desperate. *Onkel* Walter had arrived from the hospital and dealt with the officer in charge who checked our documents carefully and let us pass. Not very easy. The soldiers had to force a path through the crowd so that our little group could get through without getting trampled. We were scared, but we made it through the tall gate onto the first platform where we and a few other young mothers with children started to wait for the miracle train. Would it really come? For weeks we had not heard or seen any news, only rumors, and our interests had been reduced to the bare essentials that affected us directly. Would the front hold a little longer? Were the Russians really as bad as everybody said? Could one believe one single word that the government spoke? Who cared, as long as we did not starve or freeze, as long as there was no danger that Mutti or Marlis would be raped, and as long as we stayed together, then everything would be fine.

In the end, the train arrived, with huge red crosses painted on a white background on the sides of the tender and on the roofs and sides of the cars, slowly entering the station. Five, ten, twenty cars rolled past us, before the train stopped. Through the windows I could see the wounded soldiers in their three story bunks with their bloodied bandages; and here and there blood trickled down the windows. It was not a nice sight. This was the real war. What on earth had I imagined when I volunteered in November? We all boarded one of the few passenger cars that

105

had been reserved for women with small children. It actually was a remodeled freight car with a few windows on the sides and doors at either end, opening onto a small steel platform from which one could reach the next car. A coal stove, that had been placed in the middle of the room, kept us warm during the next ten days. Next to it were two tables and a number of chairs, where the passengers would have their meals. Of the three-tiered bunk beds, which lined the walls on both sides, our family was assigned one. Sigrid and Heidi on top, I in the middle, and Mutti and Marlis at the bottom. The car was a busy place with women and children, mostly babies and toddlers, milling about. A few boys and girls were of my and Marlis' age. A smell of baby diapers permeated the room all the time. I remember well the kids of two families who came from East Prussia and had been on the road and train for quite a while. Every family had a story to tell, and they were all very similar. As it turned out, we were the only family that came originally from the West and ultimately could go back home. Everybody else was from the East; and they would never see their homes and towns again, but who could have foresee this at the time.

Soon we had breakfast, the first meal in our new mobile world. I learned from one of the East Prussian boys that we boys had to fetch the meals from the kitchen car, a job which I enjoyed sharing with the other kids. The meals consisted mostly of thick soups, potatoes, legumes and the occasional piece of meat, and bread, margarine and jam. No doubt, we belonged to the few lucky ones, compared with the millions who had to walk for weeks or months always a short distance in front of the Soviet steamroller. Of those, only the healthy and strong ones survived. Old people frequently did not even attempt to flee, stayed behind, or killed themselves. Many fell by the wayside, babies froze to death, refugee ships or barges disappeared in the Baltic Sea. -- I read recently the review of a new book written by the German author Günter Grass. It tells the story of a passenger liner "Gustloff", overloaded with thousands of refugees, which was torpedoed by a Russian submarine. -- We listened to some of the most unbelievable stories that, after the war, proved to be true.

When the train departed I saw still hundreds of people surrounding the train station. Did they ever make it or did they fall into Russian hands? Nobody ever knew. Slowly the train rolled through the hilly, snow covered countryside towards the mountains. It did not take long to figure out the driving rhythm of the train. During the day it was parked either in a tunnel or in some quiet stretch of forest somewhat protected by the tree canopies; during the night it continued its course. This was done to avoid attacks from the air, which seemed unbelievable at the time, because we were in a Red Cross train. However, these attacks made some sense when I learned after the war that the Allied Forces harbored the suspicion that the Germans would use the Red Cross as a mantle to protect troop and equipment transports. Who knows? As a result, the Red Cross did not necessarily protect, on the contrary it might actually invite attack. Ours was truly a bona fide Red Cross train with wounded soldiers, women and children. Our journey continued through the *Riesengebirge,* the mountain range between *Schlesien* (now Poland) and *Böhmen und Mähren* (now The Czech Republic), probably on the same route that Mutti and I had taken a little more than a year earlier in the opposite direction. One rumor was apparently true, that the only escape route still open was to the South. After a few days we found ourselves in *Böhmen und Mähren* and, according to hearsay, we were on the way to Prague.

It took only a few more days until we arrived there in a huge railroad station with dozens of tracks jammed with trains of all kinds: Open and closed freight cars, military transports with soldiers from different axis countries, military trains with tanks, trucks and guns, and normal passenger trains. It looked chaotic but it seemed to work. The organizational machinery of the Third Reich remained intact until the very end, no matter how close the enemy armies had advanced and how severe the air bombardments were. We youngsters were allowed to leave our car, but had to watch with extreme care that we did not get overrun by a train when we jumped from track to track. I went immediately into the station building where I had boarded the train for *Bielorad* one and a half years ago. However, the military police would not let me venture into the city. It was off limits to all German civilians because the Czechs were no longer tolerant of their occupiers as they had been out of fear and necessity for the last seven years. The never ending rumors said that an uprising had happened or was about to happen, but the German troops were still in control of the city and the railroad station. As I learned later this had not been true at all. The uprising did not take place until April, when the Americans and Russians were already on their way towards the capital. Recently I read in the archives that Stalin considered Prague his most desirable prize, because the last centuries had taught the European rulers the adage, "who owns Prague, owns the world". Therefore, the Red Army was under special pressure to get to Prague as fast as possible. At the same time general Patton's tank battalions were racing also towards the same goal in order to save as much of Czechoslovakia as possible from the Communists. In the middle of all this, the German general Schörner defended the city and its surrounding industry "to the last man", but he had to surrender on May 11, four days after the end of the war, with one million men because they finally ran out of food, fuel, and ammunition.

In those months we had no idea what happened in the world beyond us, nor did we care. Sometimes we learned about a few events through this or that rumor, but mostly our energies were spent on survival. We did not know about the meeting and agreements in Yalta, where the borders and influence spheres of Europe had been drawn. We did not know that Stalin was the great beneficiary of those agreements. Apparently President Roosevelt had believed Stalin's assertions that all European countries that were now occupied by the Red Army would be governed democratically. That meant the actual drawing of boarders was not very important, because the governments of all European states would be self elected and sovereign democracies. The Yalta Treaty gave control over everything east of the *Elbe* to the Soviets. (Footnote 11) This included Poland, Estonia, Latvia, Lithuania, Czechoslovakia, Slovenia, Croatia, Yugoslavia, Hungary, Rumania, Bulgaria, and the East of Germany and, I believe, Austria. What an unbelievable catch for Stalin and the Communists! The Americans had only won half the war in Europe. They had defeated Hitler and his cohorts all right, but they did not consider or recognize the much bigger danger of the Communists who would overrun first East then West Europe and ultimately try to dominate the entire world. It is surprising that Roosevelt signed the agreement, although Churchill with his deep insight into European history and geography had been present and advised against it. It is one of history's ironies, that President Wilson was not able to affect the Versailles Treaty, which laid the foundation for the Second World War, and that President Roosevelt agreed to the Yalta Treaty, which laid the foundation for the Cold War, potentially leading to a Third World War. The treaty contributed to forty five years of endless fighting between the West and the Communists around the entire world.

History is full of coincidences. At about the time when our train stopped for a day or two in the Prague railroad station, my friend Günter was working somewhere in Prague for a German *Panzer* regiment, peeling potatoes and cleaning weapons. Like I, Günter had left the KLV camp to live with his mother, who had fled from the air bombardments in Mülheim to a small town in Bavaria. During the last months of the war, one of the desperate acts of the government had been the creation of a *Hitler Jugend* organization, called *Werwolf,* which was supposed to fight Russians and Americans alike with rifles and bazookas and continue an insurgency after the war. There were enough idealistic and enthusiastic teenagers who saw this as an opportunity to help the fatherland now and beyond the end of the regime. Günter joined one of these *Werwolf* groups, got a uniform, and followed the group leader through fields and forests towards the East into *Böhmen-Mähren.* Luckily that man had kept his senses, dissolved the little unit after a few days of marching, and persuaded the boys to get rid of their uniforms and weapons, obtain some civilian clothes from nearby villagers, and find their way quietly home. However, Günter and a friend were not yet ready to terminate the adventure. By truck and train they made their way to Prague and managed to report to a German *Panzer* Unit. I would guess that the commander was surprised by these two fourteen-year-old volunteers. He ordered them to help in the kitchen and with the weapons maintenance. Dutifully Günter and his friend helped the cook, cleaned kitchen utensils, kept the buildings clean, and helped to maintain the guns and other equipment. After two months, the unit made its way to the West and surrendered to the American forces near *Pilsen.* Günter who had not succeeded in fighting as a real soldier would at least now become a bona fide prisoner of war. Not so, he was foiled again, because the Americans were not about to deal with children. They sorted them out and sent them home to their parents.

The recollections of my American friend, Walter Reichelt, complete this triangle of coincidences. Walter and I became good friends when we worked together on a huge carbon dioxide laser as part of the Inertial Fusion program around 1980 at the Los Alamos National Laboratory in New Mexico. When we exchanged "war stories" I discovered that Walter also happened to be in the neighborhood of *Pilsen* at about the same time. Walter had joined the US Army with nineteen, had made it all the way through Europe and was on his way towards Prague with the advancing motorized divisions. He told me what an unbelievable experience it was to see these tens of thousands of German troops and civilians streaming towards the American lines to surrender and find shelter from the Soviet avalanche. Surrender to the Americans was by far the preferred choice for soldiers and civilians alike. Anything was better than falling into hands of the Red Army. To handle this mass of humanity Walter's regiment had to throw up temporary camps. Since they had neither time nor material, they could not contain these masses within fences. Instead they simply staked out an adequate area in a field and patrolled its perimeter with tanks and jeeps to make sure that nobody could escape. I guess the Americans could not imagine that escape was the last thought of anybody in the camps. The refugees and soldiers longed only for one thing, the end of that devastating war. They were more than happy to stay where they were, and hopefully get fed by the conquerer. I have always imagined that it was entirely plausible that Günter's *Panzer* unit was one of those that rolled in with white flags while Walter was cruising in his jeep to keep them all in. In this way, two of my best friends might have met or at least were at the same place during those turbulent weeks and months.

While our Red Cross train was parked on one of the side tracks of the Prague railroad station I started to scout our surroundings, where I happened upon a frightening scene that haunts me to this day. A freight train was very slowly pulling in and came to a stop a couple of tracks away from our train. I could vaguely discern human voices coming from the inside of the sealed cars. This was peculiar, because all other trains that transported civilians or troops had their huge side doors open, and people were often sitting in the openings letting their legs dangle from the cars. The doors of these cars, however, were locked from the outside, and even the small openings above were covered with barbed wire. Upon closer inspection, I saw human heads and arms in these openings. As I got within a few feet of one of the cars, faces were being pressed against the barbed wire and arms were squeezed through it. Whoever was in there begged desperately for water and bread. Horrified, I hastened back to our car, filled a cooking pan with water, picked up a ladle and slices of bread, and ran back. As I tried to reach up to the opening as far as I could, the hands bloodied from the barbed wire, were reaching down, ripped the bread from my hands and grabbed the water filled ladle. The shouting in what appeared to be a slavic language reached my innermost bones. After this success, I raced back to our car, got more water and bread, and flew to the second opening. I had barely given everything to this other set of arms, when two German soldiers approached in a trot and screamed at me: "Stay away from that car and get out of here as fast as you can!" I was scared to death. The soldiers were deaf to my pleas that these people needed food and drink and instead became so menacing that I fled in a panic. My report of this terrifying event raised a stir in our car with words of horror and outrage; but none of the women had the nerve to do anything about it. The lives of their children were foremost in their minds; and nobody dared to say or undertake anything against the authorities, unless they were prepared to sacrifice their families. I was left with my own terror, frustration, and thoughts. Half a year later, when I heard the first time about the unbelievable slaughter of the Jews, I realized what I had most likely witnessed was a freight train with eastern Jews.

After a day or two the signal for our departure was given, and the train extricated itself slowly from this maze of tracks. It picked up the former rhythm with days in forests or tunnels and nights of safe traveling. When somebody called out one day that the passing meadows, fields, and forests were again German, the overwhelming tension of the past weeks began to subside. We had escaped without losing as much as a hair. There had been only one incident during one night, when the train sped through a curve. Heidi fell out of her and Sigrid's bunk bed and landed with a thud on the floor. A nurse was found who inspected the child and declared it whole. Hopefully she would remain that way, which she did. Back to bed!

A rumor - always rumors - started to spread that the train would take us to *Thüringen* (Thuringia) in the heartland of Germany. This rumor was right. One beautiful morning we rolled into the small station of *Ronneburg* without the field hospital part of the train, which must have been decoupled at an earlier stop.

A reception committee had assembled already on the platform including the mayor with his staff and a large number of helpers, many still in the brown uniforms of the *Hitler Jugend* and the *Bund Deutscher Mädchen*. Everybody was very friendly and helpful and made us really feel welcome. They assisted us with the few pieces of luggage and found temporary lodging for us new arrivals. I thought I was in fantasy land. Thousands of people were killed everyday at the front and in the big cities, refugees tried to escape and stay alive, the Russians were already on the west side of the *Oder*, and the Americans had probably already crossed the *Rhein* (Actually they had not. The bridge at *Remagen* fell on the ninth of March, about three weeks later.); but here they still lived in the security of the Third *Reich*. Never mind! It was beautiful to be received so warmly and to feel secure again.

Many months after the end of the war our family realized that we and everybody else on that train had been very, very lucky, because our train had not taken the more direct route through *Sachsen* (Saxonia) with a stop in the huge railroad yards of *Dresden*. It was during the night from the thirteenth to the fourteenth of February 1945 that *Dresden* suffered the largest and most devastating air attack on a German city. Thousands of bombers in wave after wave completely destroyed the city and railroad station, and the incendiary bombs produced firestorms of wind velocities of up to the unbelievable speed of 350 miles per hour, a number that I found in the pertinent literature. Temperatures reached levels of 3000°F that actually melted steel. A second bombardment followed the first during the next day to prevent fire crews from extinguishing the holocaust. About 12,000 buildings and 80,000 apartments were erased. The number of the dead was never accurately ascertained, because city and station were inundated with refugees. Later estimates reached something like 300,000! Again, luck had remained on our side.

The End in Ronneburg

No doubt, the little town of *Ronneburg* was well prepared for the refugees who were suddenly swept onto their station. After our registration *Tante* Hanni and the Jansens were taken to their new quarters that our future hosts had prepared for the newcomers. Tante Hanni and Renate found a room in a house at the lower corner of the *Kaiser Wilhelm Strasse*; and we were lodged six houses further up the street. There, Mrs. Henning and her daughter Liselotte lived in a large very well appointed apartment on the second floor of a stately house of the turn of the century. It became obvious right away that there had been some miscommunication. The Hennings were overwhelmed at the sight of a family of five when they had expected only a mother with two small kids. After a quick consultation with the organizers of the refugee distribution, a place was found for Marlis and me with the Wurmb family two houses down the street. We moved into the bedroom of the two Wurmb children who ended up sleeping in their family living room. It is a shame that I forgot their names in spite of the fact that they had graciously ceded their bedroom to us, and we soon became good friends.

Both families, the Hennings and the Wurmbs, were very nice to us, helped wherever they could, and made sure that we felt at home. Starting our new life, Marlis and I surveyed the neighborhood and the little town. We found a three story schoolhouse at the upper end of our street where pupils were still having classes. At its lower end the *Kaiser Wilhelm Strasse* intersected with the Main Street, from where it took ten minutes to the center of town. There the street widened to a square with a beautiful old town hall, painted wine red, on one side, a large fountain in the middle and a small hotel on the other side. During the first days our family took its meals in that hotel "Gambrinus" until Mrs. Henning had found a small electric range for our cooking needs. The Main Street was paved with old fashioned cobblestones which were still in wide use in those days. Shops and businesses lined both sides of the street; and women, children, and old men went quietly about their daily business. The little town overlooked a large lake; and from its far shore one could admire the pleasant silhouette of the town's houses and churches. Ronneburg was surrounded by meadows, fields, and forests; it was the center of an agricultural region.

We did not attend the local school, because my mother wanted to go back home as soon as possible after the end of the war. Also, I did not report to the local *Jungvolk Fähnlein* because I no longer believed in their ideals. To me the whole thing had become absurd. As far as I was concerned the war was over and the Third *Reich* was finished. Uniforms, singing, marching, and flags had lost their meaning. I had already learned the hard way in *Waldenburg* how the beautiful ideology went kaputt and how the entire house of cards collapsed. I gradually came around to the recognition that all the government propaganda, which we faithfully had believed in, had been false for years. That made it easier to slowly distance myself and take leave from the Third *Reich* without sorrow, as it slipped away. With my fourteen years I did not realize the enormity of it all. It simply had come to an end. It was obvious to me that Germany had lost, no matter how terrible this thought was. Who knew how all this would end? Who would arrive here first, the Russian or the American tanks? And what might happen afterwards?

The news that filtered through from the East confirmed the worst expectations harbored by the vast army of refugees. The Red Army did not give any pardon. The Germans had to be punished for their misdeeds - and they were. Men were deported, women, no matter what age, were raped. Those who did not obey ended up in labor camps or were shot. Years later we learned about the horrors of those first weeks of the occupation from Dr. Kobel who had stayed behind with his hospital. He managed to remain free and alive by always wearing his white frock and a stethoscope around his neck. Only this made it possible for him to leave and enter his apartment at the *Cochius Strasse* at will. Even the Soviet troops respected a doctor. However, his freedom came almost to an abrupt end one fateful evening. He came home as usual, when he came upon a military patrol who wanted to arrest him on the spot. With the help of his limited Russian vocabulary and the few German words of the Russian officer he gradually discovered the reason for the arrest. When some soldiers had searched the building for food and valuables they had found a hidden Hitler picture in the basement. This was absolutely awful, because it was the Hitler picture, that the Jansen family had not destroyed and had left so "conveniently" in the basement. Poor innocent Uncle Walter got the full treatment. The officer shouted at him, accused him of being a Nazi, and wanted to take him into custody right away. This could have been easily the end of his freedom or even his life. He employed his entire power of persuasion to explain that he had nothing to do with that picture, and that some Nazis who had lived in the same house must have left it there. He finally talked and gestured himself out of that precarious situation, where the fact that he was one of the few doctors in town must have greatly contributed.

Also, his hospital did not remain unscathed by the victorious Red Army. No matter whether the women were young or old, healthy or sick, nurses or patients, they were raped like any other woman that had remained in *Waldenburg*. The horror was absolutely terrible. Tante Hanni confided to Mutti years later her husband's worst experience. A young woman who had lived with her baby and mother in the apartment above us could not or would not leave *Waldenburg* and consequently was still there when the Soviet occupiers marched in. After a few days, as the soldiers started to search all the houses for enemies and loot, they discovered these two poor women who had zero protection. Even if there had been a man he would have been taken away or shot. Apparently the news of the discovery spread fast, and the ensuing ordeal is unimaginable. How the women survived one rape after another remains a miracle. Uncle Walter had also told his wife how in their desperation women threw themselves at the officers in order to get some protection from the troops. Others committed suicide before it was too late. Because of these rumors and reports, our family pinned all its hopes on the Americans. No matter how the incessant propaganda had depicted them, -- I remember pictures of the American soldiers as werewolves devouring little babies, and other scary images -- they had to be more civilized than their Russian friends.

And what were we children up to? As I mentioned earlier, we did attend neither school nor *Hitlerjugend* duty, although both were compulsory. I do not remember how my mother got away with this; probably nothing mattered anymore in the confusion of the last war months. As it turned out, there was a more urgent matter at hand for our family. Since Papa had worked for the government as a civil servant, Mutti received a pension after his death for herself and her children. It was not great, but sufficient for us to lead a comfortable life, albeit by watching expenses carefully. The situation changed dramatically in the last turbulent months of the war, when the pension did not reach us anymore. Mutti had a choice of becoming dependent on public welfare or finding other ways of supporting the family. Because she was not the woman who would even dream about living on

115

welfare, she started to investigate business opportunities. In the course of her inquiries she learned from the owner of a stationary store that their shelves were essentially empty, and the owner would be delighted to sell anything that came into Mutti's mind. The family decided after a few brainstorming sessions to produce some art and craft articles that were simple enough that we could make them from still available materials. A new business was started with small items like bookmarks and little wall hangings. Mutti found and bought the materials: Stiff paper, cardboard, india ink, water colors, brushes, and calligraphy pens. Marlis, who was the family artist, drew and painted the decorations, and I wrote the text in gothic letters that I had learned in school. Remembering the bookmark that my mother once gave to my father, the first product became a pretty bookmark with a picture of a man who had fallen asleep over his book and the words, "Here I fell asleep." These bookmarks and others with different themes sold immediately like the proverbial hot cakes, almost faster than we could produce them. We worked day after day sitting around the large dining table in our living room. Somebody came up with the next idea to create small wall pictures with popular proverbs and accompanying drawings or paintings. Mutti scrounged glass panes which we mounted with something like black electrical tape as the frame on a cardboard backing. These proverbs dealt with the *Heimat* (homeland) and sold exceedingly well to all the refugees in town. One said, "Only when you live on foreign soil do you appreciate what homeland means," with a little house, picket fence, and a tree. Another well known German saying adorned one masterpiece, "When grass has finally covered an utter dumb event, there sure will be a dumb cow that eats it to the ground," accompanied by a cow eating eagerly a clump of grass. The next product was launched when Marlis drew a scene from a fairy tale on thin plywood, I cut the intricate contours with a coping saw, and she painted the picture in pretty colors. Beautifully embroidered toting bags were next sent to the market.

After a few weeks business was booming. Paper dolls became an exceptionally fast selling item and made an important contribution to our economic growth. Marlis drew the dolls and their clothes. Mutti managed to get rubber stencils made of the drawings and she was successful in obtaining heavy weight colored paper. I turned into a printing machine, and Sigrid and

116

Heidi filled the sets in paper envelopes. Four workers toiled with pride around the big table. Mutti organized the business and handled purchasing and marketing. Thus our little family had become independent from any pension or welfare. In retrospect, that was quite an achievement and provided us not only with a good income but also with savings for the uncertain future.

We felt the tumult of the last war months all around us. Rumors flew. Official news that we eagerly listened to on Mrs. Henning's radio were clearly no longer related to reality. Hitler still talked about the *Endsieg*, final victory, and about new weapons that would suddenly change everything. -- The V-1 and V-2 rockets had actually been such weapons, but they had not affected the outcome of the war at all. -- Goebbels kept talking about the *Totalen Krieg* (total war) where absolutely nothing but helping in the war effort was allowed. Did they really believe their own words? Instead of the troops that would attain the "Final Victory" I encountered occasionally *Volkssturm Männer* (people's army men), older men over fifty or sixty, in their civilian clothes with their rifles. They all wore armbands as the only indication of a uniform, so that the enemy would recognize and treat them as soldiers and not shoot them as guerrillas. The *Volkssturm* (people's army) had been created during the final months as the ultimate measure of activating the very last reserves. It was not clear in my mind what these old men, armed only with rifles and little ammunition, could accomplish. While Hitler promised surprise weapons, vast numbers of American bombers flew over *Ronneburg* during bright daylight without a German fighter in sight. Harry Mietusch and I stood often in the garden of the Henning house and counted the shiny planes in the sky. They always flew in formations of something like ten by ten that were arranged to form a giant armada of many hundreds. What a stupendous sight, what unopposed might! Huge flocks of death birds on their flight to Berlin, Leipzig, Dresden or other important cities. We did no longer pay any attention to the wailing sirens because we knew that those armadas were not interested in an unimportant fleck like *Ronneburg*.

Harry Mietusch had fled with his mother from Berlin. His father was fighting somewhere on the eastern front; nobody knew where or whether he was still alive. The young Mrs. Kiekbusch had also come from Berlin with her baby; the husband also in the East. That's how it was everywhere. Women and children were at home or had fled from the big cities or the East; men were still fighting somewhere, had become prisoners, were dead, or missing in action. Harry and I at the age of fourteen were the oldest boys still around. He was a little older than I, had volunteered for the army, and actually joined some *Hitlerjugend* group. They had received their army uniforms and had left with rifles to participate in the war, nobody knew how and where. After endless marches through fields and forests eastward, their leader had apparently second thoughts and dissolved the small band. They threw their rifles away, obtained civilian clothes from somebody and found their way back home in small, inconspicuous groups. Mutti told me that Harry's mother was greatly relieved when her boy showed up again fourteen days later. Harry and I became good friends and maintained that friendship for many years through an extensive correspondence and mutual visits. -- Brigit and I visited him the last time in 1961 at Cornell University where he taught German philology and literature. Then we gradually lost touch.

I took it for granted then and find it overwhelming today that the food distribution still worked flawlessly in April of 1945. Each month we received our rationing cards with which we could still buy all the essentials. Of course, there were no luxury items like chocolate, cocoa, oranges, bananas, etc. They had disappeared years ago; but we always had a reasonable supply of potatoes, turnips, bread, legumes, flour, sugar, local vegetables and fruit, as well as milk, margarine, oil, drawn butter, a few eggs, and some meat. The other miracle was that the railroads were still functioning in spite of incessant bombardments. Although the big stations were all destroyed, the system of tracks, signals, locomotives and railroad cars was repaired immediately after each air raid, so that the traffic could continue. This resiliency was, of course, only possible because of a railroad system that was based on independent steam locomotives instead of an electrified network. Such an electrified system, that existed already in Switzerland, must have been out of question for the warring parties (Russia, France, and Germany) because of its obvious vulnerability with overhead lines, transformers, switch yards, and complex control systems. A case where the new technology was well in hand since the thirties, but the old strategy proved to be superior, certainly in Germany.

Autos had disappeared almost completely from streets

and highways. Private cars that existed before the war had all been commandeered by the army. Only country doctors, police, and commercial enterprises, deemed essential for the war effort, could keep their cars and trucks. Furthermore, gasoline had become so scarce that most motor vehicles were powered by wood burners that produced methane gas. This was stored in large gas tanks, that were mounted on the back of the vehicles. The gas was generated by burning the wood slowly with a minimum of air. This did not result in a very powerful engine performance, but the vehicles moved. However, the owner had to put in fresh wood every so often, and climbing hills was slow. Our high school teacher Schmitz, who had served in a *Panzer* division, once told us that even the training *Panzer* used wood carburetors. Did they ever manage to climb a hill?

During the last weeks of April the war came rapidly to an end. Tank barriers were erected across the roads leading into *Ronneburg*. For the first time I noticed a few German soldiers here and there, wandering alone or in little groups through the landscape. I also observed occasionally low flying American fighter planes; but they never bothered us except for once in Gera, the biggest town of the region. Sometimes, I accompanied Mutti on her visit to *Gera* to buy materials for our arts and crafts business. During one of those visits we learned pretty quickly what the attacks by low flying fighters meant. As many times before, we rode into *Gera* on the milk can truck, one popular means of transportation. The dairies used those flatbed trucks to collect the raw milk from the farmers and deliver it to a central dairy. The drivers were always ready to take passengers along who squeezed themselves between or sat on top of the big metal cans. We were just visiting a store in the center of town when the sirens screamed their alarm: Low flying fighter planes. The streets emptied in seconds. Everybody dashed into houses and cellars. We raced down into a medieval, vaulted cellar that offered plenty of protection against both machine gun fire and bombs. One minute those fast fighters appeared, the next minute they were gone. Quickly out of the cellar and visit other stores. Then again rat-a-tat-a-tat, into and out of the next cellar. In spite of this racket during most of the day we completed our purchases. The thought that we had to return home under the same circumstances was not exactly encouraging. In the afternoon we made our way on foot towards *Ronneburg* which lies about five miles east of *Gera*. Luckily a dark green truck with a red cross on its roof and sides stopped and offered us a ride. Even though the driver had warned us that we had to jump out and dive into the ditch at the approach of low flying aircraft, we boarded the empty vehicle. Sure enough, after some time we heard the airplane engine noise from afar, the truck stopped, and the driver, Mutti and I were in the ditch faster then one could count to five. Nothing happened to either the truck or us, and we completed the trip whole and alive with only one other visit to the ditch.

In the following days the rumors began to fly again: "The Americans are coming. They are only thirty miles from here." The next day: "They are only ten miles away." Finally time had come to prepare for the unavoidable. The first good news was that we did not have to fear a battle, because the German Army no longer existed; it had dissolved. If I saw five or ten German soldiers in the last days that was a lot. The second good news was, the Americans came and not the Russians. Nevertheless, we were also scared of the Americans. The only knowledge we had of them had been poured into our brains during the last two years by the Goebbels' propaganda machine; and the reader can imagine that the information had not been exactly favorable. What would the American troops really do? Would they round us up and deport or kill us? Would they rape and plunder like the Soviets? Most likely not. What would they do with a fourteen year old *Hitler Junge* (boy) or with a sixteen year old *Hitler Mädchen* (girl)? Nobody could give an answer; only the rumor mill ran hot. During the last day the prominent citizens of *Ronneburg* were arguing fiercely with each other whether to complete the tank barriers outside of town or to tear them down. Purportedly the Americans had given an ultimatum: "Either the barriers come down or the town will be shelled." Luckily the older, cooler heads prevailed. They managed to persuade the young hotheads, who could not accept the end of their Third *Reich*, to finally give up to avoid a last minute destruction of their hometown. The tank barriers were removed. In the meantime we discussed with the Hennings and other neighbors the pros and cons of hanging white sheets from the windows and, more importantly, the choice of the right moment. The choice seemed to be between execution because of treason, if you hung out the sheets too early, and shelling of the house or street by the advancing troops, if they came out too late. One or the other could kill you. When should we burn all discriminating documents and books, and when to dye the brown shirts and jackets blue or green? When was the perfect moment for the "changeover"? We simply did not know how to behave, because nobody had any experience with a collapsing *Reich* on one side and an unknown conquerer on the other.

It did not take long until we could relax realizing that we had made the right moves at the right time. All house walls towards the streets were draped with white sheets hanging from the windows, and the chimneys were still smoking. The cleaners who specialized in dyeing clothes or fabrics did the best business in years. My yellow shirts and Marlis' brown jackets had changed their colors to green or blue overnight. Nobody was punished or shot for treason, because there was nobody left to enforce the law. All inhabitants of the Henning house had fled into the basement where we first hid Marlis under a pile of junk. Based on the reports from the Russian occupation of *Waldenburg* she, as a sixteen year old girl, was considered to be in the gravest danger.

Suddenly, the Americans arrived. Their Sherman tanks rattled through town making a formidable, wall shaking ruckus on the cobble stones. It did not take long until two American soldiers descended into our basement. They did not devour the babies, they did not rape the women, they did not shoot Harry and me on the spot; all they wanted to know whether German soldiers were anywhere in the house or basement. Well, there weren't any, no wonder, because the German soldiers had ceased to exist. By now they had thrown their weapons away, obtained civilian clothes from some villagers, and blended into the population. The two Americans disappeared as quickly as they had come. FOR EVERYONE IN THAT BASEMENT THE WAR WAS OVER!!! We all had waited with great anxiety for this moment for months. Without any doubt it was the biggest event of the last six years, after all the sufferings and horrors. But now when the moment arrived, we were too exhausted and numb to hug each other, to cry or laugh, let alone celebrate. We emerged from the basement enormously relieved and subdued at the same time. It was true, the war was over; but nobody could even try to imagine its unforeseeable, most likely devastating consequences.

There is Life after the War

As soon as it seemed prudent I ventured into the street with neighbor kids to survey the situation and take a closer look at these people who had defeated us. My first lasting impression was that the soldiers, victors and conquerors, were very friendly towards us kids. Huge black men grinned at us from their small open cars or from enormous trucks and said things in a language which did not remind me of the English I had learned in school for three years. They gave us chocolate, a delicacy we had not tasted for too long Then they offered something else that had a sweet taste, could be chewed, but not eaten, unless you swallowed it whole. Later, other kids explained to me that this was "chewing gum", something you were supposed to chew and spit out afterwards but not to swallow. Also later, I learned to make sense of the new English: "Wann'a chewin' gum?" A military detachment had been quartered in the school at the upper end of our street. A few soldiers had toppled a German military guard house, sat on its side, and took each others photos. They all moved about on these funny, very soft, rubber soles, which I found utterly nonmilitary. After all, I was used to nailed boots and strict military discipline. Instead of marching through town "in proper formations" they leisurely drove around in these open military vehicles that looked a little bit like the "*Kübelwagen*" of the German army. Soon I found out that they were called "Jeeps". And when they drove through town in these huge "Mack" trucks they let their arms or legs dangle from the windows. This fourteen-year-old boy could simply not comprehend that these characters had defeated the German Army. Little did I know about the vast industrial might of their country, the United States of America. To the great disappointment of all children, they immediately closed the only public open-air swimming pool. We went and watched how they scrubbed sides and bottom energetically with detergent and filled it with fresh water, just in order to have their pictures taken posing on the high dive. I do not recollect ever having seen anybody in the water, yet we who wanted to swim so badly were not allowed in "our" pool. Then they did something else that was very strange and seemed a bit ridiculous. They played ball in front of their living quarters. However, it was a most peculiar ball game that consisted of one soldier throwing a little ball very forcefully towards another soldier who tried to catch it. Apparently to make his task easier he wore a huge upholstered leather glove on the catching hand. Extraordinarily strange! And they went on for hours, changing roles and players. It seemed to be one other crazy thing these Americans were doing. How did I know that this was part of a game called "baseball", a sport we had never heard of.

However, it did not take long for us to find out that these friendly Americans meant business. A few hours after the arrival of the troops an order was posted everywhere: "All civilians have to remain in their houses from 7:00 p.m. until 6:00 a.m. If anybody is caught outside he will be imprisoned or shot on sight." Curfew! The authorities were probably concerned about insurgencies or attacks on single soldiers in the dark of the night. Of all things that was certainly the last thing on our and the neighbors' mind. Everybody was happy that finally the miserable war was over and we could breathe again, albeit under a new overlord. Sometimes Marlis and I forgot to pay attention to time and were still away from home after 7:00 p.m. Then we had to sneak from house to house through adjacent gardens always in fear of some guard suddenly shouting or even shooting. The next order was posted on all store windows and lamp posts: "All weapons and cameras have to be delivered to the town hall by 5:00 p.m. tomorrow." Mutti and I went in a hurry to deliver our small family camera that did not have much value. To my surprise a large heap of about six feet in height and diameter had already been assembled by the time we got there. What a shame; all these beautiful and expensive cameras would probably be crushed and thrown away. I did not see any weapons, no wonder, because Germans did not own guns or rifles unless they were soldiers or police. What was the commander thinking? Only years later in the US did I realize that almost every American had one or more rifles in his house for hunting and self defense. Different countries, different customs.

As Mutti was throwing the camera on the big heap, I discovered two huge photographs of about six by six feet affixed to the wall of the town hall. One showed unbelievably emaciated men in black and white striped clothes who were lying or sitting on a few bunk beds. The other showed hundreds of corpses that had been piled into big heaps. The captions explained that these men were Jews who had been brought into concentration camps

.there they worked as slave laborers, starved to death, died of diseases, or were killed outright. My mother and I were shaken by these terrible photos and at the same time infuriated that the Americans would engage in such abhorrent propaganda of the same kind as Dr. Goebbels'. There was no question in our minds that these pictures had been specially made and hung from the wall of the town hall in order to humiliate and intimidate us. There could not be any truth behind these photos; under no circumstances could Germans have committed such despicable, inhuman crimes. Back at Hennings we discussed these photos with acquaintances and neighbors; and everybody came to the definite conclusion that such horrors did not exist and that we were being exposed to the same hate propaganda that we had been bombarded with in the past. We had not the slightest idea that the day would come when we would believe the horrible truth behind these photos and accept the fact that our German government had actually committed such atrocities. However, I have German acquaintances in this country who are still, after sixty years, in denial of the facts that gradually emerged.

The whole country knew, of course, that Hitler hated Jews and that the government persecuted them in many different ways. In almost every one of Hitler's or Goebbels' speeches you heard a hateful tirade about the Jews. Sometimes you saw a poster at the door of a store, "*Juden nicht erwünscht!*" (Jews are not welcome). Mutti had told us that she was no longer allowed to buy in a Jewish store after 1936, because she was the wife of a civil servant. I remembered the *Kristallnacht* (crystal night) on November 8, 1938, when we gawked at the burned out synagogue and shattered windows of Krischel and Gelsam and another Jewish store in town. During the war I saw occasionally people wearing a yellow star on their coats. I read recently that the government had ordered this in September 1941. The propaganda machinery repeated over and over: "The Jews are the enemies of the state; we have to battle and defeat the international Zionists; they are responsible for Germany's economic misery after the First World War; they have been usurers for many centuries; they are not Aryans but of an inferior race, etc.,etc." -- I do not know why the Hitler government always made the distinction between the Aryan and the Jewish races, but never between the Christian and Jewish faiths. The racial distinction was so embedded in my memory that I became only fully aware of the other distinction, namely of the 2000-year-old religious differences, after I had met Brigit who had never thought about racial differences. -- The hate propaganda of the *Dritte Reich* was somewhat abstract for my sister, our friends and me, because we did not know any Jewish children or families neither at school, nor in the neighborhood, nor through our parents. As mentioned earlier, Mülheim, being an industrial town with a primarily blue collar population, had only a tiny Jewish community. Jews literally did not exist for us as tangible human beings. I never heard family members or friends of my parents say anything about Jews, good or bad. It was most likely too dangerous in front of us children. However, I have to assume that people discussed the fate of the Jews, but only with extremely trustworthy friends. In the fall of 1944 in *Waldenburg* I saw a number of prison workers in their black and white striped suits repairing a broken sewage line. I did not give it any thought until I discovered yellow stars on their clothes. Having been inculcated for so long with the idea that the Jews had always exploited the German people, it seemed only fair to me that, for a change, they had to do manual labor themselves.

Then came the next blow. Posters announced that all German women and girls over sixteen had to report to the town hall for a gynecological examination for venereal diseases. It is easy to imagine how upset and furious my mother and her acquaintances were. This was the worst of all humiliations to imply that German women and girls who had grown up in the puritan society of the Third *Reich* were possibly infected by syphilis or other venereal diseases. What on earth did these Americans think? Maybe they should examine their own soldiers instead. In spite of all the protests the military government proceeded with the hated examinations.

After this flare-up the little town started to settle down to a new life. Our family continued with its business that really blossomed; but we also had to reserve more time now for the shopping of groceries, because the food production and distribution that had functioned so well before had been derailed. Our wonderful rye bread was replaced by American yellow cornbread. We found this really awful, since corn was grown only for feeding livestock but not humans. We had no idea that the American people actually liked corn and corn products, and that their corn was of a different variety that had been especially bred for human consumption. Frequently we had to stand in long lines to get groceries and produce because the supply had become scarce and irregular. During the berry harvest the whole family worked in a berry plantation where we received a percentage of fruit for each picked can and, better yet, where we could eat as much as we wanted during picking. After the farmers had brought in the grain harvest, we went into the surrounding fields to fill our sacks with ears of wheat, rye, and oats that had been left on the ground. Later in the fall we collected stray potatoes after the farmers were done. It was very important to arrive on a field early before anybody else to collect most of the bounty. Marlis or I always scouted around to determine the precise day when a farmer was going to harvest his field. As one can imagine, we were not the only gatherers! We also collected apples from the highway ditches. It was the custom in *Thüringen* (Thuringia) for farmers to plant their fruit trees along the roads, and allow poor people to collect fruit from the ground but never from the trees. With these extra "harvests" we supplemented our meager diet substantially. We learned fast how and where to find extra food sources and to stand in line at the regular stores like everybody else. Queuing became a main occupation for years to come. Besides all this, we continued to spend most of our time in our business to maintain our economic independence.

These were the important events in our immediate world. For us the war had been over for a while now; but what was happening elsewhere? The first news of the END trickled through by word of mouth. We learned that the American and Russian troops had met in *Torgau* at the *Elbe* and had shaken hands on a destroyed bridge that had fallen into the river. The remainder of the German *Wehrmacht* had surrendered under Admiral Dönitz. Shortly thereafter the German capitulation was signed on the seventh of May 1945 in *Rheims.* The European war had come to an end after almost six years of endless devastation, indescribable misery, and an estimated thirty million dead. The *Tausendjährige Reich,* the empire that was supposed to last a thousand years, had ended after only twelve and had destroyed itself and the rest of Europe with it. One single man, who was not even a German, had managed through his demagogic oratory to convince eighty million Germans of his ideas and then force them to stay with him to the end. He had succeeded with "his" German *Volk* to throw all of Europe into the abyss. Not much was left of "his" *Großdeutschland* (Greater Germany, i.e. Germany, Austria, Sudetenland (northern part of Czechoslovakia), Posen (western part of Poland), and Elsass/Lothringen). Approximately five million Germans dead, the biggest and most beautiful cities flattened to the ground, the surviving population at the mercy of the allied victors, and future generations burdened with the material and emotional debt of a lost war. Before he killed himself on April 30, 1945 he lamented in front of his last associates: "Das deutsche Volk hat mich verlassen (The German people abandoned me)!"

Instead of celebrating the end of the war we continued to live in survival mode. We got used to the American occupation forces, and they to us. After some time, the curfew was lifted, and the American Military Government let Germans gradually take over the town's administration. Our "Amis" continued to use our swimming pool, play their funny ball game, and drive around in jeeps. On a lighter note, one day a supply train, that probably had been abandoned by the German Army, was discovered on a remote railroad track. It was filled with food staples, textiles and all sorts of goods. It did not take long for that news to spread; and soon most of the townspeople were on their way to the railroad depot with sacks, suitcases, shopping bags, and a few even with little carts, eager to obtain provisions for the coming tough times. Our family lugged home sacks with flour, sugar and dried legumes, cans with jam, and some textile fabrics for clothing. At last we had a feast!

I only realize now, as I study the literature about the Second World War, how little we knew about outside events and how little we were interested in them. The death of President Roosevelt, the swearing in of Vice President Truman went past us unnoticed. We did not know any details about the war in the Pacific. It was not covered in the newspapers or newsreels, and it happened in a different, far away world. Not even the dropping of the atom bombs on Hiroshima and Nagasaki, the events that shook the world, were either not reported or, if so, left no impression on me. Maybe those news never reached us, maybe we were too numbed and too occupied with our own survival.

Talking about news not reaching us, the next storm hit us totally unprepared; and this time even the rumor mill had not worked. When I went into the street on one beautiful Sunday morning in August, I did not see any American jeeps, trucks, or soldiers anywhere --- nothing. Our "Amis" had vanished, disappeared overnight without a single good-bye. What happened, what was going on? And then I heard the terrible news from some other people: "The Russians are coming!" And there they were. I could clearly discern the silhouettes of the dreaded T-34s, a well known Russian tank, as they rumbled over the nearby *Autobahn* (freeway). Full of anguish and horror I raced home to warn Mutti and my sisters. What on earth had happened? Why did we not know anything? What now? Could we possibly still escape? As there were no means of transport it would have to be on foot, although outrunning the apparently rapidly advancing Russian tanks would be impossible. Nobody knew why and how far the Americans were withdrawing, nobody knew how soon the Russian troops would follow their tanks. Slowly the certainty sank in: It was too late to flee, too late to avoid a fate that almost caught up with us in *Waldenburg*. Here, we were stuck and simply had to wait for the coming events with fear in our hearts. Would the Russians still be intent on "punishing the Germans", as their fighting troops had been in February when the war still raged? Or would their occupation troops be more civilized, because they were no longer fighting forces? Which of the many rumors was right?

A few days after the T-34s had passed and family and townspeople were still in limbo, still lamenting their fate, we heard very faint sounds coming from an easterly direction. Could this be singing? As the sounds grew stronger and it became clear that it actually was singing, Marlis, Harry, and I ran down to the main street, where we witnessed an unforgettable sight. With big eyes, we saw how regiment after regiment of Russian soldiers marched past us and all other curious onlookers. In rows of ten they marched and sang. A few rows, preceding the rest of the column, sang a verse, and then the entire unit joined in the refrain. In spite of our lingering fear, we remained rooted to the ground, overwhelmed by the beauty of these Russian songs coming from the throats of thousands of young soldiers. Their discipline was outstanding as they kept on marching through town, day after day, towards the West. That discipline and their marching and singing reminded me very much of German troops. However, I could not believe how shabbily these men were dressed. Many of them did not even wear boots and instead had rags wrapped around their feet and legs. Occasionally I would see a *Panjewagen*, a typical Russian cart drawn by one or two horses; and sometimes, unbelievable as it sounds, a bunch of soldiers would drag one of the smaller carts themselves. That was it! No jeeps, no "Mack" trucks, nothing with an engine; only an endless snake of young singing soldiers in gray uniforms. It was simultaneously scary, pathetic, and beautiful -- a sight never to be forgotten. These uniforms consisted of some kind of knickerbockers falling over the boots or foot rags, a loose tunic held together by a wide belt, and a military cap on their heads. It reminded me very much of pictures of Cossacks of the last century. In my mind I can still see how these young men in their shabby uniforms filled the town and our souls with wonderful songs from their country. Ever since, I have greatly enjoyed Russian folk songs, sung by a powerful choir.

Thank God, nothing became of the terrible fears we had harbored. These troops were totally under the control of their commanders and well disciplined. Absolutely no incidences! To the greatest joy of us children, the commander opened again our beloved outdoor swimming pool; and one could observe us mingling with the new occupiers in the same water. Unfortunately, we discovered soon that the good behavior of the troops was no indication of an improvement in our lives. The supply of foodstuff that had been halfway tolerable under the Americans decreased even further, either due to the lack of additional supplies from the Soviet Union, or due to a subtle form of "punishment". Queuing for food turned into a more time consuming task, and finding even the last wheat ear, turnip, or potato in the fields became now exceedingly important for survival. Gradually we also noticed that a new political wind was blowing into town. The Communists, Russian and German, began to govern. Men who were not "red" enough slipped down in the hierarchy of the administration or even disappeared overnight. We began to feel the weight of a new, oppressive regime.

One event impressed me at the time as the ultimate irony. The Russians had barely marched into town, when I observed here or there new flags hanging from the window sills. This time they were not white but red, to express recently discovered sympathies for the new regime. However, when I looked a bit more carefully, I could discern a darker circle in the center of the flags where the neo-communists had obviously removed the white circle with the swastika. Mutti and her kids had finally found a reason for a healthy laugh, although we should have wept. This was a perfect demonstration of the adage "turning one's flag with the wind". It also confirmed that twelve years of wind and sunshine had had their bleaching effect on the red color. It was easy for our family to have contempt for "that kind of people", because we could not have participated, even if we had wanted to, without possessing any Swastika flags in the first place.

School started again in September, however, without us. Mutti must have made up her mind already to travel back home to Mülheim, as soon as it was possible. The Wurmb children told us that they now had to learn Russian as the first foreign language. Everybody hated it. We continued to work in our business which provided the same excellent income as before. The more or less reasonable life that had still been possible under the "Amis", started to deteriorate rapidly under the "Russkis", leaving little doubt about the future. The country became economically and intellectually strangulated.

Not too long after the exodus of our "Amis", it became known that we had to thank the American Government itself for the new Communist regime. We learned that the Allies had met in Potsdam in July in order to redivide Germany. The Western Allies wanted their share of the rubble heap Berlin that was still occupied by the Soviets, who had actually conquered it at the loss of tens of thousands. It must have been an issue of prestige, or rather a symbol that the four Allies (this included now France) had won this war together. The resulting *Potsdam* Treaty divided Berlin into four "Sectors", American, British, Soviet, and French in the same manner as the country had been divided into four "Zones". The Soviet Union was compensated for its loss of the capital, its main prize, with the provinces of *Sachsen und Thüringen* (Saxonia and Thuringia). Another tremendous success for Stalin who was now in control of Eastern and Middle Europe all the way to the *Fulda* river, barely hundred miles from the *Rhein*. Why did the great minds of the West not see through the barely veiled plans of Stalin to build a Communist empire first to the Rhine and then to the Atlantic?

As I wrote earlier, life under the new government became ever more unpleasant. The Communist propaganda was revved up, very reminiscent of the National Socialistic propaganda before. Denunciation, the favorite tool of the Third *Reich,* was also the preferred tool of the new regime. It caused more men to disappear overnight; and it was a very effective method of the Communists to keep the population under control. There is no question in my mind that of all the criminal activities of the world's dictators, then and now, denunciation and torture are the worst and most despicable. Even here in the USA, in the most democratic nation of the world, denunciation was rampant during the hysterical McCarthy era. Left leaning people or former Communists frequently lost their jobs, their careers, their reputation and their good relationships with neighbors and sometimes even friends. Unfortunately, denunciation is so easy because it has its roots in jealousy, envy, and egotism of the human mind.

As the political solidification increased, the food supply decreased. Time had come for another Jansen family council: "Should we suffer any longer or should we flee to the West? If flight was preferred, how to go about it ?" Mutti started to make inquiries. Rumors alleged that crossing from East to West was in principle possible. The border, close to the *Harz* Mountains, that became later the "Green Border" and then in 1961 the "Iron Curtain", was still porous. The crossing could be dangerous; but so far nobody had been shot and many had crossed successfully. The pros and cons of our proposed flight had been thoroughly discussed with the Hennings, the Wurmbs, and Hanni Kobel. Finally the decision was made: "We are going to try it!" Since the new government had not yet curtailed railroad travel, we could certainly make it to within the proximity of the border of the Russian Zone, and from there we would muddle through.

Midnight at the Green Border

The new adventure began early in October of 1945. We left most of our meager belongings with the Hennings and packed only the most necessary things that we could carry over long distances. Thus each family member had to carry a rucksack or satchel and a small or medium suitcase. We wore warm clothes and sturdy shoes. Naturally, we did not announce our departure at town hall, although it was a requirement of the Communist authorities if one wanted to move from one city to another. After all the good-byes and best wishes we went separately to the railroad station so as not to raise suspicions. The amazing fact was that in those early weeks travel was not yet controlled. So we were able to board the train in the direction of Weimar and, unceremoniously, we were gone. The journey into the unknown - without timetables and maps - had begun. After one or two train changes we got close to our destination during the afternoon. Following the advice of fellow passengers who were familiar with the best border crossing, we left the train at a little station closest to the border. It was located approximately ten miles east of Friedland, a big refugee collection center in the British Zone. People said that we would find the border village only a few miles from here. So, we went on our way in a general direction that had been vaguely indicated. We avoided the road and purposefully marched only on field and forest paths. As it grew darker, it became obvious that this enterprise had not been planned well. When we followed the deep and straight furrows of a recently plowed field towards a forest, we saw the long white beams of a searchlight slowly making their way across the fields and meadows. A Russian border patrol! Down between the furrows until the danger was over. Up again and continued, down again and waited. Slowly we succeeded in reaching a forest where we stopped in utter darkness. As I reconnoitered ahead to find a passage through the forest I almost rolled down an embankment. That was it, we had to stop where we were and find some sleep on the ground. At the very first light of the next day we continued through the forest and actually found the village that had been described to us. It was only a mile or two from the border. We found shelter in a farmer's barn, dirty, hungry, thirsty, and dead tired. In recollection I am still impressed how valiantly Sigrid and Heidi had struggled through without a word of complaint, even though they were only nine and seven years old. To our great surprise we found ourselves in the company of a number of other refugees who were sleeping on the straw on the floor or leaning against the walls. From somewhere came warm drinks and some food. Then we too sank into a deep sleep.

When we woke up later in the day, we found out from our co-travelers what the rules of the crossing game were: "Each midnight the Russians open the border crossing, that is located about two miles from the village. And, it is true, they normally let the procession of refugees pass." As easy as that! At dusk our family with many other refugees formed a long line, which wound its way through the entire village. Most carried their belongings, some had them piled on little carts. There we waited patiently and hopefully until midnight, chatting with our neighbors about the expectations: "Yes, the Russian soldiers will let us cross the border, beginning at midnight. And, don't forget, they usually ask for some "gift"." -- Aha! -- "A British refugee camp will receive us only five miles west of the border."

Waiting, waiting, patience. Shortly before midnight began the macabre theater in which we participated as spectators and involuntary players. During the first act, Russian soldiers walked along both sides of the long column inquiring about *Schnaps,* a German hard liquor, which they knew very well and which reminded them probably of their vodka. Families who carried a *Schnaps* bottle with them, because they knew the rules of the game seemingly better than the rest, could proceed to the border crossing, deliver their "gift" and be gone. It took quite a while before the second act began. Now soldiers walked along the line asking for boots. As before, anybody who brought boots along could advance past the rest and walk through the border gate. I believe that watches came next. With every act the Jansens, who were not prepared and had nothing to offer, moved closer to the gate as the luckier families made room. By the time we got close, the border patrol had become already happy with their *Schnaps,* and controlled the traffic with gusto. Then, in the dim light of a single overhead lamp, came the last act in which we became the unhappy actors. Suddenly Mutti remembered that she carried a few pieces of jewelry in her handbag that would probably make good gifts for the soldiers. She rummaged through her bag and lifted a small foldable umbrella from the bag to find the jewelry. A soldier cried out: "A revolver." This caused quite an upheaval. Other soldiers grabbed her shouting: "You Nazi swine", beating her about her face and body. We children were desperate, ran around her to protect her, and screamed for help. Marlis disappeared quickly into the nearby trees, while I grabbed my mother's suitcase and my small sisters to escape also into the darkness. After a while the soldiers let Mutti go, as more and more refugees streamed into the circle of light and pushed her forward. In the last moment, just before I could quietly slither into the ditch one soldier ripped both our suitcases open with his bayonet. Our paltry belongings landed on the road and in the ditch. As Mutti ran away, I collected as much as I could, stuffed it back into the suitcases and tied them together with whatever I could find. Then I ran after Mutti and the girls who had already vanished into the darkness. Luck was on our side; the last act could have ended tragically.

Suddenly it was quiet again. Full of terror we kept running into the no-man's-land that stretched before us, as if the devil had been behind us. Miraculously, we managed to run and trot until we reached a small forest where other refugees had already stopped for the night. They had lit small fires, stood and sat around, and talked about the last few hours. The worst moment of my life, when my mother was beaten and kicked by drunken Russian soldiers, was over. We hugged each other and cried and laughed simultaneously, because luck had prevailed; we had escaped, and hopefully into a better future ahead.

After a few hours of rest on the soft forest ground, the small group broke camp and walked along the road towards the British border gate at the other end of the no-man's-land. There we found a British lorry that was waiting to take us to the big Friedland refugee camp. The British soldiers shoved as many people into the open lorry as possible and drove off with their load of sardines. The camp, consisting of a number of "Nissen huts", was swarming with people. (A "Nissen hut", alias "Quonset hut", looks like a huge culvert cut in half along its length with walls on either end with windows and doors.) In one of them, the "reception hut", we were registered by military and Red Cross personnel sitting behind long tables. In the square outside we were dusted with DDT, the ubiquitous bug spray of the after-war-years, to kill our bugs whether we had any or not. First head down, a load down the open collar into the back; then head up and a load down the front; afterwards belt open, a load in the front and back of the pants; now arms forward, two loads into the sleeves; and last, but probably most important, cap off and a load into the hair. Thoroughly dusted we were ready to begin our lives in the West in the British Zone.

Soup and bread were offered in the "dining hut" where people ate and drank at long tables. Straw covering was furnished in the "sleeping hut", where our little family sank exhausted into the straw. Later in the day, as I roamed through the camp, I discovered a rail line that went right past the camp; in fact, it ended here because all rail traffic across the border had ceased. I also speculated with other travelers, what might be ahead. From the usual plentiful rumors I could discern that we would go by train to the West, but probably not home. As a refugee one waited most of the time without really knowing what came next. Others made all the decisions about our well being and future. Sleeping, eating, and talking with the neighbors who all had eventful stories to tell. Some had a specific goal like we, because they had either come originally from the West or they knew relatives or friends. Most of them had left their homeland behind and depended entirely on the British Military Government for their support and future. People like this fell into the after-war category of "displaced persons" (DPs).

I mused that I who had, not too long ago, directed the endless stream of refugees at the big intersection in *Waldenburg*, I was now a refugee myself eight months later and 300 miles further west. Now I was being directed by friendly Red Cross ladies and British soldiers. Millions were still fleeing from the Communists and would continue to flee until the "Green Border" would be finally changed into the impenetrable "Iron Curtain". My friend Walter has often described this exodus as the "second *Völkerwanderung*", the equivalent of the medieval mass migrations from Far East all the way to Italy and Spain. Estimates of the displaced people range from ten to twenty million.

Friedland, located 5 to 10 miles south of Göttingen, had become a major refugee station that handled a never ending human stream. Lorries packed with people arrived from the East, and trains packed with people left for the West. After a few days it was our turn. We climbed with bags and suitcases into one of the freight cars and settled against the wall on the straw that covered the floor. The car had two huge sliding doors in the middle and four small open windows above on the left and the right. It was totally empty except for the straw covering, although I vaguely remember a stove that was not lit. Luckily it had one other important feature, a hole in the floor in one corner that served as toilet. When the car was full, which meant everybody had found a space on the straw and nobody had to stand, the train personnel closed the huge sliding doors. Another journey into the unknown began. We had learned earlier from the camp

135

personnel that this train would go to the West but not to the *Ruhrgebiet.* The latter was off limits to any refugees, because all remaining houses, apartments, and emergency dwellings were already filled to the limit. Also, the authorities were scared of epidemics because of the lack of food and heating material. The destination of the train was the little town *Aurich* at the North Sea not far from *Wlhelmshaven in East Friesland* where we would be settled temporarily. Progress was slow. Sometimes the train rolled, sometimes it was parked on a side track somewhere in a field or in a large station. Often the train backtracked, and occasionally freight cars were added or uncoupled. New questions arose during the night as the adults speculated about the near future: "Where was this freight train really going? Would we really be settled? Would they possibly herd us into some kind of concentration camp, the same way Hitler's government had kept the undesirable elements locked up? Why should we not be undesirable?" This went on and on; and slowly people worked themselves into a panic. It got so bad that a few people actually jumped off the stopped train when it was switched in some big rail yard. Later everybody became quiet again and slept or continued to wonder. I could not help thinking about that padlocked freight car in the rail yard of Prague where desperate people had reached through the barbed wire to get some food and drink. At least our doors were not locked from the outside, and the little windows were not covered with barbed wire.

As the train got closer to *Aurich,* the mood deteriorated again, and the subject of concentration camps and even gas chambers resurfaced. No wonder that nobody left our freight car when we rolled into *Aurich* on the next day. Neither the British military personnel nor the German Red Cross ladies could persuade the women -- there were only a few men in the car -- to climb out with their children. It was awful; some women became so hysterical that they shouted and screamed at the very people who wanted to help them. More officials arrived, to no avail. It was finally one Red Cross lady who used all her charm and powers of persuasion to get the women out of our car. We were trucked to a refugee camp in a school in the middle of town. Again straw on the floor, soup, bread, and water at long tables, but this time no DDT. How nice! We must have been considered already clean. When it became clear that nobody would be allowed to leave the camp in the foreseeable future, the Jansen family council met in a far corner of the school yard where nobody could overhear us. It was decided to flee from the camp. Mutti had no intention to be settled in *Aurich,* not even temporarily. She wanted to get home to Mülheim as fast as possible, although she had no idea whether our home was in ruins or not. She went to the station -- the camp was not guarded -- and discovered that trains were running, not directly to the *Ruhrgebiet,* but in a southerly direction. Next morning we split into two little groups and sneaked with our luggage out of the school without anybody noticing. The "escape" was successful, and we met again at the nearby railroad station where we waited hours for a train.

We managed to get into the first train that went south. It was already packed with people; but there was always room for more passengers. Everybody squeezed a little more together, shoved a little more, and voila we were on board. At every train change we found the platforms -- the only thing left of the railroad stations -- overflowing with people. Practically every station was completely destroyed; some concrete walls were left standing, twisted steel girders hanging from above, not a shred of glass left. The bombers had done a thorough job. The trains did not look much better either; no windows, broken doors, destroyed roofs; but they still ran on the rails. Inside, people were jammed solidly together; outside, they were standing on stairs, perched on roofs, and clinging to the bumpers. All passenger or freight cars were filled with people who were emaciated, tired, hungry, and wearing drab and often torn clothing. "Wheels must roll for the victory," was frequently still painted on the sides. After a day or so we arrived in the *Mülheim-Eppinghofen* station that was no longer there except for the platforms and several wooden structures that served as ticketing areas.

Finally we were back in our hometown which I barely recognized. We took our belongings and made our way up to the *Kahlenberg.* The city center had been pounded into rubble, a terrible sight. Of all the buildings that lined the narrow streets, only parts of the walls were still standing, and the insides were burned out. The window and door openings with their black, burned frames were a menacing sight. Mountains of rubble reached almost to the middle of the streets. Five years of air raids and the final assault on the *Ruhrgebiet* (the German troops capitulated on April 17, 1945) had essentially obliterated the city centers of all bigger towns. Fifty percent of all housing had been destroyed. As we made our way through this sad chaos I tried to remember what each street had looked like before, often without success. After we left the center, the destruction became less severe and not so complete. However, our tension mounted as we came closer. Maybe our house had survived, maybe not. Finally, we reached the corner of *Dimbeck* and *Wittekindstraße*; and -- there it was, still standing. What a relief! It had withstood all air raids like most houses in our neighborhood. Some major, some minor damage here and there, but nothing compared to downtown. Quickly to the house, pressed the bell, and waited for the next surprise. An elderly lady in an apron opened the door and inquired what we wanted and who we were. Mutti explained very softly: " I am Mrs. Jansen and these are my children. We survived intact and have finally made it back home." I still feel sorry for poor Mrs. Hesselmann who looked at us in disbelief and consternation, as if we were an apparition. But she caught herself quickly once she realized who we were. She became very friendly and understanding and bid us welcome into our own house. Back in our home and our town!! Yes, but In less than three years our world had been turned completely upside down.

Anything left of Mülheim?

Everything was still there: The town, the Wittekindstraße, the house at number eight, and the old friends. Many things had changed, but many things were still the same. Our short street did not lose one house; some houses were destroyed on the *Dimbeck* and one on the *Witthausstraße*. And this had to be the home of my friend Hans-Otto. Most of the walls were still standing; and the Bösebecks had already put a corrugated metal roof over the basement, where they lived, and a wooden structure on the first floor, where their dairy and grocery store was running again. Also Buchmüller's grocery store at the corner of *Dimbeck* street, the butcher, and the restaurant Thiesmann on the other side, as well as the bakery one block away were all open. Our neighbor on the left, Mr. Hagenguth, was back in his upholstery business, and across the street Mr. Münkemeyer in the back of the Verschoot house was still sitting on his little stool repairing shoes. The Verschoot children and the Jötten children had returned to their houses across the street. Our neighbors on the right, the Knebels, had made it through the war; and even their sons had survived but were still prisoners of war somewhere. The elderly Buchmüllers still lived in their beautiful Victorian half-timbered house directly across the street from us. Very soon Günter Rübel, Liesel Weissenborn, Hans-Otto Bösebeck and Karl-Heinz König reappeared; the neighborhood kids were all back together.

After Mrs. Hesselmann had overcome her initial shock, she invited us to a cup of coffee, roasted barley of course, and told us the house story of the last year. Four families, who had all lost their houses or apartments, had been quartered in our house. Dr. Van Üüm, the dentist who had rented the house originally, when my mother and sisters left in 1943, had moved on, but packed most of his furniture into the former office of my father. He in turn had rented the house to Mrs. Hesselmann when she lost her apartment house in the *Eppinghoferstrasse* during an air raid.

Her story was one so typical of many people who had stayed behind: "During a major air raid all inhabitants of my apartment house had rushed into the basement as usual. We were sitting down there and listening to the ruckus, hoping that some other part of town was under attack. Not so, the exploding bombs got nearer until they hit my house and many houses in the neighborhood. The house was in flames and the basement shelter got so hot that we had to escape into the basement of the adjacent house." -- As a safety measure all basements of a block had been connected by cutting holes through the separating walls, so that people could escape from one basement to the next all the way to the end of the block. -- "When the temperature in the adjacent basement became also intolerable because of the raging fires above, everybody moved on until we all reached buildings that were not burning. Trying to get out into the street from my building had been impossible because the whole street was burning - the asphalt had been ignited. We were absolutely terrified, but we got out of the last basement of the block, where the street was not yet burning. Everybody got away with their lives - and nothing else." Even years after the war the Hesselmann family still rushed into the basement during every thunderstorm.

Later Mrs. Hesselmann's oldest daughter, who had lost her husband during the war, moved into our house; and shortly thereafter her younger daughter, Maria Schröder, with her husband and two children. At the end, Miss Sonnenschein, a teacher at Marlis' *Lyzeum*, joined the company. They all had lost their dwellings. With us newcomers, there were now five families with twelve persons in the house that used to be a single family home. It became a little tight. Seen from today's perspective, it is remarkable that all these parties managed to function together without major strife. They had to share one kitchen with a gas range of four burners, one bathroom, fortunately with two entrances, one small room with a toilet and sink next to the house entrance, one connecting living and dining room, three bedrooms, and one former office. Electricity and water were always available, gas only sporadically. So, Mutti and Mrs. Hesselmann developed a plan for the use of both bathrooms and the kitchen by all parties. In the morning Mr. Schröder and I shared the downstairs restroom with a toilet and a tiny washbasin, Mrs. Hesselmann and her older daughter used the kitchen sink, and everybody else got their ten minutes or so in the upstairs bathroom. In the kitchen, each family had the right to one or two burners during fixed times of the day. Luckily Miss Sonnenschein used her own electric cooking plate upstairs. -- Brigit once asked me: "Why didn't you all prepare and eat a common meal?" The answer was very simple: " Each family had different allocations on their rationing cards depending on number and age of the children and adults; and each received sometimes extras from relatives, friends, or the black market where people traded cigarettes against butter, or coal against eggs, etc." The heating was also separated in a peculiar way. We operated the central hot water heating system with radiators in each room, whereas Mrs. Hesselmann heated the living and dining rooms with a stove. She, as the widow of a railroad employee, received good quality coal as opposed to the rest of the population which got either nothing or some coal products of poor quality. It is truly amazing that we never had a fight and all problems were discussed and solved in a civilized manner. No wonder, because times were so tough that quarrels about relatively small things had no room in our lives. Could anybody have foreseen that the temporary living arrangements would last until the year 1952, when Mrs.Hesselmann moved back into her rebuilt apartment house?

Our family finances were doing well. We had still enough money from the arts and crafts business in *Ronneburg,* and soon Papa's pension would be paid again every month. School had started up again in October shortly before we arrived. So, Mutti enrolled us all anew with Heidi starting her first grade. Marlis went to the *Lyzeum,* I attended the *Gymnasium,* and the "Little Ones" the Protestant Elementary School at the *Muhrenkamp.* To my dismay my school which was now called the *Humanistische Gymnasium* had been moved from its old stately building into the modern building of the *Naturwissenschaftliche Gymnasium* in the *Schulstraße,* because the occupation troops used our building as their headquarters. Both *Gymnasiums* could function in the same building by having classes every other day. This was changed later to alternating classes between mornings and afternoons. Naturally, we pupils loved this arrangement, since we gained entire days free of school. The classes were packed with about fifty pupils each, and only the most essential subjects were taught: German, English, Latin, and Mathematics. There were simply not enough teachers to go around. Many of the older teachers had been in the party and had to be "denazified". -- I will describe this new word in our language and the associated process below. -- Most of the younger teachers were still stuck as prisoners of war in the Soviet Union, England, France, or the US, if they had survived at all. Startup was not easy, because everybody of more or less the same age was thrown together without regard to knowledge level or actual years of previous schooling. I, for instance, had not seen a classroom in fifteen months.

I had barely attended the new/old school for two weeks, when word arrived from Erwin, that he was ready to depart for *Thüringen.* We had met this young man during our flight across the "green border", where he had joined and assisted us. We had separated in *Friedland,* from where he traveled to Frankfurt. We had agreed that I would accompany him back to Thüringen in order to retrieve the rest of our belongings. He was returning to his parents in *Weimar,* East Germany, where he planned to arrange for a truck that would take us both and our families' belongings back to the West. A daring enterprise; but he was sure that it would succeed. Mutti obtained a leave of absence from school for me for about two weeks. Erwin picked me up in

Mülheim, and off we went to the border at *Eisenach*. I could not believe it, but we had no problem with the crossing at all. The British apparently did not care, and the Russians employed a simple trade system: One German from the East for one from the West. That made it easy for Erwin and me, because the east-west travelers outnumbered their counterparts by more than ten to one. We took the train at the next railroad station, which was only a few miles away, and we were on our way back, he to *Weimar* and I to *Ronneburg*. He would write me a letter as soon as all arrangements had been completed. There were no telephone connections, at least not for the general population.

Mrs. Henning and her daughter Liselotte were perplexed, when I suddenly appeared from nowhere. They listened to my story for hours, not trusting their ears; and then I learned everything about the ominous developments in *Ronneburg*. The Soviets had installed a Communist mayor and town council. All important administrative positions had been filled by former or newly minted Communists; the new Stalin type "democracy" in full bloom. Little by little things were being "put in order". Not an enviable position to be in. People were still losing jobs, and some still disappeared. The message for the rest was loud and clear: "Toe the line!" The food supply remained erratic and below a reasonable minimum. The Wurmb kids told me that they were now learning Russian, the history of Russia and the Soviet Union, and Communist ideology. They had already learned in the history class that "the Red Army had liberated the long suffering Germans from the terror of the Nazi Regime". They also had to join the *Freie Deutsche Jugend* (Free German Youth) that was essentially a continuation of the *Hitlerjugend* with new colors, green shirts and red bandanas. People had found out quickly that one did not talk about, let alone criticize, the new rulers. Frank talk was only possible between trusted friends, exactly as it had been during the previous twelve years.

The Hennings and I had now plenty to eat, because the Jansens had not reported their departure when they left. Our family still existed on the books of the authorities, so that I could collect - albeit with great trepidation - rationing cards for five. Quite a feat, for which the ladies Henning loved me. They did prefer, however, that I remained tucked away in house and garden to avoid complications. I had my own little room with tons of books that I devoured, when I was not planning the return trip. I read my way through a collection of detective stories by Edgar Wallace. I still connect his name with that waiting period. For the trip, I organized suitcases and boxes which I filled with our belongings. There was no thought of correspondence with Mutti, because all mail connection to the West had been cut off. Two weeks later a letter arrived from Erwin in Weimar, who wrote that his parents had not yet been able to find a truck and obtain the permission to cross the western border. I always wondered what kind of extraordinary connections that family must have had that allowed them to even think about such a possibility. He invited me for a planning meeting in Weimar. Not knowing anything about the latest regulations, I went to the railroad station and joined the line in front of the ticket counter. When I got there I discovered to my horror, that only people who were workers or had some official piece of paper could use the trains. As I stood there dumbfounded, a Russian officer suddenly offered to get me a ticket. He was also traveling to Weimar. How lucky could I get! He would not even accept money when I offered to pay. Wow, there were also nice and human Russians! I had to rethink my relationship with that nation, because my sole experience was based on the terrible consequences of a brutal, tyrannical system that turned human beings into beasts, in Russia as well as in Germany. -- Much later during my professional career in the US I had the pleasure to meet occasionally Russian scientists and engineers. I always enjoyed their company and I never found a nasty or undesirable person amongst them, nor anybody who would shun me as a German. On the contrary, we often spent wonderful evenings together with more liquor than I could handle, with a lot of jokes, and the occasional song. -- In Weimar, I learned from Erwin's family that their efforts to find a truck or space in a truck needed more time. They also had heard through connections, that the Soviet and East German governments wanted to get rid of all western refugees as fast as possible. Plans were being drawn up for this extradition to begin soon. As I took leave from Erwin and his parents, I knew that from now on I was on my own. Back to *Ronneburg* with the ticket given to me by the generous, unknown Russian officer.

What to do now? I did not see how I could make my way back across the "green border" with our belongings. At best I would have been able to carry a small suitcase and a rucksack, provided I could obtain a railroad ticket. In view of the uncertainty of Erwin's truck it seemed best to wait for the soon to be expected "extradition". So, I settled down as the guest of the friendly Hennings, reading a lot, making occasional forays into town, or visiting with the Wurmb children, listening to their stories from school and the *Freie Deutsche Jugend*. Although it bothered me that I could not communicate with my family and tell them about the developments and delays, I did not give it much thought. It did not enter my mind that my mother could suffer terrible anguish when I did not return after two weeks. As I discovered later, she had become ever more desperate in the following weeks, especially when she could find little support from anyone. Instead, the school principal, the Red Cross people and the local authorities accused her of being negligent in sending her young son back East just to retrieve a few belongings: "People get shot. He may have been deported to the Soviet Union. Who knows what happened to him?" She became unhappier and more morose by the week, naturally blaming herself, if anything had happened to her son. Just then her sister Mali, from whom we had not heard since December 1944, appeared one day in Mülheim. She resurfaced at long last after her arduous trek from Silesia to the West. She arrived just in time to provide the only support that kept her sister sane. The following weeks developed into a horrible emotional torture for my mother because she had already convinced herself that I was no longer alive. At the same time in *Ronneburg* I had a lucky break when I found a long distance trucker who was willing to take a letter from me and mail it from the other side of the border. He actually did, and this saved my mother from a total collapse, when it arrived a week before me.

The rumors of the extradition of all West Germans became stronger by the week; and at the beginning of December an announcement was made that everybody from the West should prepare himself for the evacuation. Knowing that I could not carry the boxes and suitcases across the border by myself I bought myself a small hand drawn cart and loaded it with my goods. Mutti had left some jewelry behind that I was supposed to bring safely home, but did not know how. Mrs. Henning had the brilliant idea to make two little colored pom poms. She wrapped the rings in soft cotton, covered them with fabric, sewed everything together and attached them to a cord. I felt a bit stupid when she draped this arrangement under my collar around my neck, but it was tolerable and served its purpose well. All extradition paperwork for the whole family who "was still living in *Ronneburg*" had to been taken care of. And then the refugee train arrived, and it was time to bid farewell to two very good and caring friends. I drew my little cart to the station, where the freight train was already being filled. There I managed to heave my luggage and cart into one of the freight cars over the menacing growls from some passengers: "That cart takes up valuable space. Why does this boy need to take such a cart along?" Too late. I was in my freight car, and nobody could dislodge me, my baggage or my cart. Unbelievably, the train drove actually very close to the border, where we debarked and formed the same long line which our family had formed with an earlier crop of refugees. As last time the line moved slowly towards the border, however, this time in the middle of the day. Papers were carefully checked, we passed the border barrier without any drama; and the snake wound its way through the no-man's land into the British Zone. There the same lorries were ready to take us to the *Friedland* refugee camp. Again thorough dusting with DDT, soup, bread, jam, and water at long tables and sleeping on straw. Luckily, the Nissen hut was heated by a little stove, because it was already middle of December.

This time we were packed into a passenger train without window panes, a leaking roof, and generally in bad condition. Since I could not take my precious little cart along, I sold it to a local lady and heaved my numerous pieces of luggage into one of the already crowded compartments. It was filled to bursting with civilians and soldiers returning from Russian prison camps. It was obvious that they had let them go only because of their very bad health. I cannot forget the young soldier who sat across from me and slept most of the time. He was in a terrible state. The torn uniform was just hanging about his emaciated body; he smelled horribly and he had a hard time breathing and coughed all the time. He told me that he was discharged because of dysentery and probably pneumonia. After a day and a night, the train stopped in *Laasphe* in the *Sauerland*, where everybody was going to be settled temporarily. I separated myself inconspicuously from the stream of refugees, who were leaving the platform, and remained with all my luggage in the station or rather what was left of it. To my great surprise I could send most of my packages and suitcases by freight, because I did not have a

145

chance to take them with me in these overcrowded trains. They actually arrived a week later with the exception of one, a sign that the *Deutsche Reichsbahn,* (German National Railroad) functioned again. After many train changes I made it to Mülheim during the next day.

The reunion with the family and especially Mutti was heart breaking, but it was full of joy. We hugged and kissed each other, we laughed and cried, and Mutti was immensely relieved, that she had me back alive. All inhabitants of our house and all the neighbors came to greet and hug me like the long lost son. In all of this commotion I had no idea how profoundly Mutti had suffered during those two months. The biggest gift for me was a fresh, hot bath entirely for me alone. I needed hours to tell my story, and I gathered a glimpse of Mutti's agonies from their stories. Only later did I learn from Tante Mali about the full extent of her ordeal. The two most important events at home had been Tante Mali's return and the fact that Mutti had managed to obtain some sort of inferior coal to keep the house not exactly warm but from freezing. The girls had been back to school now for two months, which reminded me that by now I had missed school for a total of one and a half years.

Listening to Aunt Mali's story I realized that our two escapes had been utterly harmless compared to her ordeal. She made almost the whole flight on foot. In January 1945 her entire hamlet of *Hochweiler* had left with horse or ox drawn wagons, little hand drawn carts, or on foot, barely escaping the Red Army. The idiotic authorities had waited until the last moment with the order for the flight instead of giving the villagers the opportunity to plan ahead and start much earlier. The reason for this irresponsible behavior was the fact that the fanatics in the government of the eastern provinces were simply not willing to admit that the war was over and that it was high time to cut the losses. The extreme cold of -30 to -40°F and the deep snow turned the flight into a nightmare. Tens of thousands streamed over the same roads towards west, barely with any rest stops, because the Red Army followed on their heels. Untold numbers of old and frail people succumbed, and many babies froze to death. Since nobody had the time to bury them because of the frozen ground , they were left in the ditches on the side of the road. Also, the fleeing masses left more and more of their belongings behind, because during the weeks of the trek it all came down to sheer personal survival. Many were frost bitten or had frozen toes and fingers. It was a human disaster of major proportions. Aunt Mali finally made it to a refugee camp in Bavaria where she stayed for half a year until she had gained enough strength and will power to continue her journey, this time by train, to relatives in the *Sauerland*. From there she had just arrived in Mülheim two weeks before me.

Main train station, Mülheim. (1946)

View from the Marienkirche (1946),　Our home (1948)

Nefertiti, the jewel of the "Returned Art" Exhibition in Wiesbaden (1949)

Rowing on the Ruhr. Our "Four" (1949)

Günter, Hans-Otto and the author with our new bicycles (1948)

Class trip in the Eifel (1949), Ulm, burned out town hall (1949)

Townhall of Ulm of the 14th century, bombed out (1949)

152

The cathedral of Frankfurt, originally built in the 13th century,
bombed out together with the old town (1949)

The author on bicycle trip through Germany (1949)

The old town of Mülheim, fifty five years later (2000)

Our New Life

Our family and the entire population of the *Ruhrgebiet* were very lucky, for the winter of 1945/46 turned out to be mild. In spite of minimal nourishment and heating, we made it through the winter in good health. We four children were especially lucky, because the British military government had instituted a feeding program that kept us from serious malnutrition. The program was called: *Schulspeisung*, school meals. Every day during the long morning break, the pupils assembled in long lines on each floor of the school building. The teachers in charge ladled the soup into our aluminum pots, that were mostly of military origin, the kind in which our fathers, uncles, brothers or cousins had already received their daily soup rations. We received two kinds of soup on alternate days, a thick pea soup and an equally thick sweet corn soup. Sometime I was already so hungry during the early classes that I could only think of the soup. The two thin slices of bread with margarine and fruit jam, that Mutti prepared for breakfast, did not last long for a fifteen year old boy. Often some of the soup was left over. Therefore, I frequently hovered close by the table hoping for an extra ladle or two to be taken home. Adding to this my sisters bounty, we always made it through the day, even if little else was available.

Obtaining groceries and heating material had become one of our most important tasks. *Schlange Stehen* (standing in line or queuing) had become our "favorite" pastime. We children were sent on certain days to those grocery stores which most likely would receive new flour, bread, sugar, eggs, lard, milk, cheese, margarine, etc. Or we would queue at a produce store for potatoes, cabbage, turnips, carrots, apples, pears, etc. Turnips were almost always available, and my mother created all sorts of meals with them. During especially lucky days we could get sausages and some undefined meat at the butchers. The meat was called *Suppenfleisch,* soup meat, and it was cooked until it was no longer tough and had assumed a gray color. On most Sundays we were treated to this "delicacy". Mutti had developed her "spy system". There were times, when we heard or actually saw a *Schlange* forming at one or the other neighborhood store. Getting there in a hurry was paramount, even without knowing what was going to be sold. Who got there first, bought first. The chances of getting anything, diminished with the time at which one arrived at the store. I would hang on as long as it seemed to make sense. Sometimes unfortunately, I would get to the door of the store just when the grocer had sold the last pound of the shipment to the person before me. What a waste of valuable time! I did stand in line so many times and so long during the years after the war, that I have still not overcome "queuing phobia" until today.

It happened again in the fall of 1960 when Brigit invited me to dinner in a very nice restaurant in Summit in New Jersey. When we arrived at the restaurant during a busy time we had to wait for a table. Neither Brigit nor the other people made any comments, settled down in the waiting area or took a drink at the bar. However, I suffered a nightmarish attack. Nobody could get me to stand or sit in line, and certainly not in a country where food was not scarce at all. Suddenly the after-war-years popped into my mind; and all I wanted was to get out of there. Poor Brigit was flabbergasted. She probably thought that she had become the friend of a maniac. It took all her power of persuasion and her love to bring me back to normal, talk me into having a drink , and making our dinner a pleasant experience after all. Similar situations repeated themselves in the following years. Often we would drive to another restaurant and yet another just to avoid having to wait in a *Schlange.* The irony was, of course, that we spent the same or more time driving around instead of waiting patiently for a table like everybody else. I believe that I have mellowed over the last six decades, because I am able to wait now, -- if it is not longer than twenty minutes.

Keeping our house warm during the winter was another challenge. I heated the hot water furnace in the basement with something that we called *Schlamm* (mud) a waste product of the coal extraction and refinement. It was a sticky tar-like substance that burned very well but produced an extremely hard and dense slag on top of the ember that did not admit any air. I had to go frequently into the basement, in order to break up the slag layer to prevent the fire from suffocating. Somebody had to do this almost hourly. We could have used firewood, if we had had any. Many people went in to the neighboring forests or parks to cut wood secretly, although this was strictly forbidden. Mrs. Hesselmann and our neighbors, the Poppens, received high quality anthracite from the German Railroad, because her husband had been a train engineer, and Mr. Poppen still worked for the railroad. Both could keep their rooms warm. Our family depended on the mercy of our coal dealer who had supplied us for many years. But all he received was *Schlamm*. Many young people risked their freedom, their health or their life when they went down to the railroad and stole coal from slow moving freight trains. The irony was that Mülheim was literally sitting on top of vast coal deposits; but all the coal went to other countries, above all France, as part of the reparations; a repeat of the aftermath of the first world war. We even had a song to the melody of a popular American tune:

" And if it's cold in winter,
and you are freezing cold,
then steal a sack of good coal
from the railroad's hold,
singing hey barbareeba, etc."

Our family really suffered a shock when Mutti was informed one day by my father's former employer, the Social Security Department, that they would no longer pay our pension, because he had been a Nazi. That was a real blow! As the savings from our Ronneburg business dwindled, we would soon become dependent on welfare. There was only one way to regain the state pension; Papa had to be denazified posthumously. Not an easy task! Mutti had to prove that he had not been a very active party member, but only a *Mitläufer* (hanger-on), although he had been a *Blockwart* (block captain) during the early war years. As a *Blockwart* he was responsible for the well-being of our neighborhood. He provided support for sick or elderly people, he checked whether a house or apartment had been damaged during an air raid, and he organized neighborhood meetings. Naturally every former party member, no matter how active, now wanted to be a *Mitläufer,* because as such one had a chance of being denazified. I remember that Papa had joined the Party in 1934 or 1935, when the pressure on the ranking civil servants increased to become Party members. Since my father was utterly disinterested in politics and totally dedicated to his family, he wanted to remain neutral on one hand but also not oppose the Regime on the other hand. When his boss alluded to the possibility that not becoming a Party member could negatively affect his career and could even result in his dismissal, he began to understand the rules of the game. Both, he and my mother, decided that it would be in the best interest of the family to join. I can still see the little Party emblem that he wore on his lapel, a red button with a white center with the swastika in the middle. Later when he became *Blockwart* (the lowest rank in the Party hierarchy) he wore occasionally a brown uniform with riding breeches and long black boots, whenever he had to attend to official business.

It became quite a job for Mutti to find Papa's former colleagues, employees and acquaintances who would act as character witnesses and, more importantly, be themselves acceptable to the Denazification Committee. She visited people, wrote letters, and made telephone calls. Finally she had assembled enough colleagues, acquaintances and friends of my father who were willing to write the necessary letters of recommendation and appear before the Committee. In spite of all these combined efforts it took almost two years until Papa was denazified and our pension was reinstated. In the meantime our finances were tight; but we survived on Opa's pension and the rental income from the house. Mutti, who had always turned every penny around twice, knew only too well how to live with the bare essentials. She sewed and mended all our clothes, and we maintained a large garden. My memories of those years include a colleague of my father by the name of Heinemann. He was in charge of the *Sozialversicherung* (Social Security) of the district Oberhausen and was a very good friend of our family. We actually called him uncle, although I forgot his first name. He visited us frequently, probably a little too frequently, because he had become interested in Mutti. We found out about this one day when she told us that Uncle Heinemann had proposed to marry her. Although he was well-to-do and not bad looking, she decided against a new marriage that could possibly affect her relationship with her children. She wanted to remain independent and dedicate her life solely to our well being, our education and our future. It was years later when I realized how she had foregone her own feelings and life for the betterment of her children's lives. What a woman, my mother!

We spaded the entire garden and cultivated the last square foot in order to complement our marginal food supplies. I planted potatoes on the former front lawn, sowed *Feldsalat,* salad greens, for the spring and lettuce, spinach, radishes, parsley, chives, and diverse cabbages for the summer in beds on the side of the house. Then I planted string beans, carrots, the cabbages, kohlrabi, onions and strawberries on the former back lawn. Our apple, pear and cherry trees and the berry bushes provided fruit. After I had dug up the potatoes in the fall, I planted *Grünkohl* (green kale) and *Rosenkohl* (Brussels sprouts), which both lasted until December. Since there was not enough time during the week, I had begun to work extra hours on Sunday. However, this did not go over well with our neighbors who complained to Mutti, because in my protestant hometown Sunday was the day of rest. What to do? From then on I could be found in the garden at five in the morning and had my work completed before anybody else got up.

To produce a bountiful crop, I needed an excellent fertilizer. Where to find it? Luckily, in those days many horse-drawn carts passed through our street, and the horses obligingly provided me with manure. Every time I heard a cart approach I raced into the street, ready with my shovel and broom. I had to be fast and first, for there were a few competitors on our street who had the same intentions. Unfortunately, the occasional bucket of horse manure was not enough. I knew that there was much more of it in the pastures near the Ruhr where cows and horses grazed. So I constructed a little hand cart with which Günter and I went down to the *Hindenburg Brücke* that crossed the river high above the pastures. We descended over a dike into the meadows, where we filled our large jute sacks with first-class horse droppings -- cow manure was simply too soft. Then we hoisted these sacs with a rope onto the bridge and carted them home in the evening, a full afternoon's excursion. With this new source of fertilizer I started to produce high yielding crops. Unfortunately, we did not raise chickens or rabbits like so many neighbors and friends. They would have really improved our diet; but Mutti was adamantly opposed. I think it had to do with the fact that she never approved of her parents keeping chickens and rabbits in their yard. She, as an aspiring city girl, did not want to be reminded daily of Opa's and Oma's customs that they had brought with them from their farmer's childhood. No doubt, many people, who did not have a backyard, amplified their diet with cats which were called appropriately *Dachhasen* (roof rabbits). In those years the cat population in the city had dwindled to almost nothing . Dogs, man's best friends, did not suffer the same fate.

However, horse meat could be bought at a horse butcher by the name of Sommers. Its advantage over beef was that it required only half the ration coupons of beef. Mutti marinated it to remove the slightly sweet taste. Again, we had a song for the occasion, to be sung to the melody of "Lily Marlene":

> "Pork is seen too rarely,
> and beef, it costs a lot.
> Thus we go to Sommers,
> where we can buy trot, trot."
> (Sommers was a horse meat butcher store)

If we had gotten permission from Mutti we kids could have augmented our meals dramatically. Many other kids stole cabbage and other vegetables from the trucks that crossed Germany from Holland to the South. As these trucks had to climb a steep section of *Reichsstrasse I*, federal highway number one, only a few blocks from our home, they switched into low gear and crawled up the road. A golden opportunity for the youngsters! A group would approach the truck from behind, so that the driver and co-driver could not see them. Then one or two climbed on the truck, or preferably the trailer, if there was one, and started to throw produce or fruits down to the others who collected it in sacks. Quickly everybody disappeared in the surrounding park, before the driver could stop or do anything. Unfortunately Marlis and I could only watch -- full of envy; but Mutti would not cave in in spite of our marginal food situation. She was determined to maintain our German honesty and honor, cost it what it may. Instead we were sent into the meadows and forests to collect nettles, dandelions, elderberries and acorns. Sometimes on special occasions, boxes with vegetables and potatoes arrived from Mutti's farmer relatives in the *Sauerland*. Although the potatoes froze occasionally during transit in the winter; we ate them nonetheless.

Earlier on I mentioned the kind of songs the young people were now singing. Many of them were sung to tunes of popular American songs that one heard all the time on the radio stations of the British or American Forces. Before you knew it, somebody had composed different, German lyrics for these songs that were often not very kind to the occupying troops. In retrospect I believe that the vanquished used those little jabs as some sort of revenge on the victors. I also hope that the victors did not listen too carefully or did not understand the words. Many daring jokes circulated as well; but I do not remember a single one. Change had also come about in the choice of popular songs. The old schmaltzy German lyrics had been replaced by catchy American songs -- with the compliments of the military radio broadcasts:

> "What could a soldier be dreaming?
> He dreams about his father's house . . ."

or "Vor der Kaserne, vor dem grossen Tor . . ."
(In front of the barracks, in front of the gate)

had been replaced without much ceremony by:

> "Pardon me boy,
> is that the Chattanooga Choo Choo? . . ."

or "Mr. Whachacallum, whatcher doin' tonight?
> Hope you'r in the mood,
> 'cause I'm feeling just right."

We had to forget all those wonderful and snappy *Hitler Jugend* songs like:

> "Forward, forward
> are calling the brilliant bugles .
> Forward, forward,
> youth does not know any dangers . ."

These songs and many more became memories that my friends and I have not forgotten to this day. Talking about songs from the *Third Reich*, a most unusual occurrence in Chile comes to mind. During our journey through the South of Chile in 1966, Brigit and I stayed overnight in the small town of *Frutillar* on lake *Osorno*, which German settlers had founded in the middle of the nineteenth century and which was still essentially German. Our hostess asked me after dinner, if we would like to make a boat trip on the lake with her and her daughter. I accepted with pleasure, while Brigit went with some fellow travelers to see a movie. We had barely rowed half a mile onto the lake, when the elderly lady stopped, took her accordion out of its case and proposed to sing German songs. I enjoyed the idea. --The reader should know that the South of Chile was developed to a large part by Germans who had been invited by the Chilean Government over 150 years ago and had been given land for settlements. Interestingly enough, these German farmers and artisans had maintained their ethnic and cultural identity for more than five generations. -- Mother and daughter knew German folk songs as well as or better than I. After we had worked our way through a number of mostly older songs, both ladies insisted that I should lead them in singing songs from the *Third Reich*. Amused and utterly surprised by this development, I participated with gusto. Here I was sitting in a boat with two strange ladies on a different continent and twenty one years after the collapse of the Hitler Regime, happily chanting slightly rusty *Hitler Jugend* songs into the clear mountain air of lake *Osorno*. The ladies were so enchanted that, I am sure, they remembered this evening for a long time.

And the big picture? In 1946 the Allied Occupation Government, that had made its headquarters on top of the *Petersberg* across the Rhine from *Bad Godesberg,* began to contemplate the future of Germany. By now the break between the capitalistic USA and the communistic USSR was complete. Without any doubt, the Soviets had decided to turn the East Zone into a communistic satellite state like Poland, Czechoslovakia, and all the other countries under Stalin's control. They were demanding unbelievable reparation payments and thereby ruined the East German industry and agriculture for decades to come. The Russian Zone became a dictatorship, where all aspects of life were totally controlled by the leadership in Berlin. The economy was centralized, private property was eliminated and became state property. People had to follow the dogma of communism, or else. The Gestapo (Secret State Police) was replaced by the Stasi (State Security Service). The government and the party became one and the same. Walther Ulbricht became the first President of East Germany. He was also the first secretary of the *Sozalistische Einheits Partei Deutschlands (SED)* (Socialistic Unity Party of Germany), typical of all communistic countries, where the party and the administration are essentially the same. In the twenties Ulbricht had been the cofounder of the Communist Party of Germany which lasted until Hitler came to power. In 1938 he had to flee to the Soviet Union, from where he returned with the Red Army in 1945. As the strongest proponent of the Moscow communist course in East Germany he became the architect of the merger of the Social Democratic (SPD) and the Communist (KPD) parties into the new SED. He and his comrades, like their Soviet counterparts, truly believed that the communist way of life was better and morally superior to life in the Western democracies including the West Zones of Germany.

The West Zones under the jurisdiction of the Western Allies developed very differently along democratic lines. Only nuances separated the goals of the three military governments, depending on each historic relationship and degree of enmity with Germany. The population of the French Zone was treated harshly by a victor who had suffered most under the Hitler Regime and remembered well the years of German occupation. The French Government insisted on reparations in form of dismantled industries, industrial goods and, as after the First World War, large coal shipments from the Ruhr and the Saar. The British were not very interested in reparations except for modern tool and production machinery that had survived the war. That had a very immediate impact on the ability of the *Ruhrgebiet* to recover; but it had unforeseen positive consequences in the long run. As it turned out, the expected benefits from these reparations actually backfired. The dismantling of prewar machinery and its installation in British factories set the British industry back compared to the German industry, where the Marshall Plan and the Currency Reform had permitted the acquisition of the most modern equipment. -- When I taught Electrical Engineering at the College of Technology in Loughborough (near Leicester) in 1959, small groups of students with their professors (including me) visited occasionally British manufacturing plants. During these visits I was always perplexed to find really outdated machinery in the factory halls. Often I saw an entire hall of lathes driven with leather belts from a common shaft. I thought that I could not trust my eyes, because I had worked with the most modern, frequently electronically controlled tool machinery at Siemens in Mülheim, where I had been an engineering apprentice between 1951 and 1954. --

I became, of course, most familiar with the British occupation philosophy, because Mülheim was located in the

British Zone. The foremost quality of the occupation army was that troops and officers were always polite and correct. They were "gentlemen". They did not go out of their way to be friendly like the American soldiers in Ronneburg; but they were fair and not very visible in our city life. We heard very rarely of problems between their solders and Germans. The officers and their families lived in villas on the *Kahlenberg* or in the *Uhlenhorst*, the fancier neighborhoods of the town. A few of my friends' families had to give up their homes and find lodging elsewhere. It took years, before my friend Albrecht's family was allowed to move back. During the weeks before Christmas, our family frequently took walks past these villas because of the unusual sights. To our amazement the British families left the curtains and shutters in front of their living room windows wide open. They decorated their Christmas trees already weeks earlier and, to our great surprise, they often had parties before Christmas. Naturally we enjoyed peeking into their living rooms and admiring their beautifully decorated trees. Sometimes we saw a lively party in there, with women and children in beautiful dresses and men in their officer's uniforms. The children were playing, while the adults were standing around with a glass in their hands and talking. We really liked to watch; it was almost like a theater performance. Other countries, other customs!

The equivalent German customs were quite different. The Germans would never leave their living room windows open, Christmas or not. Somebody might look inside and intrude upon their privacy. Thus, a sheer curtain would be pulled before the window during the day, followed by a solid curtain or outdoor shutters at night. Our home actually had wooden outdoor blinds, which were rolled down after sunset. Older houses employed vertical hinge-mounted shutters. Shutters and blinds served a dual purpose: Protect the privacy and keep the burglars out. Also, the Germans did not have parties or visits before Christmas Day. The Advent month was very quiet. Every Sunday afternoon, our family lit candles mounted on a wreath on the living or dining room table, and sang Christmas songs. One additional candle was lit on each successive Advent Sunday. We children received an Advent calendar at the beginning of December. It consisted of a cardboard picture with a winter scene that had twenty four little doors cut into it backed up by pictures of dolls, children, sleds and the like. Every day we could open a little door until the last large door was opened on the 24th revealing a nativity scene. On the twenty-fourth Santa Claus managed to get into the living room without being seen. There he put up and decorated the Christmas tree, and spread the presents over tables, sofas and chairs. Nobody, but nobody was allowed anywhere near the door or, in our house, the heavy curtain that separated living and dining room until my father opened the curtain. Only then could we admire the lighted tree and search for our presents. -- During one Christmas my Aunt Hans, who was visiting us, committed the unforgivable offense of peeking through a slit in the curtain. Promptly, she did not find any presents on any table or chair. --

Talking about Christmas customs, I remember vividly a scene in the house that my friend Kurt Küffer and I had leased in 1960 in Magnolia on the northern coast of Massachusetts. We were celebrating Christmas Eve with Brigit and some Swiss friends; the tree had been beautifully decorated and was illuminated with many red candles; and we were all sitting around the piano, playing and singing songs. We had also invited our landlady and her husband who had promised a short visit. When they entered the room, Mrs. Eddington let out a shriek and pointed full of horror at the tree. The rest of us just stood there, nonplussed. What had happened? When she could speak again, she explained that "normal people" used electric candles and that lighting real candles was much too dangerous, maybe even forbidden. Wow! Brigit and I continued to light real candles on our tree, until, in the early seventies, when the commercially available Christmas trees in California were so dry that even we changed our old custom.

Back to the behavior of the occupiers in the different Zones. The generous Americans did not take any reparations out of their Zone. It is true, they had not suffered under occupation or under air raids either. Consequently they were very friendly and made every effort to get the country back on its feet. However, they had taken something very valuable and easily movable from Germany, as I found out a few years later: Many of the art treasurers that were an important part of the German culture. They had been transported to "safe" locations in the US. Was it out of concern about Russian ambitions? Or had it to do with German punishment? Curious, but they did come back five years later. The American soldiers remained mainly on their bases except for the occasional foray into German bars, where they could impress the German Fräuleins with their uniforms and wealth. -- In those days the *Deutsche Reichsmark* had almost no value left. --

The foremost interest of the Western Allies was threefold: Demilitarize Germany, minimize its industrial potential, and democratize its population. The German army, navy and air force had already ceased to exist, and there certainly were no plans to revive them. The disassembly of the German weapons industry was in progress. The real issue became what to do with the economy of the western Zones. Already in 1944, a commission consisting of the Secretary of State Hull, the Secretary of War Stimson, and the Secretary of the Treasury Morgenthau had been appointed by the US President to develop an economic plan for the after-the-war Germany. The problem was, how to fashion a new Germany that, on one hand, could maintain itself, but, on the other hand, could never again threaten the world. One of the more extreme proposals by Mr. Morgenthau was to convert it into a purely agricultural state, which luckily was rejected by President Truman.

From a political perspective, the Western Allies wanted to lead the German population away from its familiarity with autocratic regimes to an essentially unfamiliar democracy; a tall order. -- As the reader well remembers, Germany had been a democracy, albeit a very shaky one, from 1919 to 1933. The *Weimarer Republik* had suffered from its very beginning from the burdens of a lost war, a rapidly deteriorating economy, severe ideological and political unrest, and a weak and irresolute government. The extremists of the right and the military wanted to resurrect the old fatherland, the center wanted a democracy, and the extremists of the left wanted communism. The result were never ending battles between various factions of the right and left in the parliament as well as in the streets. It was an extraordinarily bad experience even for somebody who believed in democracy. -- The older Germans were used to follow the orders of the authorities. My mother, for example, referred to the government always as "they", by which she meant an unidentified body "up there" that governed us without our participation. The younger Germans had never experienced anything but the political organization of the *Third Reich*, and many were still believers. Consequently, the reeducation was a major undertaking that, surprisingly, was successful in the end;

although most Germans, our family included, remained very skeptical for quite a while. How upset were we when the first mayor of Mülheim was elected and replaced the *Bürgermeister* who had been appointed years ago by the omniscient state. The old mayor had all the necessary experience and qualifications and was an expert in city administration. The new mayor was a tradesman without any administrative and leadership experience. How could someone, who in our eyes was not qualified, govern our city, just because he had been "elected"? But that, of course, was exactly what it was all about: The majority of the voters liked him and elected him.

As the plans of our military government evolved, and decisions were made high up on the *Petersberg*, we continued to lead our lives at the lowest level. "Survival" was still the motto of each day. Part of Mutti's scheme was to fatten us up at the farm of some relatives in the *Sauerland*. Thus Marlis and I were sent during our Easter vacations 1946 to a cousin of Opa who had a beautiful farm near *Wemlighausen*, my grandfather's birthplace. With our little suitcases, we boarded the train to *Winterberg*, from where we had to walk the last ten miles. I recollect vaguely that the train could not continue, because the track went through another Zone. Grand Uncle and Aunt Dickel received us with open arms, so that we felt at home immediately. At the meals, each one of us ate for two. Food was not rationed and there was plenty of it. Whatever showed up on the table, disappeared in our hungry stomachs. We helped in the house and on the farm wherever possible, and I learned from a distant cousin how to saw and split wood. Naturally we met many relatives of my mother, of whom we had heard only vaguely before. They all invited us for dinner together with Opa who had lived there since 1943. The war had not done any damage to the village; the fields were cultivated, and cows grazed on the pastures. Everybody looked well fed, quite different from the people in the Ruhr Valley. However, there were only a few men left between the age of seventeen and thirty five, so that the older men and my once removed cousins were the only males who did the heavy work in the stables and the fields.

I want to tell here of a truly unbelievable event. During the afternoon of Easter Sunday all the children and teenagers assembled in a meadow for the annual *Eierwerfen*, the throwing of eggs. This was a traditional competition during which each

167

participant threw a <u>raw</u> egg as high in the air as possible and let it land in the grass, where, of course, most of them were smashed to pieces. The boy or girl whose egg survived the fall became the winner. Then came the next round and then another and another until all egg baskets were empty. Marlis and I were absolutely stunned. Here they smashed dozens of valuable eggs in one afternoon; while at home we were lucky to get a dozen eggs for the entire family in one month. What a world! After three weeks of farm life Marlis and I returned home, fattened like little suckling pigs ready for the market.

Following this success, Mutti sent me to *Tante,* aunt, Nisa and *Onkel,* uncle, Franz during the next two summers. Tante Nisa had moved to her father and two younger sisters in *Brühl* after the death of her little son and the divorce from her first husband. Later she married Franz Borgmann who joined the navy during the war. I always admired him in his neat navy uniform and with his mustache and goatee, and, not to be forgotten, a tattooed anchor on his forearm. The Borgmanns had sold their multifamily house in *Duisburg* before the major air raids began and had bought a large piece of property near *Orsoy* on the western shore of the Rhein. They managed to build a new home there during the early war years. How lucky they were, because their former house was a bombed-out ruin at the end of the war. Full of expectations, I took the streetcar through *Duisburg* as far as it went and then walked to the ferry that took me across the river. From there by bus to Orsoy where *Onkel* Franz picked me up. -- All bridges across the *Rhein in Köln, Düsseldorf, and Duisburg* had been blown up by the retreating German troops; and one could cross only by ferries or pontoon bridges that the Allied Forces had erected. Only during the terrible winter of 1946/47 could one cross on foot, by car or even by truck, because the *Rhein* was frozen solid. -- We walked the few miles to their home where a most memorable summer began. Seeing my favorite *Tante* Nisa again after more than three years gave me real pleasure. After she had showed me the house and my room upstairs under the roof, I had to explore their property right away. A large garden with potatoes, vegetables and all types of lettuce and other greens; behind it a big orchard with plums, Italian prunes, pears, apples, peaches and cherries. A few sheep in the pasture, and rabbits and chickens in their cages closer to the house. A miniature farm. I was in seventh heaven. At supper I could eat as much as I liked -- what a wonderful feeling. Work began the next day early in the morning. I helped *Onkel* Franz wherever I could, digging, planting, sowing, and harvesting. In the evening we fed the rabbits and chickens and cleaned the sheep pens. It did not take long before I became a full member of the small team.

Occasionally, *Onkel* Franz took me for a walk through the long property to the dike that reached into the sky for more then thirty feet. We would climb it and descend on the other side down to the immense river that was on its way to Holland and the sea. Right there on the shore a river barge was tied up that had been damaged during the war. My uncle, who knew the skipper and owner very well, said hello and introduced his nephew. I was invited to come on board and tour the barge that measured circa 150 feet in length and 15 feet in width. It was one of those freight barges that ply their way up and down the Rhine between Basel and Rotterdam. Some accomplish this under their own power, others, often two or three tied together, are pulled by a tugboat. The Rhine traffic which had come to a complete standstill towards the end of the war was picking up again. Here and there I could see a barge, however, mostly under Dutch or Swiss colors. *Onkel* Franz traded vegetables and fruit against fish that was eel today. I had never seen a live eel, only smoked eel pieces from the delicatessen store. These eels were not exactly beautiful; long, thick, gray snakes were swimming in the pail, oh horror. I was even more terrified, when my uncle killed them swiftly with his sharp knife and hung them on hooks in the tool shed. Then he pulled their skins off, while these dead eels were still wiggling wildly about. When, however, the pleasant aroma spread throughout the kitchen during the frying my appetite developed rapidly. Unfortunately for my evolving appetite, those eels continued to kick occasionally even in the hot pan, and one of these dead beasts decided to jump out. Well, my aunt terminated his ambitions by slamming the lid on the pan in one swift stroke. The life-after-death of theses eels put a new damper on my anticipation for this delicacy. However, in the end they tasted excellent with fried potatoes, cauliflower and a thick white sauce.

Next Saturday I became quickly acquainted with an age old custom that ranged from *Duisburg*, down the Lower Rhine through Holland all the way to the North Sea. On Saturday afternoons work came to an end, and house and yard were thoroughly cleaned for Sunday. It was my job to clean and rake the yard, the driveway, and the shoulder of the little country road. Sure enough, all the neighbors were doing the same, almost like a competition. Observing them carefully I understood that the crux of the competition was to rake the most artistic or unusual pattern into the sandy soil. I did my best and did better every weekend with growing experience. I am sure that there would be talk about the nicest raking design after church on Sunday. Besides helping aunt and uncle I was eager to learn more about the surrounding countryside and villages. Aunt Nisa gladly lent me her bicycle for my exploratory outings. To my surprise I discovered that her bicycle had the most unusual tires, solid rubber tires. Since obtaining tires and inflatable inner tubes had become almost impossible during the last war years, someone had the clever idea to construct a solid rubber tire. This would not have worked with the round profile of inflatable tires, because it would have been much too hard. Therefore the inventor had developed a triangular profile with one edge pointing outward where it touched the ground. This design resulted in a smooth and reasonably cushioned ride. "Necessity is the mother of invention".

The *Zwetschgen* harvest became an exciting adventure for me. --*Zwetschgen* are known by the name of "Italian prunes" in this country; they are not plums, although most people think that prunes are just dried plums. -- *Onkel* Franz and I picked the fruits day after day from a number of very tall old trees. Bucket after bucket went onto a huge heap in the basement, where they were packaged and shipped to a jam factory. After we had emptied the trees of the easy ones, somebody had to tackle the rest way up there. The somebody turned out to be I, because I was lighter and my uncle was stronger. He leaned the ladder almost vertically against a branch so as not to overload it, and I climbed up and collected what was in my reach into a small sack. Quite a balancing act as in the circus, but without net. Then I would lower the full sack, climb down, and the acrobatic act was repeated for the next branch. Being up there in the lofty height I liked to eat the ripest and biggest prunes myself; after all, had I not earned it? Unfortunately it turned out that even a young and strong teenager could only "stomach" so many *Zwetschgen*. Abruptly, one could see a young man racing faster than a rocket to the house, barely making it to the bathroom. *Tante* Nisa recommended I cut down on the prune consumption and focus instead on balancing and picking. Good idea! I still think of this hilarious event when I sit on a branch in my prune tree and prudently taste only very few outstanding specimens.

I think that it was also during this or the next summer, when Günter and I built a sailboat without having any idea about sailing. *Herr* Rübel had found in some field two reserve kerosine tanks of the kind that the bombers carried under their wings to increase their range. Once empty, they dropped them; and if the ground was soft enough they would survive with little damage. Their aerodynamic shape had predestined them to become the body of our boat. It took a lot of labor and skill to cut an opening into one of them with tools that left a lot to be desired. Günter wanted to find out if the opening was big enough and if one could sit comfortably on the bottom of the tank. So, we carried our first product to the little pond across the street, where Günter climbed eagerly into it. It capsized before I could count to three, and my best friend was hanging head down in the water. Did I scramble to rescue him! Günter's father managed to get a few iron bars, bolts, and nuts with which we connected both tanks to provide a more stable platform; and, voila, we had invented the catamaran, not the first in the Pacific, but certainly the first on the *Ruhr.* Then we constructed a mast and a rudder and tailored a sail from an old military camouflaged tent.

Finally we transported everything with Rübels' car to the Ruhr, put the contraption into the river and started our first trip. With a gentle breeze blowing up the river, we sailed quietly towards *Kettwig,* the next town upriver. What a delightful excursion!. We landed here and there on the shore, explored small side arms of the river, and enjoyed the sandwiches that Günter's mother had prepared. Shortly before *Kettwig,* we turned in order to start our trip back home. Nothing happened, the catamaran did not move. We sat in our wonder boat and wondered. No matter how hard we tried, it would not sail downstream. What kind of boat builders had we been! Neither did we have an idea, nor did we inquire how one sails against the wind, let alone understanding the significance of a keel. What a discovery; the embarrassment was full-blown: We had invented the catamaran of the *Ruh*r all right, but had forgotten the all important keel. Luckily, we had taken a long rope along, with which one of us, trotting along the shore, pulled our marvel, while the other sat in the boat and steered it. It took hours to get back to the rowing club from where we had started. Hopefully nobody had seen us in our defeat. During the next week, the crew was busily refitting the boat with a keel; and soon we were actually sailing not only before but also tacking against the wind on our river.

The summer of 1946 on the Ruhr was especially exciting, because the river had not yet been fully regulated again with dams and locks. The entire system had been destroyed in 1944 when British bombers had attacked the huge reservoirs in the *Sauerland* that fed the Ruhr. The British had developed a very clever scheme by which they dropped disk shaped torpedoes into the reservoir that skipped along the surface like flat stones. When they reached the dam they exploded and caused a breach. The water did the rest and thundered into the valley below. A huge wave raced through the *Ruhr* valley all the way to *Duisburg*. Naturally, it destroyed everything in its way. Consequently, a small unchanneled river meandered through the old riverbed in this summer, the perfect playground for us boys. However, our entertainment did not last long, because the authorities rebuild the regulating system as fast as possible.

The situation in our school started to improve during 1946. We still had classes only on alternating days, for we continued to share the building with the other *Gymnasium.* This sharing was changed later into morning and afternoon sessions; but it actually lasted until our *Abitur* (graduation) in 1951. Very fortunately we continued to receive our daily soups, the *Schulspeisung,* with the compliments of the military government. Our family needed this supplement badly. The pupils were now reorganized into classes that corresponded not to their age but to their level of knowledge. I was lucky that I was put into the same grade as most of my classmates from before the war in spite of the loss of one and a half years of schooling. The reason was that most everybody else did not receive schooling for long time periods. I belonged now to the newly formed *Obertertia* (ninth grade). The classes could be reduced, because younger teachers gradually drifted back from prisoner-of-war camps, and older teachers were denazified. My class size decreased from fifty boys to thirty, quite a change. Of the older teachers, some had never joined the Party, a surprising discovery. Others were again acceptable to the Military Commissioner of Education after they had spent months in reeducation camps. -- These camps served two purposes: Punishment and reeducation. They were very tough; and frequently older men would barely survive and occasionally not at all. Dr. Vollert, the father of Marlis' girlfriend Helga, who had served as the Director of the *Lyzeum* for decades did not come back. -- Others were dismissed, because the youth of the new Germany, who should be educated according to free and democratic principles, could not be entrusted to them. All in all, the military authorities kept a watchful eye on our education. The curriculum was carefully scrutinized and had to be approved. They wanted to make sure that we would not remain captives of the old ideology. I still see before my eyes the uniformed British education officers next to our director, our teachers and a representative from the Ministry of Education of *Nord Rhein Westfalen* serving on the panel, before which we had to pass our oral exams for the Abitur. It was the year 1951, the democratization process had begun six years ago, and Germany had become supposedly a sovereign country in 1949.

The change from the ideological demands of the National Socialists to the expectations of the the future democracy was not easy for our teachers. It was only five years ago when Dr. Heinen, our German teacher, made an unnerving prognosis for my future in 1941. An accident had left a very visible large scar on my right knee. When I returned to school after two months in the hospital, he looked at my knee and said: "It is a pity, but you will never be accepted by the *Waffen SS.*" This was a real blow for an eleven-year-old for whom a career with this elite troop was a desirable goal. After the war, when the same Dr. Heinen had returned from the reeducation camp he taught us German literature. Now he extolled the virtues of the western judeo-christian civilization to which we should aspire. We should bring up our families and make our professional contributions as part of this age old civilization. I had a hard time understanding how my teachers were able to change their outlook and view of the world from one year to the next. Difficult to digest for a fifteen-year-old! But easy to understand when one considers the position of a teacher in any society. We rarely give this much thought; but society expects its teachers to impart its values to the young. If you cannot comply with that innate requirement you cannot teach in that society. While certain freedoms exist in a free society, none exist in a dictatorship. Anybody who is under

173

constant scrutiny like a teacher runs always the risk of not only losing his job, but also his freedom or even life. Therefore in retrospect I have today a much better understanding and even empathy for Dr. Heinen and his colleagues.

In the first years after the war another change took place, quietly without any fanfare: A shift in allegiance from National Socialistic ideology to Protestant religion, which affected mainly the Hitler Youth. During the Third Reich it was no longer obligatory to attend religion class in school as it had been before. Marlis and I did not want to participate in that class and begged our parents to sign a release form. To our surprise they signed, presumably because they themselves had never shown any interest in religion. Thus I no longer attended the religion class together with a number of classmates. Also, I had not gone to the bible instruction in church and was never confirmed like other kids of my age. Everything changed after the war when the Protestant Church regained a significant presence in the country. Many families had their teenagers confirmed retroactively, but Marlis and I remained outside the church. When my younger sisters, Sigrid and Heidi, reached the age of fourteen in the early fifties they celebrated their confirmation in the Protestant Church.

It really surprised me when even my friend Hans-Otto was confirmed after the war, he who had spent two years in a *National Politische Erziehungs Anstalt* (National Political Institute of Education) where he had been thoroughly immersed in the ideology of National Socialism. These schools had been formed for the specific purpose to educate the future leaders of Germany. They provided, besides a remarkable academic education, the necessary political and ideological basis for the future bureaucrats and technocrats of the new world order. Hans-Otto's father must have had excellent connections that made it possible to obtain a place for his son in such a prestigious school.

While Hans-Otto had no serious difficulties in adjusting to the post-Hitler world, father Bösebeck himself did not survive intact the end of his beloved *Third Reich* to which he had been totally dedicated. He had been young and wide open to the new doctrine, as so many of his contemporaries, when the National Socialist Party was formed in the twenties. These survivors of the war lost their footing when the war was lost and their ideology collapsed. Those who did not commit suicide or were able to readjust their lives were left behind with deep emotional scars. Herr Bösebeck finally succumbed after years of alcoholism at a relatively early age. Other changes at school proved to be very pleasant. We did not have to assemble anymore in the school yard, class by class, until the director gave the signal to enter the building. We still had to stand up when the teacher entered our classroom, but we did no longer have to greet him with a snappy "Heil Hitler". We offered our "good morning" that was answered with "good morning, sit down". Some teachers were a little more demanding. Dr. Büser had been a major with the army and had not given up his army habits. When he came into the room in the middle of winter he sniffed audibly the air, remarked that nobody should breathe that kind of foul air, and asked us firmly to open up all the windows. The boys of the window row were allowed to find seats or stand on the other side of the class room. Furthermore it was all right to keep our overcoats on during the "airing". Ten minutes later we closed the windows, took our coats off, and shivered for the rest of the period, because the heating of the building was already minimal. Nobody had the nerve to even think about questioning Dr. Büser's orders.

Talking about overcoats, what did we actually wear? In those years, fashions like those of our teenagers today did not exist. One simply could not buy anything. Therefore we wore clothes from our fathers or dyed military or *Jungvolk* uniforms that were not exactly beautiful. Because everybody's dress was unique and was worn all the time, one could always recognize other pupils by their dress from afar. Half of the class still wore indestructible *Lederhosen* (leather shorts) during the milder months. If you had a *Lederhose,* you had to make sure that it looked used and somewhat dirty from day one. It required a bit of an art to "condition" that garment. The other boys wore long pants, which I also wore during the cold winter months. Some of us wore hats. During rainy days I, too, wore a hat that I had inherited from my grandfather. It was dark blue with a colorful twisted cord, with which my mother had replaced the old staid hat band. As I became more sophisticated I replaced the hat with a *Baskenmütze* (Beret) that I wore at a cocked angle. Later when I owned a bike, I covered myself with a gray, plastic cape that Mutti had scrounged from somewhere. That heavy plastic did not let a drop of water through, neither a molecule of air out, so that after a

175

while it was as wet on the inside as on the outside. It also channeled all the rainwater into my shoes that remained wet and squeaking for hours thereafter.

When school started up again in October 1945, Dr. Brüggemann was reinstated as the Director of our Gymnasium. He had been forcefully retired after 19 years of service at the beginning of 1944, because he continued to refuse to join the National Socialistic Party. -- I was surprised he had lasted that long. -- When he died at the end of 1946 he was replaced by Dr. Hänseler who had either not joined the Party or had been already denazified. When the ministry of education made him director they must have been scraping the bottom of the barrel. It soon became obvious that he was not very competent. Our class was already not very impressed by his teaching and knowledge, but he lost all respect on one, for him fateful, morning during the Latin lesson. In those days our teachers were seated on a podium behind a desk. The teachers desk in our classroom was already old and shabby, and one panel on the front side had become loose, or maybe one of my classmates had helped it a little. One can imagine how surprised we were to discover that Dr. Hänseler, the new director, held a dictionary on his lap, which he consulted here and there. That was his downfall as far as we, his pupils, were concerned. Finished! Interestingly enough he was moved to a different town and probably demoted shortly thereafter. This was an example of the problems the education authorities were facing. Because of the scarcity of teachers they had to employ frequently not the most qualified educators. As I mentioned earlier many of the younger teachers were still in prison camp or had been killed, and many of the older ones had yet to be denazified.

We were, however, very excited about the teachers who returned from the prisoner-of-war camps. First, they were young; second, with their first hand knowledge they could tell us a lot about foreign countries; and third, they spoke the language of their host countries very well. They knew considerably more about the practical side of those languages than their counterparts who had never left Germany. Dr. Tombers, our French teacher, had spent two years in France, and Herr Schmitz, our English teacher, a similar time in the US. Besides the teachers, also older pupils had returned. They had been soldiers or helpers on anti aircraft batteries and had spent time in prisoner-of-war camps. Since the number of survivors of age seventeen and above was very small, they were grouped in one class in which they were prepared as fast as possible for a *Kriegsabitur* (war graduation) with reduced scholastic requirements. Only the *Untersekunda* (tenth grade), one class above us, became a "normal" class. Some of the prisoners-of-war ended up in our class. When Willy Nolte joined us we learned that he had been in Russia and was three years older than we. I always wondered how he felt being amongst us youngsters who had not been at the front. Willy and others exerted certainly a wholesome influence on the rest of us, because they were very serious about their education and were eager to make up for lost time. This caused us to become also more earnest about learning and less interested in just passing our time.

Sometime during the summer of 1946, my grandfather decided to return to his daughter's family where he had lived from 1938 to 1943. He wanted to come back to us because he was not quite happy on his brother's farm in *Wemlighausen.* Now the house had to be rearranged again: Opa moved back into his room above Papa's former office, where I slept. Mutti and the girls moved into the large master bedroom, and the young Schröders into the smaller bedroom that had been vacated by Miss Sonnenschein. We were very lucky that Miss Sonnenschein found lodgings elsewhere. Mrs. Hesselmann and her other daughter continued to reside in the large living room under the master bedroom. I enjoyed working with Opa in the garden. He took frequent walks, sometimes with his grand kids, in the *Witthausbusch,* the forest-like park nearby. After dinner and supper, he helped us kids, who were on kitchen duty, to clean and dry the dishes. On Sunday he attended the *Evangelische Kirche* (the protestant-lutheran church) and dedicated the afternoon to the study of the Bible, his favorite book. Whenever *Tante* Mali visited us, she would accompany him to church. He also said again a prayer before our meals. He liked to join me when I practiced the piano. He sat there in the easy chair next to the piano and listened quietly to my playing. When I told this to my piano teacher, she taught me how to accompany the church hymns that he would sing with his beautiful baritone.

Unfortunately life with Opa was not to be of long duration. We were still hungry most of the time because there was simply not enough to eat. The lack of food did not affect us much; but one could see how he steadily lost weight, although Mutti gave him something extra here and there. I remember how Marlis and I talked about it, because we did not find it fair, for the food was normally distributed in precisely equal amounts: Two slices of bread with jam in the morning; equal servings of soup, potatoes, vegetables, and sometimes pudding for dinner; a slice of bread with molasses, occasionally covered with slices of boiled potatoes in the afternoon; and equal portions of *Bratkartoffeln* (fried potatoes) with salad and vegetables for supper. The *Bratkartoffeln* often got charred because there was so little lard in the skillet. *Suppenfleisch* (soup meat) was served with dinner on Sundays. It had to be boiled for a long time before it was soft enough, because the cow had probably been pretty old. I was so used to this kind of meat that I did not realize until much later that not all meat was served gray and that it existed in many different types and shapes.

The lack of heating affected Opa even worse, especially as the winter of 1946/47 was extremely cold in Germany. Ice and snow everywhere with very little sunshine; *Ruhr* and *Rhein* were frozen solid with trucks crossing where the bridges had been. We could barely keep the house above 60°F with our meager "coal mud" allotment. Sometimes I escaped to our neighbor Poppen who kept his apartment warm with his coal allotment from the railroad. For really cold weather Mutti had bought little bags that contained a chemical with an exothermic reaction when moistened. We would use these as hand warmers or sit on them when we did homework. -- Interestingly, there is a modern version of these bags on the market now. They are much smaller and heat up when exposed to air. Brigit puts them into her ski boots to keep the toes warm, when it gets really cold. -- We children could tolerate the cold, because we moved about a lot, went to school, saw friends, and went to stores, in contrast to my grandfather who did not move much and probably never got warm unless he was in bed or took his weekly bath. As a consequence, he got pneumonia, against which his body could no longer defend itself. He died in February of 1947. After he had been buried, Mutti told us of his last words which were truly remarkable. He thanked her for having taken him in as the only of his four children, for having given him a beautiful home, and for taking care of him during his last year and especially his illness. He had not expected this from a daughter who did not maintain the same strong Christian faith as he and his other daughter Mali. It had been a revelation to him that she had created a family that was so much healthier and happier in body and spirit than many faithful families he knew.

Mutti could not keep Opa alive, but she was very successful because of her ingenuity in keeping her children fed, clothed and healthy. A beautiful example of her inventiveness comes into my mind. No matter how scarce everything was, my mother produced a cake on every weekend. That tradition was not to be broken. Occasionally she baked a marble cake, for which a light colored dough is combined with a chocolate colored dough in some marble like pattern. She used wheat flour for one and coffee grinds, which she had collected all week, for the other. When I told Brigit this story for the first time, she made a peculiar face but did not say anything. She had been wondering how we children could have survived these caffeine shocks. The riddle was solved only years later, when I happened to tell her that those coffee grinds had come from roasted barley, the *Ersatzkaffee* of the years during and after the war. Mutti carefully saved every ounce of real coffee until she had enough for a *Kaffeeklatsch,* a comfortable get-together with her lady friends where she served the "real thing" together with cake.

I mentioned earlier that we collected nettles and dandelions for spinach and salad (cooked nettles do not sting.) If we managed to obtain fruits and vegetables during the peak of the summer, they were canned in glass jars or salted in large crocks. The glass jars filled the shelves in the basement; and the crocks with cabbage, string beans, etc. stood on its floor. Even eggs were preserved, hard boiled and kept in a sodium silicate solution. Extra tomatoes became purée, which was filled into bottles. The latter led to a funny event in our kitchen. When Mutti wanted to open one of the purée bottles during the winter, it had fermented, the lid popped and high pressure tomato purée gushed from the bottle. As Mutti tried to keep the bottle closed, turning in one or the other direction, she squirted a beautiful modern painting on wall and ceiling which could have competed with Pollock. We had to laugh so hard that she could not stop the flow; and with tears still in our eyes we scrubbed the artistic creation off walls and ceiling.

Because the gas allotment for our house was not sufficient, a number of saving methods had to be implemented.

My mother and, of course, many other families made frequently *Eintopfgerichte* (single pot meals) mostly thick soups with peas, beans, or lentils. The pot was brought to a boil on the gas range and then kept hot just below simmering in the *Kochkiste* until it was ready to be served. A *Kochkiste* was simply a wooden box filled with straw or rags shaped into two or more holes of the right pot size and covered with a lid insulated in the same way. Just about everybody I knew used these boxes. Taking a bath was also a real luxury. Each family in our house was allowed to take a bath once a week. Our bathing was organized as follows: Opa was the first, because he was the cleanest, then I, followed by Marlis and the girls, and Mutti as the last. In this way the family needed only two tub fillings. On one of these bathing evenings we suffered a terrible fright. The water had cooled off considerably by the time Sigrid and Heidi had their turn. Mutti wanted to rescue the situation by giving the bath temperature a boost with the help of a big electric immersion heater. Unfortunately she had not considered that the splashing water could get into the insulated handle. I was just ascending the stairs when I heard screams from the bathroom and saw a few seconds later the two girls, stark naked and drenched, racing through the hallway like torpedoes. The scene was so unbelievably funny that I could not stop laughing. However, learning from Mutti what had happened, I became instantly very quiet. This could have ended tragically. Never again did Mutti use an immersion heater with her children sitting in the tub.

A few other events have remained in my memory. After my grandfather had died and his belongings had been distributed amongst his children, some pieces of furniture were left over. Without much questioning I sawed them into pieces for firewood that was more urgently needed then furniture for which we had neither use nor space. Only many years later did I realize that I had also converted into heat the beautifully carved housing of a grandfather clock. It would have probably remained with the family as heirloom and antique. Another episode condemned our house to miserable cold for almost a week. I was in the basement in the process of breaking up the slag in our central furnace, when I hit the wall of the fire chamber with my long poker. Suddenly all hell broke loose. Water shot into the chamber with a terrible hiss, and a steam cloud filled the fire chamber and the entire furnace room. I fled into the laundry room nearby, for I thought the furnace would blow up. Instead hot water rushed from the furnace into the furnace room and from there into the floor drain of the adjacent laundry room. I was scared and dumbfounded, until I saw that the poker had cut a hole into the rusted back wall, and the entire heating water system was emptying out. Shucks! Mutti was having a cozy *Kaffeeklatsch,* when I broke the bad news. For days all the house mates were clothed in overcoats, shawls, woolen caps and warm shoes, until Mutti had persuaded a compassionate plumber to weld the hole shut.

Another sad episode was entirely of my own doing. As mentioned before, with my fifteen years I was permanently hungry. Anything edible became a temptation. When I spent some time every day in the basement, keeping the fire going, cleaning the family's shoes, and repairing things, I could not resist thinking about the apples that were stored on a few shelves. Finally I broke down and took one and on another day a second one and maybe even a third. Nobody would know the difference. But Mutti had most likely counted her apples and had started to wonder. One fateful day, as I succumbed again, I suddenly saw her standing on the basement stairs, looking at me. I was devastated. She did not chide me or use many words. She simply said: "I do understand that you are hungry, we all are; but we must stick together and be honest to each other. I will not say anything that I saw today to your sisters." With tears in my eyes I promised that I would never again break her trust in me. She never said a word to anybody; and I have never forgotten that. A happier food related event happened at Hans-Otto's birthday. Mrs. Bösebeck had baked a wonderful fruit pie for this occasion. She put it, topped with loads of whipped cream, -- they had a dairy business, -- on the table where Hans-Otto, Günter and I had assembled. Then she poured us some *Ersatzkaffee* and left. What a feast! We went to work without delay and took care of the entire pie. When she returned after an hour, she wondered: "What did you three do with the cardboard bottom?" -- "What cardboard bottom?"-- It turned out that the pie had been supported by a round piece of cardboard that got thoroughly soaked. Did we ever laugh! The hungry sixteen-year-olds had eaten everything "down to the plate".

Once a month my mother had her laundry day, which required the help of us all. The previous evening Mutti soaked this mountain of laundry in two concrete tubs in the laundry room. On the morning of the laundry day I made a fire under the laundry vat with paper and cardboard, which I had collected during the previous weeks. Good coal was no longer available, and the coal mud did not work. The fire was excellent, but had to be maintained all the time until the laundry that we transferred from the concrete tubs had boiled long enough. Then we moved the laundry to a wooden vat with a four-pronged stirrer that was driven by a two-stroke water motor. There the laundry was washed. Then back to the concrete tubs, where it was rinsed. Afterwards I ran every piece with muscle power through a wringer into baskets that Marlis and I carried up into the yard for drying on the clotheslines. If the weather did not cooperate we carried the baskets all the way up to the attic. It is surprising that we never had an accident when we heaved these heavy baskets up the extremely narrow and steep ladder that led from the second floor to the attic. -- Let me inject here a bit of *Ruhrgebiet* experience. Mutti always spread the bed sheets on the lawn so they could dry and bleach in the sun, in case the sun was shining. However, this only worked if the wind blew from the right direction. If it blew from the direction of the industrial part of town, the air carried enough black particles to evenly cover the beautiful white sheets. An age old custom could not withstand modern industrial pollution. -- I was always looking forward to the laundry day, not because of the hard labor but mainly because of the movie at the end of the day. Mutti had made it her custom to invite us all to a movie as compensation for our help.

The old *Reichsmark* had kept its value for such things as movie tickets and books. Everything for which rationing coupons existed, from groceries to clothing, could be bought with it. One could also pay for streetcars, buses, and trains with the old money; but for anything else it was practically useless. Extra food, cigarettes, coffee, hardware, repairs, and many services required payment in form of reciprocal services or equally scarce goods. A barter economy blossomed, and not just for luxuries but for urgently needed everyday items. Officially the barter trade was known as *Schwarzmarkt* (black market) and forbidden; but nobody paid any attention to that. People took trips to the countryside in order to exchange valuable rugs, radios, appliances or furniture against butter, eggs, ham or, maybe, half a piglet. Unfortunately, getting caught on the way back into the city meant losing everything. There blossomed also a commercial black market, organized and operated mostly by the criminal element, with questionable street vendors at deserted street corners or in the ruins. Liquor, gasoline and cigarettes were its most thought after commodities. Many of my classmates smoked "Lucky Strikes" or "Camels" that were obviously not attainable with rationing coupons. I never knew what they or their parents were trading for their fixes. German cigarettes, that Mutti could buy with her rationing card, also had value but much less than their American counterparts. She kept them for payment of the plumber and other trades people.

Since the money had lost its value, all construction had come to a halt. Nothing was built anymore except for emergency shelters in basements or on the first floor of the ruins, often miserable little huts with rusty corrugated metal roofs and sometimes cardboard walls. Big companies like Thyssen, Mannesmann, Siemens or the mining companies frequently compensated their employees with raw materials, products of the company, or goods that the companies had bartered against their own products. As mentioned earlier, our neighbor received high quality coal from the railroad. Unfortunately our family, receiving a pension from the state, did not benefit from any of these extras. Günter's family did well, for *Herr* Rübel was a representative and distributor for several food companies. Whenever I was their guest -- luckily that occurred frequently -- their supper table was well stocked with meat, sausage, eggs, butter and breads; foodstuff in which he dealt. Hans-Otto's family ate well because of their dairy and grocery store. In addition his father was a wholesale distributor of milk and other dairy products. Fate had touched us in different ways.

Rarely does one think about the lopsided demography as the result of war. But it was very evident in my hometown and certainly in the rest of Germany and in several other European countries and the Soviet Union that suffered heavy losses. Walking through town one saw almost only older men, women and children. Men between the ages of seventeen and forty had just about disappeared, until they started trickling back in small numbers from the prisoner-of-war camps. The condition of these survivors was invariably pitiful. They came back totally undernourished, racked by diseases (dysentery, pneumonia, tuberculosis), plagued by lice and fleas, and in torn,

183

dirty uniforms. Many had been wounded, some had lost a leg or an arm or worse. These men were also psychologically destroyed and demoralized. Herr Münkemeyer, a neighbor, took two years before he became fully functional again. In the years after the war the women were in charge of our world. Of our class of seventeen boys, who graduated from the Gymnasium, ten boys had lost their fathers. The ratio between women and men who were in their twenties or thirties was at least three to one, not exactly ideal for finding a male friend or husband. Marlis and her girlfriends who were between seventeen and nineteen could not find any boys or men of the same or an older age. Marlis married eventually Hartmut who was two years younger than I. I read in a school report from 1947 that 360 boys from our school had been drafted between 1939 and 1945. Of those only 60 came back. The majority of one generation of men had been swallowed by the war.

The same war had turned us boys who were now fifteen and sixteen too early into men. We missed a good part of our youth. No wonder that Günter and I played with his electric toy train when we were already sixteen. In the last years we had only known duties and work with very little time off. We had taken on important responsibilities and had to make frequently grave decisions so early that it shaped our later lives. Politically, we were totally, and I mean totally, apathetic. We only knew a totalitarian system and waited for orders from above, which used to come from Berlin and now came from the *Petersberg*. Then something strange happened one day. My friend Dieter Jakob had discovered that there was some kind of an organization of world pacifists. After he received pertinent information from them, he proposed that a group of us should join the organization, which to the best of my recollection was American. Full of curiosity and desire to do something new, a few friends and I founded the "Sunshine Chapter". We wanted to make a contribution to world peace. When the Chapter met once a week in our house, we played first a few rounds of Ping Pong and then discussed the big issues of this world. I do not believe that our tiny cell made ever any contribution to world peace; but we were all quite certain about one thing: "Never war again!" We hoped that as the result of this unbelievably terrible war the countries of this world would give up their nationalistic ambitions and join each other in a common world; and we wanted to be amongst the first world citizens. The sessions of the Sunshine Chapter ignited a very tiny spark of hope for a better future. I forgot how long the chapter lasted; but it had opened, if only slightly, the door to a bigger world beyond us.

New Doors are opening

Two more doors opened shortly after the war: The first was opened for me, the second I opened myself. Günter's parents were members of the *Wassersport Verein* (club for water sports) which started to recover from the war in 1946. Luckily the clubhouse with an indoor training basin, showers, and locker rooms below and a large hall with a restaurant upstairs had suffered only minor damage. The boathouse, however, needed significant repair; but it had protected the rowing boats more or less. Some were damaged, others dirty and unkempt. Members who found time and energy reopened the facility. They soon realized that the club needed to attract youngsters because of the war attrition. Therefore, Mr. Rübel asked his son and me one evening during supper, whether we would like to learn how to row. Of course! On the next day he took us down to the club, and we found a boat for two that was not in use because of its condition and age. It would do for us beginners. We three carried the boat to the landing dock and lowered it carefully into the water under *Herr* Rübel's direction. We climbed into the boat even more carefully, for this thing was not exactly stable. We barely avoided capsizing as we left the dock very slowly. With father Rübel as helmsman and trainer we set out into the river, cautiously putting the oars into the water stroke after stroke. Not very easy, but upon our return we felt that we had made a little progress; and our trainer said a few encouraging words. Afterwards the boat was cleaned and put back on its shelf. Then we went under the hot shower. What an indescribable joy, for I had not taken a shower since the weekly showers with *Lehrer* Meyer in 1938/39 in the basement of the *Hindenburg Schule*. What a difference between this shower and the lukewarm baths after my grandfather at home. We changed from our rowing outfit back to our street clothes and drove home with father Rübel. In those days we wore black shorts and white sleeveless shirts for rowing, as well as for gymnastics and track and field. During bad weather or in winter we wore a dark blue sweat suit on top of it. After a few outings under Günter's father's direction he allowed us to row on our own. Thus began my long lasting love for rowing. I am sure I would still be at it, if I had continued to live close to a river or lake. In the beginning we made only short trips to *Dicken am Damm* or *Mintard*; but soon we dared to row all the way upriver to *Kettwig* or down river to the locks at the *Wasserbahnhof*. There were always many members at the club on Sunday mornings so that one could find enough people for a few Fours or even Eights. Participating in an Eight was extremely demanding in terms of coordination, balancing, and keeping up with the old foxes. It took a lot of energy and meant streams of sweat.

The school teams from before the war were brought back to life during 1947. Both, the *Humanistische Gymnasium*, that I attended, and the *Naturwissenschaftliche Gymnasium* maintained their own teams. Regattas between the schools and other clubs came back to life. That meant that our leisurely rowing life was replaced by order and serious training for the races. The worst of it was that most of us were always hungry and did not have a lot of stamina. The club fixed this deficiency by furnishing the teams with healthy meals. A club member, Mr. Möhlenbeck, owned a food factory that, amongst other things, provided the *Schulspeisung* (food for school children) for the schools of Mülheim. He provided thick bean or pea soups and sometimes even a stew during the training season. As so many businessmen, he built a very nice home right after the currency reform in 1948. We teenagers dubbed it the "Soup Castle". The racing boats were usually refurbished during fall after the racing season. Everybody had to help in this demanding and time consuming job. First the old varnish was removed with shards of glass; then the surface was sanded with ever decreasing grit size, and finally three layers of varnish were carefully applied without leaving any beads behind. I also helped to built the new boathouse for better storage of additional new boats. When I visited the club again in the seventies after many years I found a modern beautiful building with boat storage, locker rooms, etc. below and the club facilities above. The old building had been sold; and a nice apartment house had been erected in its stead. The war had helped to replace the old with the new.

As teenager, I spent almost my entire social life in the

old clubhouse. We lingered often after rowing, we organized small parties or big dances, where some of us volunteered to provide the music or entertainment; and once a year at the end of the racing season the club organized a big bash for the rowing teams with equal amounts of singing and beer drinking. During the racing season drinking, smoking and hanging around with girls was an absolute no no. If you got caught you were off the team, the worst imaginable punishment.

Today's parents are worrying when their children attend a party that might include alcohol. The consumption of alcohol may be one thing, but the driving home is quite a different worry. One hears all the time about, often fatal, accidents of young intoxicated drivers. We did not know how much luckier we were than future generations. Neither our parents nor the police had to worry, because private automobiles almost did not exist and certainly none for youngsters. We walked home or took a streetcar. However, getting home after a beer party was sometimes difficult. How did Günter and I make it home under adverse conditions? On foot, of course, up the hill, and following carefully and sometimes slowly the footpath through the *Witthausbusch*. Occasionally we might miss the path; but as long as we made it uphill the direction was correct. By the time I had walked home I was usually sober again, or at least I thought so. Although Mutti apparently never worried, I had to abide by the cardinal rule: No matter how late I came home from a party I had to knock at her door and say good night. At times when I had opened the front door without the slightest noise, ascended the stairs in socks without a squeak, and knocked barely audibly at her door, she let me clearly know that it was not very considerate to bang against her door after having scratched with my key for ten minutes on the front door lock and trampled up the stairs like an elephant. One cannot win, can one?

One summer our school team had to find somebody who was willing to compete in the single scull category against Karl Grüter from the other gymnasium. Since Karl was considered unbeatable, nobody volunteered. Unfortunately the ensuing vote fell on me, the designated sacrificial lamb. I trained every day. Our school teacher and trainer Schmitz, whom we called "Gipsy" because of his informal dressing habit, was there every morning at 6:00 a.m. He even helped me to get the shell into the water, followed me with his bicycle on the tow path, and gave me good advice and moral support over his megaphone. But it was all for naught. Karl remained unbeaten; he was too good and too strong. Nevertheless I received an honorable reception when I returned to the boat landing, because I had sacrificed myself heroically.

Let me tell the story of another memorable race when our four with Günter, Alex, Alfred, me, and the cock swain Hennig became an unexpected victor. We participated in a long distance regatta on the *Rhein* in *Wesel*; and our chances for success were minimal, because we lightweights were competing with heavyweights. Four miles up and four miles down a river that had currents and waves and barreled along at several miles per hour. None of us except for Hennig had ever experienced that before. The *Ruhr* by contrast was usually flat as a mirror and had only a slow flow because of its many dams. We took at least one precaution; we raised the tholes so that the oar blades could be kept above the wave crests and could not be easily caught. As the boats were started in sequence, we could not see our competitors. Then began the struggle with waves, currents and water threatening to drown the boat. Our cock swain was busier bailing the boat than navigating around the jetties into quieter waters and at the same time keeping our boat from capsizing. Upon returning we staggered totally exhausted onto the landing platform and waited with anxiety for the arrival of our certainly faster competition. To our great surprise they did not arrive in time to beat us; then, to everybody's even greater surprise, they simply did not arrive at all. After a long wait we boys from the *Ruhr* discovered that we had beaten the experienced rivals from the *Rhein*. Of the four original boats three had been swamped or had capsized; and we achieved a victory that nobody had even dreamed of.

My final rowing story is a sad one that made a strong impression on me for the rest of my life. I was already attending college when our former four participated during semester break in the annual regatta between the Gymnasiums in Mülheim. To begin our training weeks we made our first leisurely run on the river. After only twenty minutes my classmate Hermann collapsed and almost fell out of the boat. We were stricken when we found out that he had smoked all last year; and his lungs could no longer handle the stress. I do not believe that anyone of us had imagined such a consequence of smoking. Luck had it that

Hermann who continued to smoke for decades did not succumb to cancer in his later years. I had received much earlier my personal lesson about the ill effects of smoking. Sometime in 1947 Günter had scrounged a few cigars from somewhere. So he invited Hans-Otto and me to a little smokers' get-together. We picked the basement below the destroyed government building at the *Saarlandstraße* for our rendezvous, out of the neighbors' sight. Not having any idea about smoking, in particular cigar smoking, we happily inhaled the cigar smoke until we were so sick to the stomach that we threw up and barely made it home. Never again did I smoke a cigarette, let alone a cigar; I was cured for life.

Music became my other pastime and love. It started as a hatred when my parents dragged me at an early age to a violin teacher. Although little musical interest was expected from boys, middle class parents tried at least to make them learn to play the violin. Girls were taught the piano. I had no interest in music and remembered the scratching and squeaking when Ulrich Breuer, the son of family friends, practiced on his violin. Therefore I resisted so vehemently that Mutti and the teacher gave up. A year later I was dragged to a piano teacher, Miss Molitor, who actually taught me piano later in life. The same violent performance; I simply did not want it. It was decided to try again in a few years; but the war intervened.

After the death of Aunt Hans in 1941 the family had inherited an accordion that was taken along to Waldenburg. There it stirred my interest; and I learned to play little tunes and songs. As the interest deepened and the playing got a little better, the war intervened again. We had to flee and leave the instrument behind; but I could not forget it. On our return to Mülheim I rediscovered the old upright piano that Opa had brought with him in 1938. Now I was ready, I wanted to have lessons. This was not easy, for Mutti had little money to spare; and, on top of it, the piano had been placed between the former living and dining rooms as a kind of wall between Hesselmanns and us. This meant one could only play when the other party was not in its room. Nevertheless, I was determined to learn. I begged Mutti again and again, until she finally caved in and invited Miss Molitor to talk about lessons. Thus I received my first formal instruction with eight years delay.

Miss Molitor came to our house, because she had lost

her beautiful grand piano during an air raid. I took practicing seriously and worked very hard to please my teacher. This may also have been influenced by her good looks and blond hair. Always finding a time slot for practicing in the absence of Mrs. Hesselmann I made good progress so that I had to participate in her students' semiannual recital before all parents and friends. Wow, that scared me: A public performance, playing from memory, and, worst, six-year-olds presenting the same simple pieces as I with fifteen. No protest helped. My teacher picked the *Fröhliche Landmann* by Schumann; and I practiced with determination. The whole family accompanied me to the orphanage on the Dimbeck where the recital took place. Here I was, in my blue Sunday suit with a white shirt and a tie suffering badly from stage fright. To my surprise and satisfaction I did not make one mistake and did not get stuck. However, I heard to my great embarrassment, how other kids of my age played Mozart's Turkish March, Beethoven's Für Elise, and a few Impromptus by Schubert. More reason to work harder!

With time my repertory advanced and increased: Etudes, sonatinas, rondos, bagatelles, and even sonatas. When Marlis and her friends began to dance, I tried my luck with fox trots, tangos, waltzes, boogies and blues. Miss Molitor had actually approved of popular and dance music in addition to my classical music. My favorites were the boogies; and syncopated Bach inventions had a special appeal. Once Harry Mietusch send me "In the Mood" that he had copied by hand from some sheet music of his American Army friends. After two years my teacher wanted me to practice two hours every day instead of one in order to maintain the pace of progress. Unfortunately I could not do it because of too many other conflicting demands on my time: School, tutoring to earn money, garden, house, and rowing. I could have gotten up earlier, but waking up Mrs. Hesselmann with a Schubert Impromptu would not have been a very good idea. As soon as I left home for the university the entire piano career folded. It took seventeen years when Brigit bought me a Baldwin baby grand, on which I had to start slowly again and which is still my best friend today.

I had an amusing success in 1960 during my voyage to the US on the "United States". We danced every night to a band from New York. Unfortunately they quit at midnight, although the day continued for another ninety minutes because of the time difference. So I sat at their piano and played some dance music for fun. Since people liked it, I played more the next night and the following nights. To my surprise the band leader approached me the last evening onboard and offered me a job with his band in a bar in Manhattan. I was thrilled by the prospect of a new and exciting career, but prudence prevailed and the engineering career continued for another forty years with the occasional sonata or boogie thrown in for good measure.

We have a New Currency

During 1948 rumors abounded about a final collapse of the value of the *Reichsmark.* That money had not had much value for quite a while. It was useful for all goods that could be obtained with rationing coupons; it paid for public transportation, books, and movies. That was about it. No major acquisitions like appliances or furniture could be made   (they did not exist anyway), no services could be obtained, and the money had no value on the black market. Construction had come to a standstill, and everything else, including all services, had to be bartered. I guess there was one exception, financial transactions were still made in the old money. Thus, Mutti managed to pay off the remaining mortgage on our home in *Reichsmark,* a nice gain for us, a bad loss for the lender. The economy of the West Zones had reached rock bottom, which made prospects for a recovery very dim. Unbeknownst to our family and probably most of the population the Allied Occupation Government had already decided to introduce a new currency that their governments would support, and that would be ultimately convertible on the international currency market. Preparations were kept completely secret in order to minimize speculation with goods and materials. It was rumored that the factories, the wholesalers and the retailers were already hoarding their products in expectation of a hard currency.

Then out of the blue happened the most important and furthest reaching event since the war. It was the salient event that would pull the Western Zones out of their economic misery: *DIE WÄHRUNGSRREFORM* (THE CURRENCY REFORM)! The

Bank Deutscher Länder, Bank of the German States, had already been founded in March of 1948 in Frankfurt. It was to play the role of the Federal Reserve Bank in this country. There was no doubt that the old *Reichsmark* was kaputt with 300 billion mark in circulation without any measurable exchange value. Thus American and German banking authorities began the colossal task of a massive money exchange. Everything was kept extremely secret; and the forty nine banking experts who prepared the changeover were closeted without any contact to the outside. Rumors, of course, grew from week to week. Something was in the air, but we could not imagine what and when. One million pounds of new money was printed and coined in the US and shipped to Frankfurt under the code name of "Operation Birddog". And then, on the evening of the 19th of June, 1948, the most memorable broadcast was sent over all German radio stations: "Tomorrow on Sunday, June 20 the old *Reichsmark* will be replaced by the new *Deutsche Mark."* This news came like a salvation! On the next day, the entire family went to the nearest distribution locale where each one of us received forty brand-new *Deutsche Marks.* This was followed by a distribution of additional twenty Marks in August. We could exchange the old money at the rate of 10 to 1 for the new money and convert bank deposits at the rate of 100 to 6.5. Real estate and securities kept their value. The latter decision caused an enormous social injustice, because a very large fraction of the population had lost land, homes and material goods as the result of air bombardments, flight or later forced evacuation from the East. It seemed like a bad decision from a human and political perspective, but maybe one step could only be handled at a time. It did take a few years, until the *Lastenausgleichsgesetz* (law to equalize the burdens of the war) was passed in 1952. This law taxed all property -- land, real estate, securities, and material goods -- that had survived the war and gave this money to the people who had incurred losses. In this way the losses of the war were finally shared by all West Germans (the East Zone was not involved). The new law was particularly important for the economic integration of ten million German refugees from former German land in the East, but not including the Soviet Zone. Our family owned land, a house, and all other material goods, nothing was destroyed. So we had to pay our dues. Unfortunately I do not remember how much we paid in absolute terms (Deutsche

Mark) and in percentage of our property value.

The miracle had happened!!!! On the twentieth of June 1948 we stood in line for the last time after years of food scarcity since 1945 and after nine years of rationing. It was truly unbelievable; overnight, the money had regained a real value in the form of the *Deutsche Mark*. The black market disappeared, "connections" and bartering went out of fashion; and now the amount of money and nothing else determined what and how much you could buy. The British newspaper "News Chronicle" announced, "that the currency of the cigarette, the most stable currency since the war, was destroyed overnight." A new era had begun; and for ensuing decades Germans would refer to the time "before the currency reform" and "after the currency reform".

The fundamental significance of this reform had not yet been grasped by us and most of our fellow citizens. We were totally focussed on its immediate effects. What should we do now with this new money? Would it keep its value in the future? Could the long lasting string of devaluations of the twenties repeat itself? Questions like this were uppermost in everybody's mind. Until the reform there had been no incentive for work beyond the daily needs, no desire to save, no opportunity to invest and no means for reconstruction. Suddenly all this changed. Suddenly the show windows of the stores were full of merchandise. First we were overwhelmed that such a thing could be possible after nine years of deprivation; then we were delighted that we could finally buy all the goods that we had needed for so long; and last we were angry at the merchants who had hoarded their wares for so long. My friends and I went into town as soon as we could and marveled at all the wonderful things that we saw in the show windows with their brand new price tags in DM, *Deutsche Mark*.

Hans-Otto and I wanted to buy bicycles that would give us the same freedom that Günter had since his father had given him his own old bicycle already some time ago. Now the opportunity had arrived; bicycles were available, and real money could be earned. Herr Bösebeck got us jobs with a contractor friend. On the first day of summer vacation we showed up at the construction site in *Speldorf,* a suburb of Mülheim. There the contractor was building a house for a producer of women's corsets who had apparently made already enough money to build a house. First we learned how to shovel sand, pebbles and cement into a big heap on the ground. Then we were shown how to convert these ingredients into concrete by mixing them with water. Since we were not used to that kind of heavy labor, we were already exhausted before the noon break. We sank under a tree, where we had to rest a little before we could eat. I emptied my jar with pea soup in a hurry, which filled the belly but did not last very long. We continued, energy ebbing, for the rest of the day that seemed to stretch forever. Finally we were finished and caught the streetcar back home. The next day more of the same thing and this seemed to consume the rest of our energy. But slowly we got used to our new work; and exhaustion lessened. On Saturday I received my first pay envelope with 38.40 DM, real *Deutsche Mark,* my first self earned money and the first installment for the bicycle. Hans-Otto and I were both very happy and proud. The 80 *Pfennig* per hour were not much, especially when the reader may remember that this amounted to not more than 18.82 cents at the 1946 exchange rate; but for us it was a mountain.

Our next job assignment was to support the brick layers by carrying bricks and mortar to their working site. First I learned how to carry bricks. I had to place a board with a cutout in the middle of one side on a stand like a man-sized tripod and loaded it with as many bricks as I could carry. Then I stooped under the board, lifted it with shoulders and hands, and carried it to another "tripod" stand near the brick layers. This required a careful balancing act if I did not want to drop the valuable load to the ground. Balancing became even more precarious when bricks had to be carried up a ladder to the second story. I also filled a hod, placed on the same stand, with mortar and carried it on one shoulder to be emptied into a large bucket next to the brick layers. Sometimes, when I had transported enough material, I would help laying bricks, another new experience. After the first floor was completed work became really tough. The next job was absolutely exhausting. The first story ceiling was built by pouring concrete mix into a mesh of rebars and small I-beams, with a temporary floor of wood scaffolding. To lift the concrete mix to its destination, it had to be shoveled   from the mixing station on the ground to a transfer station on a platform halfway up the first floor, and then from there to the first floor platform from where it was shoveled into the prepared forms. I had the pleasure of being the shoveler on the halfway platform. That meant I had to heave up the concrete as fast as the bottom shoveler landed it on my platform. All day long for three days. In the evenings I barely made it home. With the above exception, I enjoyed the work in the open and above all with the thought of the bicycle at the end. After five weeks Hans-Otto, Günter, and I went to the store where we had been already looking at bikes. With Günter's expert advice we each picked a very heavy -- by today's standards -- bike with a steel frame and without gears, for that was the only choice in 1948. It was painted black with two longitudinal light green stripes. We paid our 180 DM and left the store in the knowledge of our newly acquired freedom. No more streetcars, no more buses, and down to the rowing club in ten minutes instead of half an hour on foot. If I was late, I used it also occasionally to ride to school. I had bought the bicycle just in time, because a couple of weeks later a new need arose.

At the end of a French class Dr. Tombers took me aside and asked whether I would be interested in tutoring younger kids. "Of course," now that the currency reform made work worth while again. Dr. Tombers was a good friend of Mr. Mülders, owner of a construction company, who was looking for an older pupil to tutor his children and supervise their homework. After an interview Mr. and Mrs. Mülders offered to employ me for DM 1.60 per hour. That was a handsome salary, to which I agreed without hesitation. Twice as much as my wages on the construction site! I would have to work with their three boys and one girl six days a week. That was the beginning of my *Deutsche Mark* savings. I deposited my first pay at the *Stadtsparkasse* (city savings bank) on the *Victoria Platz*. From now on I would save every penny for college, which I thought I might attend after the *Gymnasium* . I actually supervised the Mülders children for about three years until my *Abitur*. Heinz was the oldest; I do not recall the names of his siblings. Since I liked tutoring and wanted the income, I added other pupils to my list whom I tutored in Mathematics and Latin, my favorite subjects.

I worked again during Easter vacation of 1949, this time in a stone quarry. One of my classmates who knew the owner arranged for a small group of class mates to work there. Albrecht, Dieter, Bruno, Helmut, Hermann, and I showed up at 6:00 a.m. sharp on our first vacation day. The foreman, who actually lived on the premises in a small house, gave us the necessary instructions and safety precautions. Off we went! Dieter and I were given the job of loading large flagstones into a tip cart. These hand-pushed carts ran on rails that could be moved to new locations as necessary. Once we had loaded a tip cart, we pushed it carefully over the wobbly rails to the loading dock, where we loaded its cargo onto a truck. It was a tough job to handle these heavy blocks or plates of stone with all their sharp corners and edges. -- Fortunately, as a result of the currency reform the entire food supply had dramatically improved since 1948. I got more to eat and was no longer at the verge of exhaustion at the end of every day. Furthermore, the rowing had done its share to strengthen muscles and body. -- During the dynamiting, that took place three or four times a day, we had to find cover behind rocks and our tip carts. That gave us always a nice break for chatting and resting. Luckily, no accident happened during those three weeks. Of course, we all had suffered minor cuts and bruises that were readily fixed. The pay was good, so that I could deposit another 144 DM at the *Stadtsparkasse.*

There were also plenty of opportunities to work for the city, that had started to clean up the totally demolished city center. The rubble removal crews would first stabilize all building walls that could be saved. Then they would swing a huge steel ball dangling on a chain from a crane to collapse the walls that were beyond saving. -- I actually had the pleasure of doing the same thing a few years later when I was working for a contractor, building a new underground riverbed for the *Rumbach* . We had to demolish a few ruins that were in the way. What an excitement, when the steel ball hammered the wall again and again, until it started to sway and in the end collapsed with a tremendous bang and dust cloud. -- Afterwards they loaded the rubble into the same tip carts that we had used in the quarry, and pushed them onto a main track where they were connected to form a train. A small steam locomotive hauled the train to locations that had been designated as part of the rebuilding plan of the city. The city engineers had laid a temporary rail track system throughout the city with feeder lines, main lines, switches and crossings. One of my classmates, Lothar Buchloh, who worked for one of the demolition contractors, had always stories to tell: From the discovery of leftover skeletons to the removal of a bomb dud by defusing experts, to a scheme for padding a contractor's income. The city estimated the volume of the rubble that had to be removed from a certain street section. The lowest bidder got and executed the job as agreed upon; but some of the contractors let the rubble conveniently disappear into a basement, when no inspector was in sight. This, of course, saved the cost of extra shoveling and hauling. Not very community minded!

I would like to relate an example of excellent civic solidarity that affected my home town profoundly. The full-scale destruction of the town had happened between 1943 and 1945, a massive clean up was in progress, but the future was uncertain. There had been much discussion in all quarters and at all levels as to what the city should look like in the future. To move forward the city government recommended that the citizens should decide on the best way for rebuilding. A choice had to be made between two very different approaches: Either rebuild the city as it had existed before by rebuilding the prewar houses on the same narrow streets, on the same lots with the same owners, or create a new city center making room for the modern means of transportation and optimized traffic patterns. The former approach was easy from a personal property point of view, because it would not require exchanges or condemnations of property with all the legal hassle. The city layout would remain the same; and all property owners would rebuild on their plats. Retaining the prewar architecture was not a decisive factor, because Mülheim being an industrial city of the late 19th century did not have much of a historical architectural value to offer. Developing an entirely new city layout would be exceedingly complex in regard to property rights, but presented a golden opportunity to create an attractive modern city. The citizens voted decisively in favor of plan number two.

Now an agreement had to be reached regarding the layout, with some of the old and some new, often much wider, streets and avenues as before, with new parks, plazas, commercial high rises and apartment buildings, potential under or over passes, and even the relocation of the railroad station. Quite an undertaking! City planners proposed layouts in form of huge drawings and moquettes that could be inspected in the town hall and commented on. Eventually the best compromise for a layout was hammered out and approved. Now began the most difficult battle, the handling of the property rights. Soon the city came to

197

an agreement with the owners of small and big parcels alike that the best solution would be to condemn all real estate property and start from scratch. The conditions for the new distribution of real estate were simple: Keep the existing location or find real estate of comparable size and value close by, if that was important to the owner. It took almost a year until all the claims were settled with surprisingly few exceptions. When everything was finally accomplished, Mülheim emerged as a new and modern city, albeit presently only on paper and as a huge moquette in the lobby of the town hall. It was exciting to follow the implementation of the plan during the next six or eight years whenever I came to visit my hometown from Aachen where I attended the *Technische Hochschule* from 1951 to 1959.

By contrast the city of Aachen, which had been literally flattened by air raids and severe battles on the ground, decided upon an entirely different course. Aachen was an old and beautiful town with a history of 1100 years, with medieval city walls and gates, with superbly crafted renaissance houses, a fabulous dome, and many handsome churches. It was rebuild exactly as it had it existed before with a modern touch here and there. One building, the St. Elizabeth Church, was rebuilt in a most inventive way. The architect left as much of the old church as possible standing; then he completed the building in a striking modern style with imaginatively designed colored glass windows. I think that most German cities were rebuild as a compromise between keeping their old image and the necessities of modernity. During a visit of the former East Germany in 2000 I found that Dresden and Nürnberg were prime examples of that compromise.

The currency reform meant that our family could now make long needed repairs on the house and particularly on the roof that suffered considerable damage from air raids. We also needed a new central furnace, which could burn anthracite coal or coke, which were both again freely available. We bought paint for kitchen and bathrooms and fabrics for new clothes or even a ready made piece of clothing here and there. People began to rebuild there houses. The Bösebecks who had lived first in the basement and a later in a makeshift dwelling on the first floor could now rebuild their first and second floor and later the entire house. Some of our house mates found apartments so that after 1949 only Mrs. Hesselmann and the Schröder family remained with us until she had finished rebuilding her apartment house in 1952.

Teenagers without Fathers

Today in the age of single mothers, society gradually recognizes that children are better served with a mother and a father. I believe that this is particularly true for boys. Although little was commonly known about such psychological insights, I am sure that my classmates and I, who lost their fathers, felt instinctively the need for a father. Right after the war I attached myself to Mr. Poppen, our neighbor. He was probably between thirty and thirty five years old, had returned from prison camp in 1946, and was now working as a mechanical engineer for the *Deutsche Reichsbahn*. His main job was the rebuilding and repairing of the rolling stock, in particular locomotives. He was a born craftsman and thus installed his own little workshop in the shop of his father-in-law, an upholsterer. There he created many objects from wood or metal. I admired his electric saw, his drill press, his small lathe, and other quality tools. I enjoyed visiting in the evening and helping wherever I could. In this way I learned to work with wood and metal; he taught me to glue properly, to varnish or lacquer, to solder, braze, and weld. After some trial and error I was even allowed to use his lathe. He and I spent once half a year building a toy railroad for Udo, his small son. We fabricated everything from turning the car wheels on the lathe, to fashioning locomotive, tender and cars from metal parts, and also to building the tracks from curtain rails. Through him I learned to design and build simple electrical circuits and devices.

With his help I constructed a small radio consisting of a crystal with a needle as diode with coils and capacitors as tuners. I mounted the parts in a cigar box; and the "radio" was completed with a pair of head phones, which I had found in his attic. We strung an antenna between our neighboring houses, and I ran a cable from the antenna through the little window in the small entrance lobby all the way to my new detector next to my bed. Getting a radio station took some doing, tuning to the right frequency and then patiently moving the sharp needle over the crystal until I could get a reasonable reception. In this way I could listen to the news before I fell asleep. I remember the transmissions from Cologne of the first *Karneval* (the Mardi Gras of the Rhineland) after the war and the speeches of a certain Konrad Adenauer who was talking about a future for Germany under a democratic government.

Two years later I met another father figure. One day in school my friend Albrecht (also without father) mentioned that his family had known Mr. Liekfeld for many years, an elderly bachelor who was a juvenile judge in Mülheim. He had asked Albrecht whether he wanted to accompany him to a concert performance. If he liked the idea he could also bring a few friends along, who were interested in classical music. When Albrecht asked Hermann Schwarz (no father) and me, we accepted without hesitation. What an opportunity for me to become acquainted with orchestral music. I had now played the piano for two years, but I had never been to a concert. I did not have the money for that kind of extravaganza. The next Wednesday I put on my only dark blue suit with a white shirt and tie. Albrecht and I picked up Mr. Liekfeld and Hermann on the way to the *Altenhof* that contained the concert hall. The *Altenhof* (old farm) had its name from a farm house that had stood in this location for hundreds of years. It was now a cultural center that housed meeting rooms and the concert hall. Mr. Liekfeld gave us an introduction to the concert pieces to be played. We followed him like his disciples. The orchestra played amongst other things Bach's Violin Concerto Nr. 1 in A-Minor and the Concerto Nr. 2 in E-Major. Those two concerts gave me such a pleasure that I have listened to them many times and still enjoy them today. For me, they opened the doors to half a century of concert visits, and they became the foundation for my, and later Brigit's, love for classical music.

After the concert, *Herr* Liekfeld invited us three to a beer in the restaurant *Handelshof.* That was already exciting; but it really impressed me that he treated us as adults, although we were only seventeen. We talked about music, rowing, and school. He told us about his job experiences as juvenile judge, a world I did not know anything about. He explained that his exposure to young people was very lopsided, because he only dealt with law offenders. Therefore he had decided to become acquainted with normal teenagers in order to balance his view of the young people of those years. He invited us many more times to concert evenings; frequently followed by conversations and discussions over the customary glass of beer. In a few years I became acquainted with works by many masters from Bach, to Beethoven, to Mahler. Soon, Herr Liekfeld invited Albrecht and me to his house on the *Friedrichstraße,* where we had profound conversations about music, literature, school, sports, the emerging new government, and the choice of a future profession. Each afternoon or evening broadened my horizon. Sometimes I would take a walk with him through the *Witthausbusch* or along the *Ruhr,* where he delighted in taking pictures with his small *Leica.* I learned much from him, that I probably would have picked up from my father, had he lived. During my student years I became such a good friend of him that I called him *Onkel* Hans. Our friendship lasted through several paralyzing strokes to his death at the age of eighty. When Brigit met him in 1963 during her first visit to *Mülheim,* she also greatly enjoyed his company.

I am also counting professor Löbl amongst my father figures. He was a guest professor in Aachen during the fifties, where he lectured on high power electric machinery and particularly on rectifiers. I assisted during his lectures, graded the exam papers of the students, and acted as the liaison to my resident professor Brüderlink. After his afternoon lecture he always invited me to dinner — what a treat — , where we had the most interesting conversations over a glass of wine. Naturally we talked about professional issues, but occasionally also about his fascinating life experiences. After my graduation, I worked for him for half a year at the RWE, the biggest West German power company, where he acted as the scientific advisor to the president. Professor Löbl was mostly responsible for my later decision to come to this country for a year or two. He believed very strongly that a young man had to see the world and become exposed to other ways of living and thinking. Professor Löbl was half Jewish and had actually managed to stay unscathed in Germany during the war, because he was a well known engineer and scientist, had good friends in the Party, and was very much needed. He worked all the time in the electric power industry in Berlin. He introduced me in 1959 to Mr. Besag, a lecturer at the College of Technology in Loughborough near Nottingham, who offered me my first job as lecturer at the College. Emil Besag's life history was typical for the fate of many Jewish families in Germany. He had grown up in Frankfurt as a Jewish boy and had experienced the ever growing repression of his family and friends. When the rotten deeds of the Nazi Regime became more widely known and when rumors abounded in the Jewish community about the concentration camps, his family like so many others split into two factions. His parents and two siblings argued for staying in the country of their ancestors; after all, their family had been German for centuries. It was true that there had always been ups and downs in the relationship between German Jews and Christians; but nothing was so bad in their memory that they should leave the country. Unfriendly monarchs had come and gone. He and his sister saw more clearly and with less emotion what was coming and desperately tried to persuade the others to leave as long as that was still possible and actually desired by the regime. Emil and his sister left for England for a new and not very easy life; the rest stayed behind and perished. I enjoyed many hours in the company of the Besag family who, like all British families I met, treated me openly and generously in spite of my German provenance.

My Best School Years

With the new school year, that began in the fall of 1947, school life had become almost normal again. Our Humanistic *Gymnasium* was still sharing one building with the Natural Sciences *Gymnasium*, because the occupation authorities continued to reside in our old building. We still alternated between morning and afternoon classes from week to week; but class sizes had shrunk to acceptable levels. So many teachers had returned and had been denazified that our class had been reduced to seventeen pupils, who all remained together until the *Abitur* (graduation) in 1951. I must say that I truly enjoyed those last school years. We classmates knew each other very well and helped each other in the school as well as outside. Most of us had been in the same class since 1941. We also had reached the age when we were eager for new knowledge and ideas. I believe that the new ideas were paramount, because the one old idea, National Socialism, had been demolished. Furthermore, we had had for years so little school instruction and only in very few subjects that we were sponges wanting to be filled with knowledge.

I have a fond memory of those teachers who had the greatest impact on my life: Dr. Tombers taught French and Latin, Dr. Heinen enriched our lives with German literature, *Herr* Schmitz imparted English literature and German history to us and immersed us in the present-day world by making us read and discuss political articles in the Manchester Guardian, *Herr* Engmann was responsible for Mathematics, Physics and during the last year Physical Education. He was also our *Klassenlehrer,* which meant he had the overall responsibility for the class. Another favorite teacher was *Herr* Rickert who instructed us in art and art appreciation and above all art history. He was a painter in his private live.

I think that German literature was the favorite subject of the class as a whole. We read and recited prose and poetry in school as well as at home from the minstrel songs of Wolfram von Eschenbach to the *Teufel's General* of Carl Zuckmayer. Many of us, myself included, favored Hermann Hesse, of whose novels I liked *Narziss and Goldmund* best. The school organized also visits to theater performances in Mülheim and the surrounding cities. Goethe's *Egmont,* Schiller's *Don Carlos* ("Sire, give me freedom of thought!"), *Kabale und Liebe,* and *Wallenstein,* and Kleist's *Der Prinz von Homburg* were very popular. They dealt with freedom, class injustice, oppression, usurpation of power, and the consequences of not obeying military orders. All these topics were very important to us on our tortuous path from dictatorship to democracy. One of the most impressive plays that stimulated a good deal of thought, animated discussions, and elaborate essays was Lessing's *Nathan der Weise.* It deals with the conflict between the three western religions: Jewish, Christian and Islam. At its climax Nathan tells the *Ringparabel,* the parable of the rings, representing the three disunited religions that should be united like three interlocking rings. In addition to German literature, we studied poetry, prose and plays in English and French. We worked our way through a number of Shakespeare's plays. This was not exactly easy because of the old English, but became a delight under the patient guidance of *Herr* Schmitz. He also acquainted us not only with Milton, Chaucer, and Dickens, but also with modern American writers like

John Steinbeck, Sinclair Lewis, and John Dos Passos. Every week, we spent hours reading and translating the Manchester Guardian. He used editorials and special reports of current events to bring our history lessons up to date. By contrast, our regular history curriculum went only as far as the Weimarer Republic. It took more than one generation after me, before the Hitler and war years became part of West German school instruction. Starting with the *Obersekunda* (eleventh grade) we had to compose lengthy essays in class for which we were typically given five hours. My friend Dieter always excelled with his elegant style and remarkable ideas, while the rest wrote in a conventional schoolboy style. He walked away with an "A" each time, for which I admired and envied him.

Of all the other subjects I liked Latin and Mathematics the most. I assume the reason was that both are complicated but very logically constructed so that they presented the greatest challenge for the brain and the power of concentration. I enjoyed translating Roman authors as much as solving mathematical problems. Unfortunately, I did not continue to read Latin after the school years. It has mostly disappeared from my memory by now. In contrast, Mr. Schmitz, our neighbor who was a mining engineer, pursued his love for Latin throughout his life. Very impressive! However, as my interest in the relationships between the European languages grew with time, Latin started to surface again because of its etymological importance for these tongues. Throughout my school years, I felt very comfortable with Mathematics and always enjoyed solving complex problems. Naturally, it became an essential part of my engineering career. Physics was in the same category. One application of modern Physics that interested me most was the possibility of producing nuclear energy. It meant that Germany would no longer have to depend on its coal that would not last for ever. The future actually proved me right. Coal mining that had been the mainstay of the entire economy of the highly industrialized *Ruhrgebiet* declined and finally stopped altogether. The last coal mine in *Mülheim* was closed during the seventies, because the remaining coal was too far underground and consequently to costly to produce. I was close to studying nuclear engineering, a brand-new discipline during the fifties, but luckily I chose electrical engineering instead. Otherwise I would have been out of a job twenty years later, when this country did no longer increase its nuclear power production.

There were two other subjects that excited me and many of my classmates: Art history and art appreciation, both taught by Mr. Rickert. I looked always forward to his lessons, because he was a wonderful teacher, and his materiel was excellent. With a never ending supply of slides, he introduced us to art and architecture created by painters, sculptors, and builders from ancient to modern times. For me, he laid the foundation for a lifelong interest in these disciplines. Mr. Rickert's art classes reached a climax, when we visited an art exhibition in *Wiesbaden* in the fall of 1950. The art museum of Wiesbaden showed a unique collection of all major art works that had belonged to German museums before the war. These masterpieces had been stored in bunkers and mining shafts during the war and thus had not been damaged. After the war the Americans had transported this treasure trove to the US for safe keeping. -- It was never clear, from whom these gems were actually kept safe. -- As the relationship between this country and the new Germany improved, the US Government decided to return the masterpieces to their respective German museums. We spent days in the exhibition halls to admire in natura these exquisite paintings and sculptures, which we had seen only on the screen. The pinnacle of the exhibition was the head of Nefertiti, resting on a solitary pedestal in the middle of a large hall that housed Egyptian art. Having seen often photographs and slides of this exquisite sculpture was nothing compared to a close-up view of the original from the fourteenth century BC. - - Brigit and I were lucky enough to admire her again during a visit to Berlin in 2000, where she was exhibited in a simple illuminated glass cabinet in the middle of a totally blackened room - -.

During the last three years of school, the doors to the knowledge and wonders of the world were truly opened for us seventeen pupils. I am still very grateful to this team of teachers, with whom we had a wonderful cordial relationship. The class did maintain this relationship for many years afterwards; and I enjoyed their company for the last time during a class reunion in 1991.

Germany again a Democracy

As I enjoyed my last school years and as I was focussed primarily on family, friends, school, sports, and music , a new Germany was being shaped. My classmates and I were politically totally uninterested and did not pay much attention to German or world issues, although Herr Schmitz tried valiantly to arouse our interest in current history. At least he made us read about world events in the Manchester Guardian, as I pointed out earlier.

At the Yalta Conference, the Allied Powers had agreed to divide Europe and Germany after the war. The Soviet Union would extend its hegemony all the way to the *Elbe*. Of the former German provinces East Prussia would become a Russian province, and Pomerania and Silesia would become part of Poland. The former eastern Poland beyond the Brest-Litovsk line would fall to Russia. This so called "movement to the West" had been approved "with reservations" by the Western Powers. Germany would be divided into four Zones to be administered by each of the victors, including the French. After the war, the Soviets and the French began immediately to exploit their Zones. The Soviets took everything that could be dismantled including even all railroad tracks on lines that had two or more. The French went primarily after the coal of the Saar and the Ruhr. The position of the Americans was that "Germany was a conquered enemy state". Any fraternizing with German citizens was not allowed, although that was not strictly enforced because of interests that the GIs exhibited for German Fräuleins. As I mentioned earlier, American plans had been developed to convert Germany into an agricultural state. Thanks to President Truman they were scuttled. The British followed their colonial policies that had been successful in the past, by integrating the German with the British Administration after the principle of "indirect rule". In this way each Zone developed differently.

I was quite surprised when I discovered during my recent study of the archives that the Americans as well as the British permitted the founding of German political parties already between June and September of 1945. I found this even more surprising in view of an American Directive JCS 1067 that forbade any German political activity. Konrad Adenauer, whom the Allies had reinstated as mayor of Cologne in March 1945, became the leader of the recently founded Christian Democratic Union (CDU) in January of 1946. I found it most remarkable that a handful of pre-Hitler politicians got together to contemplate and actively pursue a future for Germany in spite of the utter defeat and destruction. Furthermore, this happened at a time when our family and probably the vast majority of Germans could not even think about politics and a future. -- The German cities were heaps of rubble and ruins; only eight million apartments remained for fourteen million households countrywide, with a much worse ratio in the big cities. The mayor of Frankfurt estimated "that it would take thirty years to remove the wreckage". By October 1946 the Red Cross had received ten million search inquiries for missing persons. There was little to eat and even less to heat with. Men between eighteen and thirty five were difficult to find; and those who had returned from prison camps were often sick in body and mind. -- Men like Adenauer, Schuhmacher, Kaiser, and Böckler fought against all odds for a way out of this misery to a better future. They all had suffered badly under the Nazi Regime, from job loss to concentration camp. Others had paid for their beliefs with their lives. Others who did cooperate with the regime had to suffer now, because the Allies were determined to punish those Germans who were guilty of the Nazi war crimes. The punishments ranged from loss of job, of civil rights, of property, of pension, to reeducation in tough rehabilitation camps, to imprisonment, and, for the worst offenders, to death. If somebody could prove -- like my father posthumously -- that he had been only a *Mitläufer* (insignificant follower), he could be denazified.

The standard of living had sunk so low that it could not be maintained for long. Ration cards had been issued for the hundredth time in February 1947 since August 1939. I am citing an announcement by the department for rationing that was typical for those times. It said: "Two clothing coupons will be allotted during the next period. They may be used for a pair of suspenders, two handkerchiefs, three collars -- men wore removable collars on their shirts in those years -- , or one replacement pants seat." I found especially the "replacement pants seat" extraordinary. The black market blossomed; and the "Ami" cigarette was the only reliable currency. One pack of Lucky Strike cost six *Reichsmark* at the end of the war and thirty *Reichsmark* eighteen months later. The Control Council, which was made up of all four occupiers and resided in Berlin, had developed the first plan for the German industry in 1945. The allowed industrial capacity had to be reduced to approximately 50% of its value in 1938. This meant that all production facilities in excess of this number had to be destroyed or disassembled and transported into the countries of the victors. The Soviet Union and France received most of it, for they had suffered the worst losses from the Germans. Affected industries were primarily weapons, ships, ball bearings, heavy trucks and tractors, most heavy machinery, and chemical plants. The huge chemical concern *IG Farben* was broken up into a number of small companies, to reduce its competitive potential. The second plan for the German industry was issued during 1947. It ordered the further destruction or disassembly of another 918 large production plants. Times were tough, and people could only think of survival. Their lives were influenced by forces and events, which they could not control and mostly did not even know about. For instance, I had no idea of Churchill's speech that he gave on March 5, 1946 in Fulton, Missouri with the famous pronouncement, "From *Stettin* on the Baltic Sea to Trieste on the Adriatic Sea, an iron curtain has been lowered over the European continent." I had no knowledge of Truman's speech a year later, "The United States will employ all means to support all nations whose freedom is threatened from within or without." -- And that included Germany! -- I had, however, ample knowledge of the formation of the *Bizone,* two joined Zones, in December of 1946, when the American and British Zones were integrated economically.

Our family and our friends again knew nothing about the most far reaching turning point in our existence, which would determine the future of Germany and all of Europe in the long run. The new American Secretary of State, George Marshall, announced on June 5, 1947 that the USA would offer Dollar credits for the reconstruction of all European nations -- including Germany --. Approximately one year later, President Truman signed the plan, which provided more than five billion Dollars in help for Europe. The American Government had become concerned that the increasing misery and desperation of the population would lead to a strengthening of the Communistic parties and thereby to the opening of Europe to the Soviet Union. Interestingly, the credit offer had been made to <u>all</u>

European nations, west and east alike; but Stalin rejected the offer for the Soviet Union and its satellite states. However, during the last conference of the allied foreign ministers in November 1947 he insisted on an economically integrated Germany. In that case Russia would have participated in all decisions about the German economy and, especially, about the reparations. It certainly would have changed the future of the *Ruhrgebiet* in a big way. "The Communists would have been in Cologne," said the French foreign minister Bidault. In February 1948, the three western foreign ministers decided to integrate economically all three western Zones with the intention to create eventually a new German state. The *Bizone* was expanded to a *Trizone*. This was baptized immediately "Trizonesia" by the population that had not given up its sense of humor in spite of all the hardships. We sang with great enthusiasm a Karneval song that had become the big hit of the year:

"We are the happy natives of Trizonesia,
heidi thschimmela tschimmela tschimmela bum.
With gorgeous girls from Rhineland and Westphalia,
heidi tschimmela tschimmela tschimmela bum.
We are no frightful cannibals,
but rather kiss the pretty gals.
We are the natives of Trizonesia,
heidi tschimmela tschimmela tschimmela bum."

There was also an internal battle raging for Germany's economic future. The big political issue in 1948 dealt with the question whether the future West Germany should continue with the centrally planned economy, or whether it should be built upon a free market economy. The country had lived for the last ten years with central planning, the East Zone had not made a change, and the British and French pleaded for a socialized economy in line with their own economies. The Americans, of course, argued for a free capitalistic system as in the USA. The recently appointed head of the West German department of economics, Professor Ludwig Erhard, also fought resolutely against the continuation of a socialistic market economy, because he and many other economists were convinced that only a free economy could support a rapid recovery. Fortunately for West Germany, he won the battle against an array of British,

French, and German socialistic politicians. A new law was enacted: A free economy and abandonment of price controls. This forced also the gradual elimination of rent control. The latter announcement caused an explosion; many people fumed and lamented, and the socialistic press went wild, " The rents will go up; the poor renters will suffer; the rich owners will reap the harvest." Nobody could envisage how the removal of the rent control would accelerate the building construction that was desperately needed. Neither could anybody imagine that an unshackled housing market would ultimately offer better and often cheaper living quarters. Professor Erhard was right in the long run. The German *Wirtschaftswunder* (economic miracle) began. West Germany experienced an unforgettable boom, while England, France and East Germany suffered for many more years under their controlled economies. -- As I mentioned earlier, when I lived in England in 1959, I could not believe that people were still queuing for meat at the butcher. I hardly trusted my eyes, when I saw in a factory for electric machinery that age-old lathes were still driven from a central shaft with long leather belts - -.

Little by little, the recently created concept of a West Germany as a sovereign nation moved closer to its realization. On July 1, 1948 the Western Allies presented the so called "London Decisions" to the premiers of the newly formed *Länder* (States). Each *Land* was allowed to form a Constitutional Assembly under the condition, that the form of government was federal, and that the rights and freedom of the individual were guaranteed. It amounted to a conditional sovereignty that could be removed by the Military Government at any time if things did not work out.

The Currency Reform in July 1948 had one unexpected result. As soon as it was announced, the Soviets closed off all traffic across the East Zone border as "self defense against the aggressive Currency Reform of the Western Powers". I think that this draconian measure was actually justified, because the useless *Reichsmark* that was still circulating freely in the West would have flooded East Berlin and the Soviet Zone and thereby would have raised havoc with the shaky economy of the East. Thus, the *Währungsreform* put the final seal on the long feared division of Germany. -- It took forty one years until the country was united again. This was a miracle for all Germans, who had given up hope a long time ago. Even I was utterly overcome by emotion, although I had lived in this country for thirty years, eight thousand miles away. -- When the de facto division happened, the Western Allies acted fast and supported the creation of a Constitutional Assembly for all of *Trizonesien,* which was rapidly evolving into a sovereign country. A Parliamentary Council produced a *Grundgesetz* (fundamental law) which was given this name, because everybody was reluctant to use its real name: Constitution. By calling it a constitution, the founding fathers would have admitted that they were creating a partial state, and that there would exist from now on two Germanys. Nobody was yet ready to take such an unthinkable step.

Of all the cities that were considered for the seat of the Parliamentary Council, Bonn, a small sleepy university town on the *Rhein,* was picked; and the festive opening session took place on September 1, 1948. Konrad Adenauer became the Council President. He was accepted by the Allies without much ado as the most desirable of all candidates because of his history and unquestionable allegiance to the West. "He was," stated a high ranking Allied official, "cooperative, but not submissive; dignified, but not arrogant." Furthermore, he showed that he was not only willing to work with the Western Powers, but also willing to criticize them. He began this historic session with his famous words, "Thus, we want to begin this work together, deeply bowed, but not broken." And it was in that spirit how he succeeded in bringing the devastated nation back on its feet.

Nine months later on May 8, 1949, the new *Grundgesetz* was accepted by the Parliamentary Council and it was announced to all West Germans on May 23. Each council member signed the document with the exception of the Communist representative Heinz Remer who said: "I will not sign the division of Germany". In quick succession Theodor Heuss was elected as the new President of the Federation, Bonn was confirmed as the capital, and Konrad Adenauer was elected with an absolute majority as the first Chancellor of the new Nation. A new Germany was born: It had a constitution, a parliament, a capital, and a new black-red-golden flag.

Across my Shattered Country

During these eventful months, Günter and I began to plan a bicycle tour through the South of our new old country. Our friend Hans-Otto could not join us, for he had to help his father during this summer. We had undertaken many trips since we had bought our bicycles; but they did not lead us very far from Mülheim. This was going to be The Big Trip. Günter's father and his friends obtained everything that we needed for the tour: Two triangular military tarps, blankets, ponchos, saddlebags for the luggage carrier, rucksacks, military eating utensils, one salami sausage, and some bread and margarine. When we had loaded everything the bicycles were so heavy that we barely could lift them. Somebody even found a map, a rarity. The adventure began; we followed the road along the *Rhein* through *Düsseldorf, Leverkusen,* and *Köln* to *Bonn;* easy traveling in flat country without any traffic on the roads. In 1949, there were literally no cars on the roads; and we met only occasionally a truck or some military vehicles or convoys. We felt wonderful; the roads were ours, an unexpected benefit from the aftermath of the war.

Shortly after *Leverkusen,* we caught up with an older cyclist, who was also on his way to *Köln.* As we chatted I discovered that he had only one leg left. The other had become a victim of the war. This handicap did not prevent this man from traveling by bicycle. He had fashioned a mechanism that pulled up the pedal with a strong spring after each down stroke. In this way he could ride his bike almost as good as we, albeit a little slower. I was greatly impressed by this encounter. It taught me that if someone wanted to overcome his personal aftermath of the war and move on in spite of his handicap he could make it. Our co-traveller obviously belonged to the type of person who would not easily accept defeat, but took his own initiative to improve his lot.

During the postwar years I could always differentiate between two human attitudes: One group could not stop bemoaning the devastation of the war and their personal fate. They wrung their hands and waited for the government or some other body to get them out of their misery. The other group put the disaster behind them, took the initiative and improved their lot as speedily as possible. I observed the same contrast after the

Currency Reform, after the new burdens of the Equalization-of-the-War law, and after the new Free Market Economy was launched. -- Not surprisingly, we encountered an exact repetition of this phenomenon, when in the year 2000 Brigit and I visited the places where I had lived during the war. We spent exciting hours with people, young and old, who had launched businesses or started a small hotel. But we spent also depressing hours with people who were still waiting for help from above ten years after the fall of the Berlin Wall. -

Shortly after this encounter the tall spire of the *Kölner Dom* (Cologne Cathedral) emerged on the other side of the river. It took another hour to find our way through *Deutz,* across the barely repaired Rhine bridge to the center of *Köln* and the *Dom.* Even Günter and I, who had been hardened by the destruction of Mülheim and its surrounding cities, were totally shaken by what we saw. Here, everything, and I mean everything, had been turned into rubble; no stone had been left on top of another. Blackened pieces of walls reached into the sky. Mounds of rubble covered not only the sidewalks but reached almost the middle of the streets. A narrow path served pedestrians and cyclists. -- This reminds me of my first year in Aachen, when I cycled every morning from *Burtscheid,* a suburb where I lived, to the *Technische Hochschule.* There, too, a small path in the middle of most streets had been cleared of rubble; but so much mud flowed from the rubble mounds into the street that on a rainy day I arrived at the university always spattered with mud. And this was still the situation in 1952, seven years after the triple devastation of that city. -- In Cologne like in Mülheim, people still lived in the middle of the ruins, some in basements that had not collapsed, and others in makeshift dwellings on the first floor. Oh wonder, the cathedral still stood in the center of the wreckage. A number of bombs had fallen into it, and the huge choir was so damaged that we could not enter. But the remaining vast structure took our breath away; we had never seen anything like it. We became unusually quiet when we advanced slowly through this marvel of gothic architecture. When the bells rang, it seemed miraculous that they could still ring above this sea of destruction.

An hour later, we arrived in *Bonn,* where we visited my Aunt Mali. Eighteen months ago, she had become the matron of the *Humboldtstift,* a residence hall for students of theology. We were given a room to ourselves, because many students had left for home for the summer break. As we were taking all our meals with Aunt Mali, the house pastor, and a few students, we had plenty of opportunities to converse about the new Germany, the new constitution, the government and the democracy. I learned for the first time of all the hardships that the Protestant Church and its pastors had endured during the Nazi Regime. Men like Bonhoeffer had resisted the takeover by the government to the last; and he had paid with his life for it. The Protestant Church had been much more vulnerable than the Catholic Church, because it did not have the equivalent of the Pope in Rome. We visited the old university, once beautiful renaissance buildings that had been severely damaged. The students had to collect bricks from the ruins and chisel them clean so the buildings could be gradually rebuilt. They also had to work ten hours per week in the reconstruction. -- We pupils of the *Gymnasium* in Mülheim, too, collected bricks. Not only pupils and students, but also the workers of the large factories, as for instance Siemens, participated voluntarily without pay in the rebuilding of their destroyed work places. When I worked in 1951 for Siemens, I became acquainted with many *Kruppianer,* employees who had worked for Krupp all their lives, and who were temporarily working for Siemens. They were all waiting for the signal to begin the reconstruction of the huge Krupp Works in *Essen*, where they wanted to participate in the rebuilding like their colleagues at Siemens. The famous *Wirtschaftswunder* was accomplished mainly by hard work and long hours. -- Bonn had not suffered too badly from the air bombardments, because it was too small and insignificant. But now over night it had become important, when the new Federal Government made it into the Capital of West Germany. Buildings were springing up everywhere, especially near the Rhine shore south of town, where the new Parliament and Administration was being located. They were impressive but simple.

After Günter and I had hoped in vain to see the new Chancellor, we packed our bags -- Aunt Mali had furnished us with food for the next leg of our trip -- and continued through the beautiful *Rhein* valley, which we had already enjoyed during our train trip to the KLV camp in the May of 1943. Here was this immense river again, with barges of many nations on it, vineyards up both sides of the valley, and here and there an old castle on top of the steep embankments. The high point was the Lorelei Rock, on top of which Lorelei had sat and combed her golden hair, causing the doom of many a fisherman. -- My late friend Max Fowler still demonstrated with his 86 years that he had learned in his German lessons *"Ich weiß nicht was soll es bedeuten"* by singing every verse of Heine's Lorelei with his beautiful bass. Much better than I! -- The next stop was in *St. Goar*, a pretty old town on the western shore of the *Rhein* with medieval walls and gates and lovely half timbered houses, wedged between river, road, railroad and vineyards. We visited Hermann Schwarz, who spent his summer vacations with his grandmother. She invited us for a few nice days during which we accompanied Herman through the old, narrow cobblestone streets up into the vineyards and down to the river. We sat for hours on the shore watching the river barges floating easily down river or working hard against the fast moving current upriver. They flew Dutch, French, Swiss, and sometimes the new German flags. After these enjoyable days we continued past the *Pfalz von Kaub,* where *Blücher* had crossed the Rhine in 1814 in pursuit of Napoleon's army. Then the *Binger Loch* and the *Mäuseturm*, the narrowest passage of the river. It is so narrow, the currents are so swift, and the rocky river bottom is so treacherous that every barge has to bring a pilot on board who guides it safely past the lurking dangers. A little further south, the narrow valley opens wide to orchards, fields and meadows.

The Rhine meadows near *Worms* witnessed our first and last attempt at camping. We picked a place in a meadow near the river, unfolded our triangular tarps, and fashioned a tent from them with the help of a rope, a tree and its branches. After a few sandwiches, we wrapped ourselves into the blankets and fell asleep on the soft grass. Good night! And what night it became, colder and wetter by the hour. At four at the very first glimpse of dawn we were up soaked and shivering. We packed as fast as we could and cycled off as hard as we could in order to get warm and dry. Well, we ignoramuses had no idea that a tent needs a bottom, especially when one pitches it near the river where the dew soaks everything in sight. It took a few hours before we had pedaled ourselves warm and we could stop and dry our clothes and blankets in the sun. Unfortunately, the cathedral in *Worms,* where Martin Luther had to defend his theses on April 18, 1521 before the *Reichstag,* the assembly of German nobility and clergy, was still locked, when we came through at too early an hour.

Next, we spent several days in Heidelberg staying with a friend of Mutti, who received us cordially, fed us well, and quartered us in an empty storage room just big enough for the two of us to sleep. The town had not been damaged; no wonder, for it had no strategic significance. We strolled through the old narrow streets and walked along the philosophers' way, we visited the famous university and the castle with the huge wine cask. Heidelberg was still the university town it had always been. We continued the trip along the lazily flowing *Neckar* through a pleasant countryside to Stuttgart where the Coermanns, a cousin of my father and her husband, resided. Although they lived in a tiny attic apartment, -- their house had been demolished --, they found a corner for us to sleep in. We took our main meal together with them and a group of others in a private house at a large table d'hote; an arrangement that the church had made for elderly people. We listened to their war experiences, and they asked about the conditions in the *Ruhrgebiet* and were fascinated by our adventurous bicycle trip. Nobody traveled in those years unless he had to go to a specific place for business or personal reasons. However, we met on and off cyclists of our age who were also exploring their homeland. Stuttgart was badly destroyed, the entire valley was one maze of ruins. It had been a favorite air target because of its automobile industry. I learned an interesting detail at the dinner table about the removal of hundreds of thousands of tons of debris. The city had decided to simply create a new mountain actually not far from the city center. The citizens called it appropriately and with a sense of humor *Monte Scherbellino* (shard mountain -- the German word *Scherbe* means shard). -- When Brigit and I visited Stuttgart recently we actually saw *Scherbellino;* it looked like all the other hills surrounding the city, covered with meadows and trees. -- In general, the removal of the huge volumes of rubble was a problem for all big cities. Mülheim solved it by filling old quarries, filling in land during river corrections and even stuffing abandoned mine shafts and tunnels, which had caused a problem for decades. Collapsed abandoned mining tunnels had caused the earth above to sink. People had learned to reinforce their houses that had been built within the vicinity of a mine by installing heavy horizontal iron rods with huge washers and nuts at their ends outside. It was a common sight in my hometown where houses were often held together with half a dozen rods. -- A few days later we arrived at the beautiful *Bodensee* (Lake Constance) that borders Switzerland, Austria, and Germany, and is the natural regulating reservoir of the *Rhein*. We chose a youth hostel in *Lindau* as our lodging for the night. It was one of the few youth hostels in which we could stay during our trip, for most of the prewar hostels were still closed. Prior to the war the Ministry of Youth had fostered the development of a network of youth hostels that covered the whole country. The idea was that young people should be able to travel through their homeland on foot or by bicycle with minimal expenses. The distance between hostels was generally so short that it could be traveled in one day. All one had to do was to obtain a membership card for a small fee and present this upon arrival at a hostel. The rules for residency were very strict. Above all, the rooms had to be kept clean and quiet. Upon arrival, every guest received an assignment from the *Herbergs Mutter or Vater,* hostel mother or father. The chores ranged from work in the kitchen to room cleaning or bathroom duty. A simple dinner could be bought for a very nominal amount. After dinner the hostel parents frequently invited everybody to participate in singing and story telling around a camp fire. Of course, no alcohol and absolute quiet after ten. When you wanted to leave in the morning and get your membership card back you had to demonstrate the completion of the originally assigned job.

If we could not find a youth hostel at our destination, we invariably found a farmer who would be willing to put us up in the barn or stable. The farmer families were almost all friendly and interested in our trip experiences and the conditions in the demolished *Ruhr* cities. We talked about the war, the American occupation, the new German government in Bonn and everyday events. Sometimes a farmer would not give us lodging, for he had made bad experiences with other youths and was afraid of fire. If the farmer admitted us, we had to swear that we would not smoke anywhere on the premises. No problem for me, but Günter had to forgo his evening cigarette. On occasion the farmer's wife brought us something to eat; mostly we cooked ourselves. Since we both had no idea how to cook, we created some interesting meals, however, mostly soups. One night we tried noodles. We boiled water in our cooking pot and poured what appeared to be the right amount of noodles into it. During cooking the noodles grew and grew. Pretty soon they were overflowing the pot so that we had to ladle them quickly into another vessel; but they kept overflowing more and had to be taken off again. I guess that we had used enough dry noodles for a family of six. The farmer's wife who had watched the procedure could not quit laughing; but she also gave us good advice for future meals. We ate noodles for two days. -- This episode reminded me of one of The Brother Grimm's Tales *"Der süße Brei"* (the sweet porridge), where a magic pot with millet porridge overflowed, because the mother, who knew the word to start it, but not the word to stop it, could not arrest the flow. The porridge flowed from the house into the street and filled all the town's streets. Finally the daughter, who knew the magic word, came home and stopped the porridge avalanche. --

We learned fast that sleeping in a barn on hay was nice and soft, but gave us nasty headaches. Straw was hard but without aftereffects. There were a few times when we slept on the straw in a stable together with a dozen cows. It was not easy to adjust to the odor and the variety of noises the cows made during the night, but it was comfortable and warm. Once we were offered a tiny shed with barely enough room to stretch out. Not too uncomfortable, until it started raining and we found out that the roof was not exactly tight. We constructed a slanted roof with ropes and our tent tarps so that the water could run off and we sank again into dry slumber. Language became a rather unexpected problem. I had already made my experiences with the Silesian dialect, which, it turned out, was harmless compared to the Swabian and Bavarian dialects. Half the time I could only guess what these people were saying or what they meant.

On our return trip we stopped in *Ulm,* another destroyed city. Even its beautiful gothic cathedral had suffered badly. But all of this was nothing compared to our next destination, the utterly devastated *Nürnberg.* The inner city had essentially disappeared, and the two towers of the *Frauenkirche* loomed silent and heavily damaged over a huge rubble field; but to our great surprise, the *Schöne Brunnen,* the beautiful fountain, with its elegant, intricate gothic architecture was still intact on the opposite side of the market square. Somebody told us that it had been surrounded with a bunker-like structure that had been removed after the war. -- Almost all of the famous masterpieces of German art had survived. Where possible they had been covered with concrete structures or had been removed from museums, castles, and churches to be stored in safe places, frequently old mine shafts and tunnels. In most cases the irreplaceable stained glass windows had been taken from the cathedrals and moved to safety. -- The *Nüremburg*, the medieval fortress above the old town, had survived most of the bombing with some destroyed walls, roofs and windows. The *Dürer Haus*, Albrecht Dürer's residence and workshop next to the *Burg*, was still there and looked fine, although I believe that it had already been repaired. When Brigit and I visited *Nürnberg* in 2000 we found a beautiful, completely rebuilt city. The old town had been mostly reconstructed exactly as before. The remaining buildings of lesser historical and architectural significance had been replaced by modern buildings that were so similar in style and appearance that from afar it was sometimes difficult to decide which was which.

Günter and I followed the *Main* river through beautiful vineyards, pretty intact little towns and villages. Suddenly we came upon the ruins of *Schweinfurt* that had been the frequent target of Allied bombings because of its well known ball bearing factories. In Frankfurt, we found again a youth hostel and explored the city. It was difficult for us to imagine what the city might have looked like before. Now it consisted of huge mounds of rubble that were already overgrown. The ruins of the cathedral stood there above it all with what was left of spire, roofs and walls. Would any of these destroyed cities ever be rebuilt? Our last stretch took us along the eastern shore of the *Rhein* through little pleasant towns that are famous because of their wines, past steep vineyards and the occasional castle ruin above. This time we pedaled through a tunnel under Lorelei's rock , past the famous bridge of *Remagen,* and finally below the *Petersberg,* where the three Allied High Commanders still had an eye on the evolving German democracy. -- The people from the *Rheinland,* with their indefatigable sense of humor, had baptized them the *Drei Heiligen of the Petersberg* (the Three Holy Saints of the Petersberg). --

One last night at Aunt Mali's in Bonn, and then in record time back to *Mülheim* where the new school year started two days later. Our grand journey through the South of our shattered homeland had come to an end. Although overwhelmed by all the rubble and devastation we had glimpsed a better future in the words of the dying *Attinghausen in Schiller's Wilhelm Tell:*

> "*Das Alte stürzt, es ändert sich die Zeit,*
> *und neues Leben blüht aus den Ruinen.*"

> "the old things fall, the time has changed,
> **and new life blossoms from the ruins.**"

It was the first day of September 1949, ten years after the beginning of the war and the most turbulent and impressive ten years of my life. What a fate, and yet so lucky! What would things be like if this horrible war had never happened? Approximately five million Germans dead, all major cities devastated, the once flourishing industry on its knees, not much left from the proud *Großdeutschland*. Worse, most of Europe in shambles, half of it no longer free, almost thirty million that did not survive, a complete economical and cultural collapse. It seemed that decades would pass before everything would be reborn. And all this because of one man and his disciples who probably never imagined this result of their insane ambitions. Since the beginning of mankind, fanatics have rarely considered the potential consequences of their decisions. They have been and always will be so convinced of their ideologies and carried away by their presumed power that reason and wisdom lose their rightful place.

I wrote this book as a memoir about the most incredible years of my life that left their imprint on my mind and soul forever. I wrote it as a reminder that mankind is able to destroy itself. I wrote it for the young generation as a warning that in a modern war everybody, young or old, military or civilian, will suffer the consequences. I wrote it also to show that it was possible to lead an entire country first from democracy to tyranny and then back to democracy. And lastly I wrote it from the viewpoint of a boy who was sucked into the torrent like everybody else, who simply did what was expected of him, and who was lucky enough to emerge unscathed together with his beloved mother and sisters.

Epilogue

Fifty Five Years Later

Heavy dark clouds greeted us when we left the garage of the Frankfurt Airport on the way to the *Autobahn.* Rain all the way to Eisenach the starting point of our journey into the past. Ever since the *Wende* (the turning point) in 1989 -- this is how the East Germans had called the end of the Communist Regime -- I had mentioned to Brigit frequently that I would enjoy to revisit all the places where I had spent my war years. Now on the first of April of 2000 we had crossed the former Iron Curtain and were on our way to Ronneburg. As we were entering the town I did not recognize the Ronneburg of 1945 until we arrived at the market square and saw the old town hall on one side and the hotel "Gambrinus" on the other side of the square. The pretty fountain was gone. The town hall looked brand new because it had been painted recently in a beautiful wine red color. Unfortunately it was one of very few buildings that had been restored and painted. The rest of the houses, the entire little town was in a deplorable state. Nobody had touched the house walls, the window frames, the doors, or the roofs in more than fifty years. The plaster was falling off and the paint was peeling; it hurt to see this total neglect. After a while we found the Kaiser-Wilhelm Strasse, which had been renamed Martin-Luther-Strasse. We found the houses where we had lived but not the former inhabitants who had either died or moved. The school at the upper end of our street, where the American soldiers had taken pictures sitting and laying on a toppled German guard house, was as dilapidated as everything else. Forty five years of Communist rule had left deep scars behind.

These were not the only scars. Driving a few miles outside of Ronneburg we noticed a number of fairly tall hills that had not existed in 1945. Talking to the local librarian we learned that these hills had been created from the tailings of several gigantic uranium mines. It turned out that the Soviets had discovered uranium close to the earth's surface and had mined the ore in two or three pit mines next to town. The onrush of workers had changed the entire economic fabric of the little town, and now after the Soviets had pulled out in 1990 and the workers had gone they left the little town and its economy in shambles. When we visited, the German Federal Government was in the process of cleaning up this terrible mess.

All over former East Germany the Soviet Government had ruthlessly exploited the people and the economy without ever maintaining or repairing anything. The factories were totally out of date; they belched clouds of pollution into the air. Buildings everywhere, not just in Ronneburg, where dilapidated; streets were in a pitiful condition; railroad stations were in worse condition than in 1945. The East German Government had built large, ugly five story apartment houses on the outskirts of every town. That had been their way of housing the "comrades". These buildings were in an awful condition. Sometimes people were still living in them, frequently they were deserted. In contrast to this misery, the center of most cities had been already renovated during the last ten years. In places like Erfurt, Weimar, Leipzig and even Dresden the old renaissance buildings had been carefully restored and their facades beautifully painted. Parks and squares invited one to stroll or sit.

Brigit and I talked with many young and old people about their experiences under the Communists as well as about their new freedom. A large percentage of the younger people was happy with the new democratic world. They obviously had adjusted to the newly won political and economic freedom and were running shops, small hotels and other businesses. They clearly were proud of their achievements. In Potsdam one young couple had acquired a small river barge, tied it to a deserted dock and converted it into a bed & breakfast. When we stayed there overnight they told us how they got together with friends to buy and restore the boat. They had to learn about loans, setting up a business and running it independently from the state and its bureaucracy. A totally new experience; but they had obviously succeeded. By contrast, we met many older people who were very unhappy and often wished the old regime back. Under that regime life had not been good, but everything was taken care of by the government. They had had their food, their housing, and their employment. Now it all had become very confusing, they had to find new jobs on their own, nobody told them any longer what to do and the entire cradle-to-grave coddling had vanished. Many had given up and were living on seemingly permanent unemployment benefits. The toppling of the Berlin Wall in 1989 had raised great expectations for everyone; but the realities of everyday life had crushed hopes for many.

Our impressions of the former East Germany were essentially repeated in former Silesia, which is now a province of Poland; with the difference that the country was poorer and the people worse off. The centers of the cities had been restored to a large degree, the facades were colorfully painted, the market squares were inviting with trees, flowers and benches; but the rest was in a worse state of neglect and decay than in East Germany. We met entrepreneurs and we met recipients of unemployment benefits. I think one of the reasons that much less reconstruction had taken place than in former East Germany was the fact that all the Poles living now in the former Silesia had been moved here after the war from East Poland that had become part of Russia. For years they had been under the illusion that they would move back to their former homeland. Therefore they had considered their life in this foreign country as temporary and done little to rebuild the old towns and make them beautiful again.

I had a hard time recognizing Waldenburg upon first blush; but slowly I found my way around, found the old school, rediscovered the central market square, but could not find the house in the Cochius Strasse where we had lived. Maybe it had been razed to make room for a new ceramic factory. However, the old post office and even the movie theater, where we went with my mother so many times, were still there. But, all in all, Waldenburg was dilapidated and a sad sight.

Breslau presented itself in quite a different light. Most of the city center had been rebuilt (it was completely destroyed during the long Russian siege in 1945). I was very impressed how beautifully its famous market square had been restored. All house facades were freshly painted, and the gorgeous cathedral in the center of the square with its beautiful astronomical clock looked like new. The parks along the Oder had all been replanted and were frequented by young and old. The old churches and cathedrals had been rebuilt or repaired. During our visits we found out that they served now a catholic instead of the previous protestant population. Poland was and is a catholic country, whereas *Schlesien* , Silesia, was a protestant province of Prussia. We found this remaking of the churches to be true in all towns of the former *Schlesien*. We met frequently groups of German tourists who were visiting old German sites, like churches, cemeteries, town halls, castles and other prominent buildings. It turned out that these elderly travelers were former Silesians who had either fled at the end of the war or who had been deported later on. To our surprise, some of them had bought vacation homes in the nicer areas, which was now possible under the laws of the European Union. Occasionally we ran into a group that was part of a German protestant church organization, whose purpose was to restore and maintain the most beautiful protestant churches and cemeteries that the Poles had abandoned. We visited a cemetery in *Schweidnitz* that was completely overgrown with grass, weeds, bushes and trees. Quite a sight! The last gravestone inscribed in German was from 1945.

We made our last visit to Bielorad in the Czech Republic, my KLV home in 1943. Nothing had changed; it was still the same sleepy little town with an equally sleepy hotel section. Our hotel was still there, a little modernized. The only difference was that the hotels were now utilized by the Czech Medicare System for convalescents. The owners and their two daughters of the small bed&breakfast where we stayed overnight wanted to know all about America. With eager faces they listened to every word that came from our lips. Before we returned home from the trip into the past we spent a few days in Prague. It was still as beautiful and inspiring as it had been in 1943, in the middle of the war. Nothing had been destroyed -- Prague did not get touched by any wars since the Thirty Year War in the seventeenth century -- , all buildings in the old town were in splendid shape, the astronomical clock was surrounded by multitudes, the Charles Bridge was busy with tourists, and the *Hradçany* still dominated the other side of the Vlatava. However, when we inquired about a visit to the treasure chamber we were told that it was no longer open to tourists because of the damage that would be done to the irreplaceable jewels by tens of thousands tromping through. What a change from the day in 1943 when the guard was only too eager to open the vault with his huge key and show these heavenly crowns, diadems, rings, necklaces, chalices and bishop's staffs to two curious German boys.

Our journey into the past became a complete success. People were very friendly and eager to communicate. They opened their arms to us wherever we went, so that I buried quickly my early anxieties as a former German. What we saw and heard was fascinating, marvelous, and enlightening; but it could not hide the deep scars that the murderous war and the ensuing inhuman Communist Regime left behind.

Footnotes

(1) There exists often a confusion about the meaning of the title of the German national anthem. People often think that *Deutschland über Alles* (Germany over everything) means that Germany should reign over all other countries. This interpretation is unfortunately generally believed; but it is actually totally wrong. The melody was composed by Franz Josef Haydn in 1797 with the lyrics: "Gott erhalte Franz den Kaiser" (God, preserve Franz the Emperor). In 1841, Heinrich Hoffmann von Fallersleben wrote new lyrics:" Deutschland über Alles".

As a consequence of the French revolution a desire grew in the German speaking states to shake off the shackles of monarchical absolutism and to increase liberalism. This culminated in the creation of a German National Assembly in 1848 and the writing of a constitution. This was an extraordinary event for all Germans i.e. German speaking people. It was for the first time in approximately 600 years that untold numbers of large and small principalities had been united again under one umbrella. There had been kingdoms, dukedoms, counties, and other feudal realms with never ending hostilities between them There had been custom barriers between these realms; often they coined their own money; but there had not been a country called Germany. Now custom boundaries were broken, people and goods could move freely, and as a consequence industry and trade had a chance to blossom.

Von Fallersleben was very active in the liberal circles which agitated for change. He wanted "unity, rights, and freedom" for the German people, and with his lyrics he exhorted the Germans to stand together against all the individual fiefdoms and monarchies. He and his liberal friends wanted that the Germans should put the idea of one Germany "above everything else". As the result of his agitations he actually lost his professorship, but his lyrics survived and became the anthem of the new Germany that was finally created in 1871.

(2) The modern Czechoslovakia had seen a turbulent history of occupation and domination throughout the centuries. No wonder as it was sandwiched between a few powerful nations. The Hungarians invaded Moravia during the 6. and 7. century, and it became part of Hungary in the 10. century. The dukes of Bohemia joined the German Empire between 929 and 950. At the beginning of the 11. century Bohemia and Moravia were combined and their dukes became kings during the 12. and 13. century. When their lines died out in the 14. century Heinrich IV. and later Karl IV. took over the reign of both kingdoms. The entire region fell to the Habsburgs during the 15. century, then to the Polish kings and back to the Habsburgs (Ferdinand II.). The northern part, known as the Sudetenland, became part of Germany, the South and Moravia became part of the Austro-Hungarian Empire. This lasted until the defeat of Germany and Austria-Hungary at the end of the First World War. As part of the Treaty of Versailles in 1919 a new country was created with the name of Czechoslovakia.

(3) An Austrian National Socialist Party had come into being in the same time frame as the German NSDAP (German National Socialist Workers Party). It was strengthened over the years through infiltration by German National Socialists. In the summer of 1934 Hitler and the Austrian National Socialists actually attempted a coup that failed. However, the Austrian Chancellor Engelbert Dollfuß was murdered and succeeded by Kurt von Schuschnigg. During all this time Mussolini's troops were ready at the southern Austrian border. The Austrian National Socialist hotheads still were not satisfied with Dollfuß' successor and continued to make plans for the next coup. In the meantime, Hitler committed himself to the Austrian Chancellor von Schuschnigg (July 11, 1936) "not to interfere with Austria's internal affairs". However, when von Schuschnigg forbade parades of the Austrian National Socialists through Vienna, Hitler directed them to ignore the ban. At the same time he demanded a union of Germany and Austria (*der Anschluß*) in a meeting with von Schuschnigg on February 12, 1938. When Schuschnigg ordered a plebiscite for March 13, Hitler demanded a postponement of the plebiscite and the resignation of

Schuschnigg, whereupon Schuschnigg and his cabinet stepped down. The Secretary of the Interior, a National Socialist, took over the government and asked the German government to send troops "to maintain order". The German army occupied Austria on March 12, 1938, and the country became part of the *Großdeutsche Reich* (the Greater Germany). In a plebiscite on April 10, 1938 the Austrian and the German populations voted with overwhelming majorities for the *Anschluß*.

(4) Field Marshal Paul von Hindenburg was already retired, when Kaiser Wilhelm II. called him back in August of 1914 as chief commander of the German East Army. The Russian Army had beaten the Austrian troops in Galicia, had invaded East Prussia, and was advancing on Königsberg, the capital of East Prussia. After Hindenburg had taken over the command he demolished the Narev Army at Tannenberg, beat the Njemen Army at the Masuren Lakes, and managed to stop the Russian "steamroller" altogether with the help of the Austrian Army. After the collapse of Germany at the end of the war and after the death of the first president Friedrich Ebert, Hindenburg was elected as *Reichspräsident* in 1925. After his reelection in 1932, when he was already eighty three, he finally acceded to Hitler's desire and appointed him Chancellor on January 30, 1933. He died as a German hero in 1934.

(5) Alfred Graf von Schlieffen, who became Field Marshal in 1911, had developed a plan in 1905 how to handle a war on two fronts. The plan foresaw a massive attack in the West coupled with a holding pattern in the East. In order to achieve the defeat of France as fast as possible, the German forces would had to advance through Holland and Belgium all the way to the coast and then turn south with the intent to encircle the French Army and push through to Paris. Speed was of the utmost essence. Once France was defeated, Russia could be fought with reinforcements from the western front.

In the early weeks of the First World War Field Marshal von Moltke did not exactly follow the plan. The German armies turned southward too early and, in addition, were weakened by von Moltke's decision to attack at the same time through Lorraine. The attack from the North did not succeed and degenerated into the "trench war" that lasted until the end in 1918.

In contrast to this, the German armies of the Second World War followed the Schlieffen plan exactly. They raced through Holland and Belgium all the way to the coast and only then turned south. It took only five weeks from the attack on Holland and Belgium until Paris was occupied.

(6) The struggle over Alsace-Lorraine has been going on for almost 2000 years. First, the Alemanni and the Romans opposed each other. Then, after the Huns had retreated in 451, the Alemanni moved again into the region and established the linguistic boundary which, surprisingly, still exists today. Charlemagne (768-814) extended the Holy Roman Empire of German Nation from the Pyrenees in the West to the Oder river, Moravia and Croatia in the East, and from the North Sea in the North to south of Rome in the South. After his death his sons divided the empire in the Treaty of Verdun (843) into three parts: A Germanic East, a Romanic West, and the mixed Middle Reich under Lothar. When Lothar's family died out in 870, the Middle Reich was divided again between East and West. The new border was defined by the rivers Rhone, Saone, Maas, and Schelde; and Elsaß-Lothringen (Alsace-Lorraine) became part of the East Reich.

This political, geographic division remained in place until the *Westfälische Frieden* (peace of Westphalia) of 1648 at the end of the Thirty Year War. The peace treaty assigned Metz, Toul, Verdun, and the *Oberelsaß* (Upper Alsace) to France; and Straßburg and the *Unterelsaß* (Lower Alsace) to Germany. Thirty three years later Louis XiV. conquered all of Elsaß-Lothringen. The new Alsace-Lorraine was called "Provinces d'etranger effectif", and it was given special privileges in regard to language, religion, and commerce. In spite of many territorial changes after the final defeat of Napoleon in 1815, Alsace-Lorraine remained with France as the result of the Second Peace of Paris. Then it changed hands again after the Franco-Prussian war of 1870/71, when the Second German Reich was inaugurated by Fürst Bismarck in the halls of Versailles. The Peace Treaty of Versailles (1919) assigned the province back to France as part of the occupation of the *Rheinland*, the *Saarland*, and in 1923 the *Ruhrgebiet*. After the defeat of France in 1940 Alsace-Lorraine fell back to Germany and in 1945 back to France.

(7) Friedrich Krupp founded the company in 1812 with the intent

to win substantial prize money from the Emperor Napoleon, who had offered a prize for the first firm that could produce cast steel on the continent. The British blockade had made it impossible to obtain cast steel any longer from England. Friedrich was an incompetent businessman, and the company could only continue without the prize money under the direction of relatives and later his son Alfred. After Friedrich's death the company began to produce cast steel around 1830. Alfred worked day and night already as a teenager to avoid becoming another failure like his father. He employed 214 workers by 1850 and had his first big success with seamless steel rims for railroad wheels. (Steel rims that were customarily welded together always broke after relatively short usage.) He also built railroad axles, church bells, and guns from cast steel. At the 1851 World Fair in London he impressed the industrial world with a two ton steel block and a cast steel gun barrel.

A few years later at the 1855 World Fair in Paris he exhibited an even heavier block of steel and a cast steel gun barrel that was exactly the same as the famous French "Canon de l'Empereur" made from bronze. Napoleon III. got very excited, because this barrel could fire 3000 rounds without wear. He bestowed a gold medal and the Cross of the Legion d'Honneur on Alfred Krupp, but he was not able to give any orders to a foreign firm against the strong resistance of the French war industry. Consequently the French army with its bronze guns was totally overpowered by the Prussian superior steel guns, and France lost the war in 1871.

By 1864 the Krupp Steel Works had 6750 employees, by 1914 80,000 and by 1918 167,000. It had become the most powerful steel and weapons maker of Europe.

(8) Barbarossa (Red Beard) is the name of the German King Friedrich I. who lived from 1152 to 1190. His reign is often lauded as the height of the glory of the medieval Holy Roman Empire, which still encompassed the same area as the East Reich (footnote 5). Equally distinguished as diplomat, politician, and warrior he represented the essence of the knightly ideal of that time. When Sultan Saladin conquered Jerusalem, Friedrich led the third crusade in 1189 to liberate the Holy City with the English and French kings under his command. Before the armies reached their goal he drowned in the river Saleph. During the

siege of Akkon, hostilities broke out between the participating nations, and Jerusalem remained in the hands of Saladin. German legend has it that the Emperor Barbarossa went to sleep in the Kyffhäuser Mountain in Thüringen and will reappear one day to restore his mighty German empire.

(9) Catherine the Great, the daughter of Prince Christian August of Anhalt-Zerbst, married Peter III., the grandson of Peter the Great and became Tsarina after his death. She settled large groups of Germans in the Ukraine, along the Volga, in Galicia, and in the Bukovina between 1763 and 1767 . Earlier in the 13th century German settlers had already been invited by the Hungarian kings to colonize *Siebenbürgen* (Transylvania), and later during the 17th century the Banat. During the 19th century Alexander I. brought more German settlers to Romania, Besarabia, Dobrudscha, Wolhynien, Latvia and to other areas.

(10) Synthetic fuel was invented in 1927. There were two processes in use in Germany during the war. The Fischer-Tropsch method (named after its inventors) converts coal into paraffin with the help of catalysts. The paraffin is then converted into gasoline. I believe that this method was mainly used by the German chemical industry. The second process, named after its inventor Bergius, converts coal at high temperatures and pressures directly into gasoline, again with the help of catalysts.

(11) Stalin had pursued a strategy of expansion and exploitation from the day the Red Army marched into the neighboring countries. His goal was to occupy as many countries as fast as possible before the Western armies got there. Consequently he became very annoyed when the Western Allies invaded France, which meant that their armies would spoil his plans for the domination of Europe. He immediately accelerated the pace of the war and occupied within one year Poland, Bulgaria, Rumania, Hungary, and the eastern parts of Czechoslovakia, Austria and Germany He achieved this at a horrendous expense of Russian life. -- I remember very well newsreels from the eastern front that showed German machine gun emplacements that were covering open fields, while Soviet soldiers burst from a forest and tried to race across the open space. Wave after wave was mowed down until mounds of corpses covered the fields. One always heard

that the officers threatened to shoot their own soldiers who had the choice between German or Russian bullets. -- Communism was going to reign in Europe and ultimately in the world. The Allied strategy was entirely different. It consisted of defeating Hitler without much thought about the European political landscape after the war. Roosevelt said in Yalta that the American troops would not stay longer than two years in Germany. Stalin was reported to have said at the same time: "We Russians will never leave Germany." Germany was destined to become a Communist satellite like all the other countries.